GRAZERS

THE BRITANNICA GUIDE TO PREDATORS AND PREY

GRAZERS

EDITED BY JOHN P. RAFFERTY, ASSOCIATE EDITOR, EARTH AND LIFE SCIENCES

Britannica
Educational Publishing

IN ASSOCIATION WITH

ROSEN
EDUCATIONAL SERVICES

Published in 2011 by Britannica Educational Publishing
(a trademark of Encyclopædia Britannica, Inc.)
in association with Rosen Educational Services, LLC
29 East 21st Street, New York, NY 10010.

Copyright © 2011 Encyclopædia Britannica, Inc. Britannica, Encyclopædia Britannica, and the Thistle logo are registered trademarks of Encyclopædia Britannica, Inc. All rights reserved.

Rosen Educational Services materials copyright © 2011 Rosen Educational Services, LLC. All rights reserved.

Distributed exclusively by Rosen Educational Services.
For a listing of additional Britannica Educational Publishing titles, call toll free (800) 237-9932.

First Edition

Britannica Educational Publishing
Michael I. Levy: Executive Editor
J.E. Luebering: Senior Manager
Marilyn L. Barton: Senior Coordinator, Production Control
Steven Bosco: Director, Editorial Technologies
Lisa S. Braucher: Senior Producer and Data Editor
Yvette Charboneau: Senior Copy Editor
Kathy Nakamura: Manager, Media Acquisition
John P. Rafferty: Associate Editor, Earth and Sciences

Rosen Educational Services
Heather M. Moore Niver: Editor
Nelson Sá: Art Director
Cindy Reiman: Photography Manager
Matthew Cauli: Designer, Cover Design
Introduction by Greg Roza

Library of Congress Cataloging-in-Publication Data

Rafferty, John P.
Grazers / edited by John P. Rafferty.—1st ed.
   p. cm.—(The Britannica guide to predators and prey)
"In association with Britannica Educational Publishing, Rosen Educational Services."
ISBN 978-1-61530-336-6 (library binding)
   1. Herbivores—Ecology. 2. Ungulates—Ecology. 3. Mammals—Ecology. 4. Animal-plant relationships. I. Rafferty, John P. II. Title.
QH549.5.R34 2011
599.6—dc22

                                                        2010032169

Manufactured in the United States of America

On the cover: Two male gemsbok (*Oryx gazella gazella*) battle it out on the Etosha plains. *Shutterstock.com*

On page v: © Photos.com/Jupiterimages Corporation

On page xii: Reticulated giraffe (Giraffa camelopardalis reticulata), Kenya. © CorbisOn page xx: Burchell's zebra (Equus burchellii). © Digital Vision/Getty Image

On pages 1, 35, 70, 127, 156, 179, 203, 224, 267, 280: Herd of guanacos in eastern Patagonia, Valdés Peninsula, Argentina. © Victor Englebert; Banner. © www.istockphoto.com/Exkalibur

CONTENTS

158

178

193

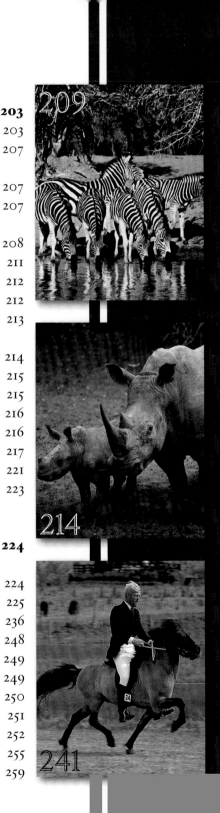

209

214

241

270

292

308

312

All over the world—on grasslands, in forests, and even on farms—grazers are ardent consumers of Earth's plants. Grazers are animals that roam from one "victim" to another. They feed from plants, but in most cases, they do not kill them. There are hundreds of grazer species categorized into a number of groups. Most have specialized front teeth designed for cutting, slicing, or tearing morsels from plants and thick back teeth for grinding them up.

Many grazing species spend at least part of their lives in medium to large groups called herds. Herds serve several purposes in the animal world. Perhaps the most notable advantage is protection from predators. Although a herd of animals is a highly visible target for predators, grouping reduces the risk of attack on each individual herd member. Another advantage is that older animals can lead younger animals to feeding grounds, breeding grounds, and water sources.

However, not all grazers form large herds. Some prefer to live in small groups led by dominant males or females. Gazelles, for example, typically form two types of small groups: females and their young, and males. These groups mix during migration and breeding, during which times dominant males govern the herd.

Still other grazers prefer to lead solitary lives, coming together only to breed and raise young. For example, individuals in four of the five species of rhinoceros prefer to live alone. Baby rhinos live with their mother in a small herd. Male rhinos, however, leave their mother to find their own territories, when they reach two and one-half years old or older, mixing with other rhinos only during mating season. White rhinoceroses, however, often live in herds of up to 10 members.

Grazers include the mammalian orders Artiodactyla (even-toed ungulates), Perissodactyla (odd-toed ungulates), Proboscidea (elephants), and Lagomorpha (rabbits, hares, and pikas), and also a number of species in the mammalian infraclass Metatheria, also known as Marsupialia (marsupials).

The largest group of grazers is made up of the artiodactyls, or even-toed ungulates, which contains about 150 species. An ungulate is an animal that walks on its toes, which are usually covered in a hard layer of skin or are combined into hooves. Even-toed ungulates have two or four toes on each foot. The group includes deer, pigs, camels, sheep, antelopes, goats, cattle, giraffes, and hippopotamuses. Most artiodactyls are medium- to large-sized animals. Ruminants are the largest group of artiodactyls. Other groups include pigs and peccaries, camels, and hippos.

Even-toed ungulates support their weight with two main toes. Those with two large toes are called "cloven-hoofed" animals. Others have four toes, and they support their weight with the larger middle two toes. The weight-bearing toes are referred to as the third and fourth toes. This is because—over many years of evolution—the first, second, and fifth toes became either reduced in size or disappeared altogether.

Most even-toed ungulates are rather well known to humans, having played an important economic and cultural role in the development and maintenance of civilizations. Artiodactyls have long been used for their milk, meat, wool, and hides. Goats and sheep were first domesticated in the Near East around 7000 BCE, whereas cattle and pigs were most likely domesticated before 3000 BCE. Artiodactyls are the most extensively hunted group of mammals on Earth, and hunting pressure has sometimes led to the extinction or near extinction of entire species. Only Australia and the polar regions are devoid of native artiodactyls.

Many artiodactyl grazers roam between breeding and feeding areas. This allows them to take advantage of seasonal bounties of food and water, and many spend their entire lives in large herds. This behaviour occurs in wild as well as domesticated animals. Some herd species, such as the gazelles and wildebeests, may number in the tens of thousands.

Social order within herds is often based around a hierarchy of dominant males. In smaller herds, however, the maternal unit is the most cohesive, with females caring for and living with the young. Smaller herds may or may not contain older males. The territories in species with solitary males can range from vast open spaces to small sections of a forest or savanna.

The survival of most artiodactyl species is closely tied to the resources in the environments they inhabit. The abundance of food and water dictates when and where grazing animals roam. Although finding plants to eat is generally easier than finding meat, plant matter is more difficult to digest. As a result, even-toed ungulates usually have larger stomachs and longer intestines than other mammals. In addition, the ancestors of many artiodactyls were omnivores that mainly ate plants. Some pigs are still omnivores.

More advanced artiodactyls called ruminants — such as sheep, goats, deer, camels, giraffes, and llamas — swallow partially chewed food which can be regurgitated and chewed more thoroughly later. This process is advantageous because it allows for the digestion of cellulose and the production of both vitamin B and vitamin K in the digestive tract. Ruminants accomplish rumination with the use of stomachs with multiple chambers.

In contrast, perissodactyls are odd-toed ungulates, who (as their name implies) have an odd number of toes on each foot (either one or three). Odd-toed ungulates and even-toed ungulates probably evolved from the same ancestor. One main difference between the two groups is that a perissodactyl's weight is supported by one main, middle toe, which is usually larger than the other toes. Odd-toed ungulate groups include six species of horses, four species of tapirs, and five species of rhinoceroses.

Perissodactyls's toes are protected by hardened body parts called hooves, which are made of keratin (which is the same substance that makes up human fingernails). Equids—that is, horses, asses, and zebras—have hooves made up of one main toe on each foot. They are the only mammals to walk on the tips of a single digit in each of their feet. Tapirs have four hoofed toes on their front feet, and three on their back feet. Rhinoceroses, the largest of the perissodactyls, have three hoofed toes on each foot.

Grass plays a major role in the diet of the herbaceous perissodactyls. Perissodactyls are found all over the world, but they are usually absent in heavily wooded areas. Like the artiodactyls, perissodactyls often migrate to reach sources of food and water. However, browsing perissodactyls (that is, those that consume foliage from shrubs and trees) usually don't need to migrate. Rhinoceroses generally live in areas where there is enough plant life to sustain them all year long. Unlike the artiodactyls, perissodactyls have small, undivided stomachs.

Socially, perissodactyls are similar to artiodactyls, although perissodactyl herds are generally much smaller. Dominant males are often the leaders of herds, but the males of some species prefer to live alone. Scientists have observed that wild horses form small herds composed of several females and their young lead by a single dominant male; bachelor males live alone or in small herds. Most species of rhinoceros live alone on large expanses of land that they mark out using dung and urine. Although little is known about the social hierarchy of tapirs, all tapir species are usually observed alone or in pairs.

The elephant is the only living member of the order Proboscidea. Extinct members include the mastodon and the woolly mammoth. Scientists have identified about 160 species within the proboscidea order from fossils, but only the African bush elephant, the African forest elephant, and the Indian Elephant survive today.

Elephants live in small family groups led by females. The groups join together to form larger herds when food is easy to find. Males usually live in bachelor herds separate from the females and young elephants. Elephants migrate seasonally to find food and water. They are able to remember the locations of water sources along migration routes.

Just like artiodactyls and perissodactyls, elephants walk on their toes. Elephant toes are buried within the thick flesh of their feet, but only some of the toes have a hard protective nail. African elephants have three toes on their back feet and four toes on their front feet, whereas Asian elephants have five toes on their front feet and four toes on their back feet.

The mammalian order Lagomorpha contains the families Leporidae (hares and rabbits) and Ochotonidae (pikas). Hares and rabbits have small, fury tails, and elongated ears and hind feet. Pikas look more like rodents with rounded ears and short limbs. All lagomorphs are similar to rodents in that they have two large, continually growing incisors used for gnawing plant matter. However, lagomorphs also have a second pair of short, peglike incisors positioned directly behind the larger incisors.

Lagomorphs eat grasses. They pass two types of feces. First they pass soft black or green pellets that still contain many undigested nutrients. They eat these immediately after passing them to obtain additional nutrients. Once the matter passes through their digestive system again, lagomorphs pass hard, round pellets. This process, known as coprophagy, ensures that lagomorphs digest as many nutrients as possible from the plants they eat. They have large digestive tracts and must eat a lot of plant matter every day to meet their nutritional requirements.

Primarily solitary animals, some species of lagomorphs live in groups of up to 20. Many come together only to breed or forage for food. Hares are the most widespread of the lagomorphs, occupying most of North America, Europe, Asia, and Africa. They are also the largest lagomorphs. Picas are much smaller than hares and rabbits.

Marsupials are mammals whose young are born premature and develop in pouches on their mother's lower belly. Although some marsupials are carnivorous (such as the Tasmanian devil), most are grazers. Grazing marsupials include kangaroos, wallabies, wombats, and koala bears. Most marsupials live in Australia, New Guinea, and the surrounding islands. About 70 species live in South and Central America. One species, the Virginia opossum, lives in the United States and Canada.

Although many people probably picture kangaroos when they think of marsupials, they actually come in many shapes and sizes. Some look like rodents, rabbits, or cats, while others resemble dogs, deer, or bears. These distinctions between marsupials are attributed to convergent evolution—the development of similar adaptations in unrelated species.

Many marsupials have a mixed diet. The American opossum, for example, eats plants and insects, making it an omnivore. Several notable marsupials exhibit behaviour typical of grazers. Although marsupials exhibit scant social organization, the six species of kangaroos form herdlike groups called mobs for the purposes of feeding and traveling. Just as in other herds, kangaroos in a mob benefit from increased protection from predators. Multiple eyes and ears scanning for danger increases the probability of predator detection, thereby reducing the effectiveness of predator surprise. However, mobs are not truly social groups like other herds. Individual mob members come and go rather than forming lasting bonds with the other members.

Internally, the digestive tracts of kangaroos are similar to those of the ruminants, with multichambered stomachs. Although a kangaroo's diet varies by species and environment, all kangaroos are grazers that mainly consume grasses. Kangaroos have complicated high-crowned teeth, including strong molars that they use to cut their food. The red kangaroo—the largest species of kangaroo—lives in the grasslands and deserts of central Australia. It mainly eats grasses and shrub foliage.

Wombats are also grazing marsupials, but they are quite different from kangaroos. With thick, tailless bodies and short legs, wombats look like small bears. Wombat teeth also differ from kangaroo teeth. They have long front teeth for gnawing, which are similar to those of rodents. These teeth grow continuously and allow wombats to eat tough bark and roots. They are primarily solitary animals, although they may live and graze in small groups.

From the mighty elephant to the tiny marsupial mouse, grazers serve as valuable links in the food chains they are a part of, transferring the solar energy captured by plants to the carnivores that prey upon them. Although some species prefer to live in one place, many others roam widely in search of food and water that will sustain them. Some groups of grazers, such as goats, cattle, and swine, have even aided in the development of human civilization. This book highlights the varied groups of grazers and their contributions to Earth's ecosystems and human society.

CHAPTER 1

ARTIODACTYLS: EVEN-TOED UNGULATES

An artiodactyl is by definition any member of Artiodactyla, the mammalian order of even-toed ungulates—that is, hoofed animals with an even number of toes on each foot. Artiodactyla includes the pigs, peccaries, hippopotamuses, camels, chevrotains, deer, giraffes, pronghorn, antelopes, sheep, goats, and cattle. It is one of the larger mammal orders, containing about 150 species, a total that may be somewhat reduced as the classification of these animals continues to be revised. Many artiodactyls are well-known to humans, and the order as a whole is of more economic and cultural benefit than any other group of mammals. By contrast, the much larger order of rodents (Rodentia) affects humans primarily in a negative way, by competing with them or impeding their economic and cultural progress.

ABUNDANCE AND DISTRIBUTION

Artiodactyls were once the dominant herbivores (plant-eating mammals) of almost every continent. They are an important link in the chain by which the Sun's energy, having been used by green plants, is made available to other forms of life. They tend to be medium- or large-sized animals. If they were any smaller they would compete with rabbits and the larger rodents, and if they were larger they would compete with elephants and rhinoceroses, the largest of terrestrial herbivores. The success of artiodactyls has depended on skeletal adaptations for running and on the development of digestive mechanisms capable of dealing with plant foods. None of these animals is adapted to flying, burrowing, or swimming. The individual species tend to be fairly narrowly adapted, in comparison with other mammals. Nonetheless, many have broad distributions.

Native artiodactyls are absent only from the polar regions and from Australasia, but many have been introduced into Australia and New Zealand. In Australia, the ecological position of medium and large herbivores is occupied by kangaroos. Through most of its evolutionary history, the order was absent from South America. Only within the last few million years have some groups entered that continent. The occurrence of most living artiodactyls in the Old World is a recent phenomenon. A considerable variety once inhabited North America.

The order Artiodactyla contains nine families of living mammals, of which the Bovidae (antelopes, cattle, sheep, and goats) is by far the largest, containing nearly one hundred species. The family Bovidae is primarily African and Eurasian, with a few members in North America. Its members, known as bovids, are advanced artiodactyls, many of which live in open grassland and semi-arid areas. There are five Eurasian and four African species of pigs (family Suidae) and two Central and South American species of piglike peccaries (Tayassuidae). The two hippopotamus species (Hippopotamidae) are African. The more familiar large species were until recently widespread throughout Africa south of the Sahara and in the Nile Valley, but the pygmy hippopotamus has a restricted distribution in West Africa. The camel group (Camelidae) was formerly abundant in North America, the now extinct North American stocks having produced the camelids of South America (wild guanaco and vicuña, domestic llama and alpaca) and the Old World dromedary and Bactrian camel.

The remaining artiodactyls (i.e., the suborder Ruminantia) are all ruminants (cud chewers), the most primitive of which are the chevrotains (Tragulidae), with three species in Asia and one, the water chevrotain, in West Africa. The chevrotains are clearly remnants of a group that was once more numerous and widespread. Deer (Cervidae) are basically Eurasian and have not spread into sub-Saharan Africa, although they have reached the Americas. There are about 30 species, the greatest number being concentrated in South America and tropical Asia. The giraffe and the okapi (Giraffidae), two distinctive African species, are closely related to deer. The pronghorn (Antilocapridae), although sometimes called pronghorn antelope, is not a true antelope. It is the only survivor of a stock of ruminants that was particularly successful in the Neogene Period in North America (from 23 million to 2.6 million years ago).

IMPORTANCE TO HUMANS

Artiodactyls have long been exploited by humans for economic purposes. Olduvai Gorge in East Africa displays clear evidence of the use of antelopes for food almost 2 million years ago. In Europe during Paleolithic times (about 30,000 years ago) Cro-Magnon man heavily depended on the reindeer. By this time the use of animals other than as food had become established. Skins were used as clothing and footwear, and bones were used as tools, weapons, and accessories.

The domestication of animals was a major advance in human history. Domestication of herd animals probably arose gradually, perhaps before agriculture. Domesticated goats and sheep are first known from the Near East at some date close to 7000 BCE. Cattle and pigs were domesticated at some subsequent date but certainly before 3000 BCE. In South America the llama, now used for transport, and the alpaca, which provides a source of wool, were developed from guanacos by the Incas or their predecessors. The dromedary (*Camelus dromedarius*), domesticated in Arabia, was introduced into the Southwestern United States, southwestern Africa, and inland Australia in the 19th century. A large feral population now exists in Australia.

In addition to providing meat, milk, hides, and wool, artiodactyls have served humans many other ways. In Kashmir, the underfleece, or pashm, of the Siberian ibex (*Capra ibex*) and of local domesticated goats has been used as the basis for the manufacture of cashmere shawls. In southwestern France, pigs have been used to locate underground truffles (the fruiting bodies of certain edible fungi).

No group of mammals is more extensively hunted than the artiodactyls. Sport hunting of various deer supports a multimillion-dollar industry in North America and Europe. In many cultures hunting has been reserved for monarchs or the aristocracy. In the centuries after the Norman Conquest of England, the forest law provided severe punishment for the slaughter of deer and boars. Père David's deer (*Elaphurus davidianus*) of China now survives only because it was preserved first in the hunting park of the emperors of China and later by the Duke of Bedford after the slaughter of the Chinese herds at the end of the 19th century.

Wild ungulates were the primary source of meat for human populations long before the appearance of modern settlements. Prehistoric men hunted the large mammals of their environment with an ever increasing effectiveness that was certainly instrumental in the survival of human beings. The extent to which humans were involved in the extinction of some of the larger Pleistocene animals (i.e., those that were abundant 11,700 to 2.6 million years ago) is still under investigation. There is now known to have been a wave of extinctions of large mammals, including artiodactyls, in the late Pleistocene. In North America this wave reached its zenith about 9000 BCE. Many animals also became extinct in Africa, where long-horned buffalo and large relatives of hartebeests survived until very recently. More of the large mammals have survived in Africa than elsewhere, but the reason for their survival is not known. A second, probably final, wave of extermination of the larger mammals has taken place with the spread of European culture and firearms in the past three hundred years. It has been marked by wanton slaughter and has ultimately produced an interest in conservation. It now seems, however, that the unprecedented demands on the environment being made by rapidly expanding human populations will result in a nearly complete extinction of large wild mammals.

NATURAL HISTORY

The skeletal adaptations for movement and the ability to digest a number of plant foods have resulted in a broad range of behaviours among artiodactyls.

MIGRATION

Many artiodactyls undertake seasonal migrations between their breeding grounds and feeding areas or between different feeding areas. They can then take advantage of the seasonal changes in different areas. This means that larger populations, and hence a larger biomass (i.e., the total weight of all individuals in an area), can be supported than if all passed their lives in one area. The North American mule deer (*Odocoileus hemionus*) comes from its summer pastures at high altitudes as the first snow falls and returns at the end of winter, several weeks after the snow has melted.

SOCIAL BEHAVIOUR

Although the popular image of artiodactyls is one of great herds numbering thousands of individuals, some species are solitary, and many others form only small family groups. The maternal family unit, in fact, is the most cohesive one, providing the basis for herd formation. Most artiodactyls are more or less social, and grazing forms may be found in especially large aggregations. It appears that the practice of aggregating gives protection, favouring those members of the species that are the most active contributors to the gene pool (thus the most available to natural selection), because the individuals most frequently taken by predators are old, solitary males, males maintaining territories, and animals of either sex separated from the herd.

Social facilitation (the instigation of collective behaviour) takes place in herds. After one animal flees, all the others flee, and the predator may thus not catch any. Social facilitation may also promote a restricted season for births, which helps survival of the young by denying these easy-prey individuals to predators through much of the year and keeps the predator population lower than if young were available throughout the year. Another advantage of herding is that the older generation in a herd can guide migrations to water, feeding areas, or mating grounds.

Females and young are usually in herds separate from those of the younger males, but territorial (the older, proven) males may accompany the females. There are some variations of this behaviour. In the Eurasian roe deer (*Capreolus capreolus*), for example, the basic unit includes the doe, her litter of two, and often the young of the previous year. During the rutting (mating) season males associate with females in heat but do not gather harems. The female herds of red deer (*Cervus elephas*) are separate from the males except in the breeding season, when

Mountain goat (Oreamnos americanus). Earl Kubis/Root Resources

the stag will defend his female herd against other males. Among cattle and related species, the males associate with the females and young, but the bulls are ranked below a so-called master bull, each defending its place within the rank order. Female hippopotamuses and their young form a group in water and have a favourite resting and basking sandbank. The males have their resting places around this area. Each male's rank in the social hierarchy determines how close to the females he may be.

There can be some flexibility of social organization within a species. During the rutting season the male mountain goat (*Oreamnos americanus*) makes little effort to herd females within a fixed area if there is little snow, but he does drive off other males. When there is much snow, he neither fights other males nor defends individual females.

Forest-dwelling artiodactyls often live singly, as does the okapi (*Okapia johnstoni*) of central Africa. Individuals meet only for mating. Female moose (*Alces alces*) with calves are intolerant of their own young of the previous year and of adults, so even small herds do not form.

The territory of an animal is an area from which the possessor attempts to exclude other individuals of the same species (and occasionally other species). An animal in an area lacking its own scent is more timid and ready to flee. Among solitary artiodactyls the territory holder defends an area sufficient to meet his needs for food and shelter. Among social artiodactyls the territorial system is interwoven with breeding activities, and territories are normally defended only by certain males. Other males are driven off, and a percentage of males are prevented from mating.

The most simple territorial organization among artiodactyls is that of the common boar (*Sus scrofa*), which lives within a home range including resting, feeding, drinking, and wallowing places. There is little sign of territorial defense, and the herd (called the sounder) may move to a new area. At the other extreme, male Uganda kob antelopes (*Kobus kob thomasi*) hold territories, for breeding only, that are as small as 15 to 30 metres (50 to 100 feet) in diameter. There are 30 to 40 territories on the breeding ground of a herd, and groups of females and young move about the territories despite the efforts of individual males to detain them. The semi-arid Serengeti plains of northern Tanzania contain nomadic aggregations of blue wildebeest (*Connochaetes taurinus taurinus*), males of which defend temporary territories only while an aggregation remains stationary.

In territorial defense an aggressive encounter between males is generally preceded by visual signalling of intentions. Chital deer (*Cervus axis*), for example, have several sorts of threatening displays. When sharp, potentially lethal horns appeared in early ruminants, intimidating displays rather than combats would doubtless have been favoured. Horns or antlers eventually functioned to maintain head contact during struggles rather than to bruise, slash, or gore. This stylized fighting, in which the competing males interlock horns or antlers and try to "outwrestle" each other, minimizes the danger of killing an opponent of the same species (conspecific). It evolved in two ways: further development of the wrestling, found in stags and some of the antelopes, and ramming, as in sheep. In sheep the horns are the sole organs of display. They increase in size throughout life and parallel the dominance order of the males, so that unnecessary fighting is minimized. Ramming may have intermediate forms. Goats, for example, butt with a sideways hooking motion. In the fighting of hornless artiodactyls, such as pigs, the combatants may be badly mauled or even killed. The fighting behaviour of camels retains primitive elements of biting, kicking, and neck wrestling.

REPRODUCTION

Many advanced artiodactyls have elaborate courtship behaviour, a regular component of which is for the male to sniff or lick the female's urine, and afterward to raise his head slightly with upcurled lips. This behaviour, which has been called *flehmen*, apparently enables the male to recognize females in heat. In the mating ceremonies of tragelaphine antelopes (kudus, bushbucks, and others) the male follows the female, nuzzling her neck several times. When he mounts, he lays his neck along hers so that their heads touch. In Thomson's gazelle (*Gazella thomsoni*), following the *flehmen* behaviour, the male runs close behind the female and finally taps her hindleg with his foreleg. Similar leg contact also occurs in some other antelopes. Its function could be to test the female's readiness to mate, to habituate her to contact, or to heighten her readiness to mate. It appears to be equivalent to the neck contact of tragelaphines. During mounting, the male Thomson's gazelle holds his head high and does not touch the female's flanks with his forelegs. The pair may continue walking. This is probably a more advanced pattern of events than that in tragelaphines. The kob antelope has elaborate displays after mating. These and the specialized sexual displays seem to be a consequence of this species' tightly clustered territories on the mating grounds. Another pattern occurs in the normally solitary Indian hog deer (*Cervus porcinus*): as many as 20 or 30 aggregate loosely in a certain area, then females and males leave in pairs and usually remain together until they have mated. Mating in artiodactyls often intensifies toward dawn and dusk.

Gestation periods vary and are related in part to the size of the animal. They range from four months in the small chevrotain to 14 months in the Bactrian camel (*Camelus bactrianus*) and over 14 months in the giraffe. Females of normally gregarious species become solitary a few days before giving birth. The female chital, or axis deer, for example, remains near a patch of dense bush and high grass to which she can retreat if endangered. The female collared peccary (*Pecari tajacu*) withdraws to a burrow. The European boar gives birth in a rough nest.

In temperate regions, birth takes place in spring or early summer, and in tropical areas there are often more births during or just after the rainy season. The absence of a well-defined breeding season in a species may indicate less rigorous environmental conditions, which sometimes vary in different parts of a species' range. Warthogs have one restricted breeding season in most of eastern and southern Africa, while elsewhere two seasons or year-round breeding have been recorded. The breeding season of the common waterbuck (*Kobus ellipsiprymnus*) is continuous in Uganda, but in Zambia its breeding season shows a sharp peak at the height of the rains.

Most modern artiodactyls have one young at each birth, but there are some well-known exceptions among ruminants. The Chinese water deer (*Hydropotes inermis*) bears twins or triplets but during gestation carries even more fetuses, early records (now known to be incorrect) of large litters were based on observations of dead pregnant females containing the large number of fetuses. The mule deer, white-tailed deer (*Odocoileus virginianus*), roe deer, pronghorn (*Antilocapra americana*), nilgai (*Boselaphus tragocamelus*), four-horned antelope (*Tetracerus quadricornis*), and saiga (*Saiga tatarica*) commonly bear twins. In the white-tailed and mule deer and in the saiga, a higher percentage of twins are borne by the older females, and this is probably true in other species. The number of young is usually three in the warthog, five in the European boar, and two in peccaries.

The female boar almost ignores her young, which free themselves from their birth membranes and seek a teat. Female camels show comparatively little maternal attention and do not eat the afterbirth (the fetal membranes and placenta). Ruminants generally eat the afterbirth, as well as the dung and urine of the young, to help prevent discovery of the young by predators. Licking of the young tends to facilitate its recognition by the mother. An artiodactyl is normally precocious (well developed) at birth and may weigh one-tenth as much as its mother. An extreme example of precocity is the wildebeest calf, which rises within five minutes of birth, follows its mother within another five minutes, and can move as fast as an adult in 24 hours. Young deer fawns "freeze" during danger but rejoin the herd when the danger is long past or when retrieved by the mother.

Pigs and hippopotamuses are weaned after a few months, but among higher artiodactyls, lactation lasts longer. Wildebeest, for example, suckle for almost a year, although they start to eat grass when only a few days old. This may either maintain a bond between parent and offspring and form the base for larger social groupings or help to "develop" the four-chambered stomach. Higher artiodactyls eat soil when they begin to eat solid food, probably to establish a normal flora and fauna in the rumen (the first of the four stomach chambers).

LOCOMOTION

Artiodactyls are preyed upon by carnivores and therefore need speed and agility to escape death. They have an added disadvantage in the sheer weight of their very large stomachs, which they need to digest plant food. Running ability reaches an extreme in advanced artiodactyls living in open country. The hippopotamus, with an adult weight of 2,500 to 3,000 kg (5,500 to 6,600 pounds), is the only living artiodactyl big enough to need heavy, pillar-like limbs for support. The maximum speeds of some artiodactyls are: warthog, 48 km (30 miles) per hour; camel, 14–16 km (9–10 miles) per hour; giraffe, a little over 48 km (30 miles) per hour; Cape buffalo (*Syncerus caffer*), 56 km (35 miles) per hour; Thomson's gazelle, 80 km (50 miles) per hour.

In the normal walking of artiodactyls the legs move in the following order: (a) left front, (b) right rear, (c) right front, (d) left rear. This basic pattern is masked in faster walking or trotting by each foot being lifted off the ground before the one ahead of it in the sequence reaches the ground, resulting in telescoping the first (a and b) and second (c and d) pairs of movements. In galloping or fast running the two front legs leave the ground one immediately after the other, then the two back legs. The chief propulsive force in locomotion comes from the back legs,

*Cape, or African, buffalo (*Syncerus caffer*).* Mark Boulton—The National Audubon Society Collection/Photo Researchers

except in the giraffe (*Giraffa camelopardalis*), in which the front legs provide the main propulsive power.

Camels often amble, both legs of each side moving together, and the giraffe and the okapi always use this walking gait. Here the middle two (b and c) and the first and last (a and d) actions of the normal walking pattern occur together. The giraffe, having a short body and great height, could not adopt the normal ruminant gait without tripping. The long neck moves back and forth in time with the strides and helps smooth the movement. Galloping by the giraffe is of the normal ungulate type.

Artiodactyls living among bush or rocky cover may develop a bounding sort of gait in which the legs are pulled up sharply during each stride. Deer and some antelopes are examples. When walking, species in such habitats are supported by the diagonally opposite legs for a greater length of time in each stride than are fast-running, open-country ruminants. This is a more primitive stable position and allows an easier leap from hidden danger. Some bovids, notably goats in Eurasia and the klipspringer (*Oreotragus oreotragus*) of Africa, are especially agile on rocky slopes and precipitous ground.

FOOD HABITS

Most artiodactyls are closely tied to the resources of their environment. They are dependent, for example, on feeding areas not being covered by too much snow or shrivelled under a drought, and on the regulating effects of fire or other herbivores on the seasonal succession of vegetation. Various grazing species feed on grass at different heights. Browsers, those that feed on the foliage of shrubs and trees, show more extreme variation in feeding height, the maximum being that of the giraffe.

Herbivorous animals need less initiative and intelligence to collect food than do the meat-eating, hunting carnivores, but digestion is more difficult. Advanced artiodactyls have evolved the ability to bolt food and to ruminate it (chew it more thoroughly) at a later time or while resting in an area where they may be less obvious to predators and can conserve energy. Tropical artiodactyls frequently have adaptations for water conservation, having developed to a high degree internal physiological regulation (homeostasis).

Primitive artiodactyls were probably omnivorous but favoured plant foods, a characteristic still found in pigs. The latter dig with the snout and, to a lesser extent, with the front legs and upper tusks (canine teeth). The warthog of Africa (*Phacochoerus aethiopicus*) has a modified method of gathering food. When food is scarce it forages for young grass shoots under very low bushes. Its tusks and localized thickening on its skin protect the eyes and muscles from thorn damage, and small incisors enable it to pluck food.

Although they spend a great deal of time submerged in lakes or rivers, Hippopotamuses (*Hippopotamus amphibius*) do not feed in the water. They graze at night, wandering over well-used trails, sometimes far from water, often damaging crops.

Most members of the camel family are found in arid habitats. The vicuña (*Lama vicugna*) of the South American Andes lives at high altitudes where it grazes on soft grasses and herbs. It has much the same food requirements as domestic sheep.

Chevrotains live in dense undergrowth close to water or in marshes, where they browse on soft vegetation, roots, and tubers, following a way of life probably not unlike that of their ancestors.

The other ruminants browse or graze. They may take many plant species in the course of the year, but at any one season a large part of the diet consists of only five or six plants. Some ruminants are strongly specialized. The reindeer of the Arctic (*Rangifer tarandus*), for example, eats a variety of sedges, grasses, and herbaceous plants in summer but, as the long winter approaches, gradually shifts to a diet of lichens. It uses its front feet to scrape snow away from lichens to a depth of about 60 cm (2 feet). The females are unique among deer in possessing antlers, which are thought to help them get scarce food in late winter by driving off the males that have by then shed their antlers. Reindeer may eat lemmings. Conversely, the red deer has catholic feeding habits. In woods it browses on lichens, berries, fungi, and the leaves of most deciduous trees; and in open country it eats grass, heather, berries, and lichens. Shrubs and trees are used more in winter. When the red deer lives in the same areas as other ruminants, it can be a serious competitor for food.

Grasses form a substantial part of the diet of many ruminants. Young grass consists of about 5 percent protein, 1 percent fat, 3 percent minerals, and 20 percent carbohydrates; the remaining percentage is water. The most noticeable changes as grass ages are an increase in carbohydrate content to 75 percent and a large decrease in the amount of water. Such food, especially when coated with silica, as are many grasses, or when covered with dust, would be impossible for nearly all nonruminant herbivores to eat or digest. The major evolutionary trend in ruminants has been to make use of grasses and grasslands, and the higher ruminants have evolved largely in adaptive balance with one another. This adaptive balance was shown during a study of the change from plains to thickets of scrub growth in an area in the eastern Congo over a period of about 10 years. There was an accompanying decrease in numbers of antelopes and warthogs, no change in buffalo, and an increase in elephants and hippopotamuses.

There is not usually a one-to-one dependence of any artiodactyl species on one plant. The plant species that constitute the major part of the diet may vary with the season, and similar parts of different plants may be eaten in preference to other parts of the same plant. Food resources in an area are thus parcelled out among the various artiodactyls present. Sometimes behavioral differences minimize competition between closely related species in the same area. A study has shown that in central Africa the roan antelope (*Hippotragus equinus*), a grazer, favours open areas with taller, ranker perennial grasses and is more or less sedentary within a small area. The sable antelope (*H. niger*), also a grazer, prefers savanna woodland or the edges of open areas, and herds follow a more or less cyclic annual route over an area of about 500 square km (200 square miles). When pasturage is restricted, sheep will cut grass extremely short, and goats will damage trees and bushes. American zoologist George B. Schaller has observed that, in Kanha Park in central India in the hot season, blackbuck (*Antilope cervicapra*) continue to graze on grass shoots in open areas; chital deer seek out tender grass blades, especially along forest edges, and also feed on leaves and fruits; barasingha (*Cervus duvauceli*) eat dry and moderately coarse grass along ravines; sambar deer (*Cervus unicolor*) browse on leaves and crop coarse grasses in the forest; and gaur (*Bos gaurus*) graze on tall, coarse grass and break down saplings to get at the leaves. The choice of habitat also varies: chital avoid steep terrain and forests with an unbroken canopy; blackbuck require less water than the others and thus remain in drier regions; sambar and gaur are less specialized in habitat requirements, and both are active primarily at night; barasingha prefer reed beds but also enter forests and climb hills.

It has also become evident that grazing successions are one of the mechanisms that enable the maximum use to be made of environmental resources. On the Serengeti Plain, for example, the wildebeest grazes on ground already covered by the zebra and leaves the grazed grass in a condition suitable for the Thomson's gazelle. Interactions take place between artiodactyls and some plant species. It has been noted in the Tarangire area of northern Tanzania that *Acacia* seedlings germinate only where the impala (*Aepyceros melampus*) has left its dung. In parts of southern Peru plants growing on or close to the dung of the vicuña are different from those of the surrounding pasture.

Artiodactyls often favour the boundary zone between habitats. In Rhodesia, Lichtenstein's hartebeest (*Alcelaphus buselaphus lichtensteinii*) is usually found at the edge of clearings adjacent to woodland.

AREAS OF DISTRIBUTION

Some artiodactyls have surprisingly small ranges. Hunter's hartebeest (*Beatragus hunteri*) and the dibatag (*Ammodorcas clarkei*), for example, are found in two especially restricted areas in eastern Africa. Others have extremely large ranges, such as the roe deer, which lives from the western shores of Europe to the eastern shores of Asia, or the red deer, which is found in a similar band across Eurasia and is regarded by many as conspecific with the North American elk (*Cervus elaphus canadensis*). Sometimes a considerable area may be occupied by a chain of related species. One such example is that of the oryx: the beisa and gemsbok (races of *Oryx gazella*) occur in South and East Africa, the scimitar-horned oryx (*O. dammah*) in West Africa, and the Arabian oryx (*O. leucoryx*) in Arabia.

It is well known that climate is one of the factors limiting the ranges of artiodactyls. Many South African antelopes differ, at the species level, from their ecological counterparts farther north in Africa. The bontebok and blesbok, subspecies of *Damaliscus pygargus*, are found in the south and the topi (*D. lunatus*) farther north. The black wildebeest (*Connochaetes gnou*) occurs in the south and the blue wildebeest (*C. taurinus taurinus*) farther north. This probably is a result of climatic or climatically influenced factors. Each species evidently functions best in a certain temperature and aridity range. Wide distributions can occur more easily along lines of latitude than they can by spanning the tropics to temperate or polar regions. Species that cross lines of latitude are often associated with mountain chains, examples being the mountain goat, with its wide latitudinal range in western North America, and the Himalayan goral (*Naemorhedus goral*), found from Indochina to the Amur River. Climatic effects on distributions sometimes occur with regard to altitude. In Central Asia, the goa (*Gazella picticaudata*) is found in valleys from 3,000 to 3,660 metres (10,000 to 12,000 feet) above sea level, the chiru (*Panthalops hodgsoni*) and the wild yak (*Bos mutus*) are on the very high steppe between 5,500 and 6,100 metres (18,000 and 20,000 feet).

South America has a more impoverished artiodactyl fauna than Africa, being limited to deer and camelids. This arises in part from the late arrival of the artiodactyls (deer in early to middle Pliocene, about 4 million years ago, camelids perhaps a little later) and in part because a number of large rodents compensate for the shortage of large herbivores. The cervids in South America have not shown the same capacity for radiation in open country as have bovids in the Old World.

The areas of distribution and numbers of individuals are determined by complicated interweaving of effects not yet completely understood. Bloodsucking flies are thought to be the main reason that red deer in Scotland ascend to higher feeding grounds in June, and reindeer are afflicted by horse flies (*Tabanus*) and other dipteran pests. It is questionable whether the level of artiodactyl populations is controlled by predation, availability of food, reproductive rate, disease, climate, or competition, insofar as these can be regarded as separate factors. It is known that undernourishment increases the susceptibility of an animal to the effects of parasites. If such an infected animal, say a pig, is caught by a leopard, it would be an oversimplification to assign a single reason for its death: it could have died from starvation, parasites, or predation. There is no evidence that artiodactyls are affected more than marginally by predators during most of their mature lives. Mortality is greatest among juvenile and aged animals. In a study of central African warthogs, it was estimated that a 60 percent loss occurred during the first six months of life in an expanding population and 95 percent in a declining one. Although predation was thought to be the main cause, another was the fact that the piglets had only limited control over their body temperatures and were thus more at the mercy of environmental temperature change. Food supply may sometimes be decisive, either directly or through the indirect action of intermediate agencies such as drought. Disease has generally been considered to have only a secondary importance in regulating numbers.

Thickness of the snow cover in winter is a crucial factor for Asian artiodactyls. The saiga, for example, cannot move in snow deeper than about 40 cm (16 inches), and the argali (*Ovis ammon*) in snow deeper than 60 cm (24 inches), at the most. The snow may have other effects. A layer of ice on top of snow may damage an animal's legs and weaken the animal to the extent that it is caught by a predator. Saiga may be unable to dig through even a shallow layer of compacted snow. Hoarfrost on vegetation is especially dangerous when prolonged or when it occurs in consecutive winters, but elk may escape the worst effects by feeding in winter on bark and high shoots. Massive periodic mortalities among Palearctic (Eurasian) ungulates in winter have been known since ancient times. The saiga has adapted to these crises by migrating great distances in a short time away from snowstorms or from areas where fodder is short. It also has a particularly rapid maturation to a reproductive state, ensuring that populations will build up after heavy mortalities.

Population density over the range of a species is affected by social behaviour, such as the effects of territoriality, dispersal of the young, and whether the species lives in herds. Fecundity may be reduced in overcrowded conditions by effects on reproductive control mechanisms, reduced viability of the young, or retarded maturation.

FORM AND FUNCTION

Artiodactyls have larger stomachs and longer intestines than carnivorous animals because plant food is less easily digested than meat. The necessity of escaping predators and the handicap of a heavy digestive system have resulted in limb bone adaptations.

In all artiodactyls the main weight-bearing axis of the leg passes through the third and fourth toes together. This has been called paraxonic support and is contrasted with the mesaxonic limb support of the other great order of herbivorous mammals, the perissodactyls (rhinoceroses, horses, tapirs), in which the weight-bearing axis passes through the third or central toe alone. As artiodactyls evolved there was increasing development of the third and fourth toes and a parallel decline of the second and fifth toes flanking them. Progressive simplification of limb extremities has characterized the evolution of the artiodactyls, and even in the earliest known artiodactyls, the pollex and hallux (corresponding to the big toe and thumb of humans) were already rare.

The other main morphological characteristic of artiodactyls is that the astragalus, one of the bones in the ankle, has upper and lower rounded articulations (areas of contact of bones) and no constricted neck, instead of simply one rounded articulation above a neck, as in other mammals. This character is so basic to artiodactyls that it has not developed very much within the known history of the order, having already been present in long extinct members. The artiodactyl astragalus also has an articulation on its rear surface for the calcaneum (heel bone). The three articulations are in nearly parallel planes, allowing the astragalus to rotate vertically.

Other features of the limbs, skull, and dentition distinguish artiodactyls. The ulna (posterior forearm bone) and fibula (posterior bone of the lower leg) have become reduced. The humerus, the upper bone of the foreleg, is large and has a large protrusion, the greater trochanter, to which muscles are attached. The femur, the upper bone of the hindleg, has a large greater trochanter and a second, lesser trochanter, but lacks the third trochanter characteristic of perissodactyls. There are typically 19 thoracic and lumbar (upper and lower back) vertebrae. The separate lumbar region of the spine is retained with its forwardly directed transverse processes (lateral projections on the vertebrae). There is no clavicle, or collarbone, in the shoulder girdle. The hip girdle shows fore-and-aft elongation and a well-developed ischium (upper anterior bone of the pelvis). There is never a penis bone.

The large tongue is very mobile and can be thrust forward. The brain is moderately developed, with folding of the surface of the cerebral hemispheres variably developed, often less in small artiodactyls than in large ones. The olfactory region of the brain is well developed and hearing is acute. The brains of earlier artiodactyls, such as the extinct entelodonts, were smaller than those of later forms. There are often scent glands on the head and body.

SPECIALIZATIONS OF THE HEAD

The skulls of pigs and peccaries lack a complete bony bar behind the eye (postorbital bar) as in most suiform artiodactyls and the early camels. The hippopotamuses, most camels, all ruminants, and two fossil suiform groups (entelodonts and oreodonts) have a complete postorbital bar. Any surface exposure of the periotic bone (bone around the ear) on the skull is called the mastoid, and skulls without such a surface exposure are described as being amastoid. Amastoid skulls are found in most suiform groups (including entelodonts, anthracotheres, and all living suiform groups). Mastoid skulls occur in some early suiform groups, oreodonts, and all remaining artiodactyls that have lived since the end of the Eocene Epoch (about 33.9 million years ago). Hippopotamuses have many modifications for aquatic life—large lungs, eyes and nostrils on top of the head, nostrils that can be closed by muscular control, and small ears. They can remain submerged for at least five minutes.

HORNS AND ANTLERS

Pigs, peccaries, hippopotamuses, camels, and chevrotains have no horns or antlers. In the early Miocene, Old World ruminants related to giraffes and deer first developed such appendages. Most deer have antlers, defined as solid, bony, branched outgrowths of the frontal bones, present only in the males (but also in female reindeer) and

Moose (Alces alces) with fully developed antlers. Tom & Pat Leeson— The National Audubon Society Collection/Photo Researchers

HORNS, ANTLERS, OR NEITHER?

In zoology, horn and antlers are the pair of hard processes that grow from the upper portion of the head of many hoofed mammals. In common speech, the term *horn* is loosely applied to antlers and to similar structures present on certain lizards, birds, dinosaurs, and insects, but true horns—simple unbranched structures that are never shed—are found only in cattle, sheep, goats, and antelopes. Horn consists of a core of bone surrounded by a layer of horn (keratin) that is in turn covered by keratinized epidermis.

The antlers of deer are not horns. Antlers are composed entirely of bone, though they bear a velvety epidermal covering during the growth period. They are shed yearly and become increasingly branched with age. The "horn" of a rhinoceros, meanwhile, is actually neither a horn nor an antler: it is simply an extremely effective offensive instrument composed of fused, heavily keratinized hairlike epidermis. In any case, both horns and antlers serve as weapons of defense against predators and of offense in battles between males for breeding access to females.

shed seasonally. They are not covered by a horny sheath but, during a growth period of about four months, have a fine-haired skin or "velvet." The antlers have two basic branches, the anterior or brow tine, and the posterior branch or beam. The brow tine is unbranched, except in Pére David's deer, in which both it and the beam are branched, the brow tine forming the dominant part of the antler. Antlers are specialized sex characters used for fighting by males in the rutting season and to scrape or slash at trees and bushes for territorial marking.

A study of the chital deer showed that antlers increase in size up to the seventh year, remain at a constant size until the ninth year, then decline. The horn of bovids consists of a hollow, unbranched horny sheath (formed of modified skin like fingernails and toenails) that fits over a bony core. Horns are often present on both sexes. If such a horn is accidentally lost, it is not regenerated. This is unlike the situation in deer, in which normal shedding is followed by regrowth. In the giraffe, but not in the okapi, horn growth is mainly from the parietal bone. The pronghorn has horns in both sexes. The sheaths are shed each year after the breeding season, and new ones develop under the old ones. The sheath is two pronged, but the underlying bony core is unbranched.

TEETH

There is a complete set of teeth in early artiodactyls and in modern pigs of the genus *Sus*, consisting on each side of three upper and lower incisors, an upper and lower canine, four upper and lower premolars, and three upper and lower molars. There has been a tendency toward reduction of the front teeth and development of a gap (diastema) between them and the back teeth. The premolars tend not to molarize, and the first premolar often disappears. Early forms had five-cusped upper molars, but the fifth cusp (protoconule) disappeared early.

Members of the suborder Suiformes have the full complement of incisors and canines, except for peccaries, which lack the lateral pair of upper incisors. Hippopotamuses have continuously growing incisors and canines, the lower canines being very large.

The canines of pigs grow continuously. In this group the canines are weapons for offense and defense, the sharp cutting edges of the lower canines being maintained by wear against the uppers. Young camels retain the full complement of front teeth, with three incisors and one canine in the upper and lower jaws. The upper incisors are extremely small. In the upper jaw of the adult only the rear incisor and canine are present. The vicuña has continuously growing lower incisors.

Pig molars are low crowned (except those of the warthog) and have many cusps, whereas those of peccaries are more simple. Peccaries have one less premolar than pigs, and camels also have reduced premolars. Chevrotains have rather flattened lower premolars but have incipiently selenodont molars (i.e., in which the cusps are drawn out into longitudinal crescents). Premolars of ruminants are wider, and the molars definitely selenodont. In many bovids and the pronghorn, but not in giraffes or deer, the molars are markedly high crowned.

LIMB ADAPTATIONS

Adaptations for fast running reach an extreme in advanced artiodactyls living in open country. In addition to the increased rotation of the astragalus, which increases the propulsive thrust at the ankle and enables a quicker recovery at the end of a stride before starting the next one, there are other features that help to increase the speed of striding. The legs of most camels and ruminants have lengthened, especially in the lower parts. The number of toes, or digits, in the feet is reduced from the original mammalian five, and ruminants walk on the tips of their toes. The muscles are inserted high on the legs. Only tendons pass lower, so that a large mass is not concentrated near the tip of the limb, where its inertia would restrict speed of movement. Muscle contraction is fast. The movement of each leg is almost limited to a fore-and-aft plane. Emphasis on the fore-and-aft articulations between the limb bones is especially pronounced in many bovids, the alternating bones in the wrist (carpus) and ankle (tarsus) taking the strain of impact on uneven ground.

Pigs have four toes on each foot, but only two of them touch the ground. Their limbs are short and not very advanced. Peccaries have lost the outer accessory hind hoof in the back leg. All four toes of each foot of hippopotamuses touch the ground, and the terminal phalanges have nail-like hoofs. The toe bones of camels are completely enclosed in hardened, horny hoofs, and lateral toes spread across the broad pad which aids in walking on desert sands. Chevrotains have four hoofed toes on each foot. Deer often retain the first and second phalanges (sections) of their lateral toes, but all bovids have lost the bones of their lateral toes.

The fibula bone in the back leg and the ulna in the front leg have been reduced in different artiodactyl lineages. Both are still complete in pigs and hippopotamuses, although the fibula is slender. In most other artiodactyls, the lower end of the fibula has survived, and the upper end is occasionally found, but always less noticeably. In camels the ulna has fused with the radius. Pigs, hippopotamuses, and camels have separate navicular and cuboid bones in the ankle, and magnum and trapezoid bones in the wrist. Other artiodactyls have a fused naviculo-cuboid and magnum-trapezoid. In chevrotains and some deer, the adjacent ectocuneiform is sometimes joined with the naviculo-cuboid.

The artiodactyl method of limb support through the third and fourth toes, with the attendant lengthening of lower limb bones, has frequently led to a fusion of the two principal metacarpal and metatarsal (midfoot) bones in the forelegs and hindlegs, respectively, forming cannon bones. The nearest approach to a cannon bone in the living Suiformes is the proximal fusion (i.e., at the upper ends) of the two central metatarsals in peccaries. Camels have front and rear cannon bones, but the fusion does not extend right to the bottom, the lower articular surfaces being less pulley-like than in ruminants. There is a hind cannon bone in all chevrotains and, in addition, a front one in Asiatic species (*Tragulus*). All other living artiodactyls have front and rear cannon bones. Lateral metatarsals and metacarpals survive in chevrotains; splints of lateral metacarpals often survive in bovids; and either upper or lower splints of metacarpals in deer.

SKIN MODIFICATIONS

Pigs are covered with rather sparse, coarse hairs, and peccaries with a denser coat of coarse hairs. Except for those of the warthog and the babirusa (*Babyrousa babyrussa*), piglets have longitudinal stripes or flecks. Hippopotamuses are naked. Tragulids have light-coloured flecks and stripes in their fur. The coats of camelids and deer are much thicker in species living toward the polar regions, at great heights, or in deserts, but are not noted for striking colours or patterns. Many young deer and the adults of a few species have pale flecks and stripes, and some South American deer have reddish fur. Antelopes have a wider range of coat colours, and some are strikingly marked (e.g., the oryxes, bontebok, and blesbok of southern Africa).

SCENT GLANDS

External glands occur in various places on artiodactyls. Preorbital glands, immediately in front of the eyes, are present in the giant forest hog (*Hylochoerus meinertzhageni*), in all cervids except the roe deer, and, among the bovids, in duikers, many neotragines, gazelles and their allies, and the hartebeest group. These glands are apparently required in small forest forms and have disappeared in many, but not all, open-country forms. In some, the glands are definitely connected with territorial marking. A firm object is marked by rubbing, soft vegetation by swinging the head gently from side to side. Foot, or pedal, glands are present in the African bush pig (*Potamochoerus porcus*), camels, tragulids, the pronghorn, some bovids, and on the back legs only of most American deer.

Inguinal (belly) glands are found in bovids, there being two in sheep, saiga, chiru, gazelles, duikers, and blackbuck, and four in members of the tribes Reduncini and Tragelaphini. Carpal (wrist) glands are present in some pigs, some gazelles and allies, and the oribi (*Ourebia ourebi*). Glands in other positions are rather less frequent, but postcornual ones (behind the horns) occur in the mountain goat, the pronghorn, and the chamois (*Rupicapra rupicapra*), supraorbital ones in muntjacs (several species of *Muntiacus*). There are jaw glands in the pronghorn; neck glands in camels; dorsal glands on the back of peccaries, pronghorn, and springbok; and preputial glands (in front of the genital region) in several pigs, grysbok (*Raphicerus melanotis*), and the musk deer. Tail glands are found in musk deer, pronghorn, and goats; tarsal glands in pronghorn and American deer; and metatarsal glands in camels, some deer, and the impala. Pronghorn, blackbuck, gazelles, and oribi are thus particularly well equipped with glands. The use of such glands, apart from the use of preorbital glands in some species for territorial marking, is a matter for conjecture. Chital deer, when alarmed, thump the ground several times with their hind feet, which possess glands; the scent remaining on the ground may function as a danger signal. In general, mammals often mark with their glands when they are threatening other individuals of their own species.

DIGESTIVE SYSTEM

The higher artiodactyls feed only on plant matter, which consists largely of cellulose and other carbohydrates and water. This necessitates adaptations of the structure and functioning of the stomach and intestines. Even pigs have enlarged stomachs—they have a pouch near the cardiac orifice (the upper opening) of the stomach—and in peccaries the stomach is more complicated. In hippopotamuses the stomach is divided into four compartments, and micro-organisms ferment food as part of the digestive process. Unlike pigs, hippopotamuses have lost the cecum (a blind pouch) further on in the gut.

In the most advanced ruminants, the much enlarged stomach consists of four parts. These include the large rumen (or paunch), the reticulum, the omasum (psalterium or manyplies)—which are all believed to be derived from the esophagus—and the abomasum (or reed), which corresponds to the stomach of other mammals. The omasum is almost absent in chevrotains. Camels have a three-chambered stomach, lacking the separation of omasum and abomasum, and the rumen and reticulum are equipped with glandular pockets separated by muscular walls having sphincters (valves) and glands. The esophagus opens into the rumen, not into the area between rumen and reticulum. These and other differences suggest that camels evolved the ruminating habit independently of the true ruminants. The total stomach of the domestic ox (*Bos taurus*) occupies nearly three-quarters of the abdominal cavity, and, even in medium-sized cattle, the rumen alone can have a capacity of 95 to 285 litres (25 to 75 gallons), having undergone a tremendous growth in early life, with the changeover from a milk diet.

Food taken into the rumen is later regurgitated into the mouth and completely masticated, then swallowed

RUMINANT

A ruminant is any mammal of the suborder Ruminantia (order Artiodactyla), which includes the pronghorns, giraffes, okapis, deer, chevrotains, cattle, antelopes, sheep, and goats. Most ruminants have four-chambered stomachs and a two-toed foot. The upper incisors are reduced or sometimes absent. Camels and chevrotains, however, have a three-chambered stomach. Ruminants eat quickly, storing masses of grass or foliage in the first chamber of the stomach, the rumen, where it softens. They later regurgitate this material, called cud, and chew it again to further break down its cellulose content, which is difficult to digest. The chewed cud goes directly to the other chambers of the stomach (the reticulum, omasum, and abomasum), where it is further digested with the aid of various essential microorganisms that live in the stomach.

Giraffes (Giraffa camelopardalis). © Digital Vision/Getty Images

again and passed to the reticulum, omasum, and aboma-sum. The regurgitation and chewing in the mouth is called rumination.

In the rumen many different species of minute proto-zoans (animals) and bacteria live without free oxygen. The digestion of the cellulose of plant cell walls is the main function of the fauna and flora in the rumen, because mammalian digestive juices are incapable of digesting cel-lulose. The contents of the plant cells are thus released for digestion. Large volumes of saliva are secreted into the rumen to help digestion. Soluble products of micro-bial action, mainly fatty acids, are absorbed through the rumen wall. In the omasum, some fatty acids and 60–70 percent of the water are absorbed. Gastric juice contain-ing hydrochloric acid is secreted in the abomasum, as in an ordinary mammalian stomach.

In the rumen any ingested protein is degraded into fatty acids and ammonia. The ammonia and other simple nitrogen-containing substances are used by the micro-organisms for their own cell-protein synthesis. These organisms are ultimately digested in the abomasum and small intestine, thus providing the ruminant with protein.

Many artiodactyls are adapted to living in condi-tions of water shortage. The best known and one of the most spectacular examples of this is the camel. Its body temperature can fluctuate according to the outside tem-perature, thus minimizing water loss through sweating. The camel excretes rather dry dung and a concentrated urine (i.e., high in urea and low in water) and is not seri-ously weakened by as much as a 25 percent dehydration in its body, because water is not withdrawn from the bloodstream and the continuing circulation avoids any buildup of excessive internal temperatures. The thick coat hinders the inward transference of heat from the environment (the temperature of which may often exceed the animal's body temperature). A thirsty camel can take in water quite rapidly. Oryxes and gazelles are antelopes noted for needing little water, the dorcas gazelle (*Gazella dorcas*) in the Sudan depending on leaves of *Acacia* bushes for its water. The zebu (a form of domesticated cattle) needs less water than most temperate climate breeds.

REPRODUCTIVE SPECIALIZATIONS

The testes of male artiodactyls descend outside the body cavity but may regress into the abdomen in the nonbreeding season. Female pigs have many teats, but ruminants have only two to four (although domestic cattle occasionally have as many as six). Among the bovids, the alcelaphines (hartebeests, wildebeests, and relatives), gazelles, and some caprines (sheep, goats, and relatives) have two, the rest have four.

The unborn mammal within its mother breathes, feeds, and excretes through an organ called the placenta, which is connected with the tissues of the mother's uterus (womb) wall. Hippopotamuses and pigs have an epitheliochorial placenta, a layer of fetal tissue merely pressed close against the uterus wall, but camels and ruminants possess a syndesmochorial placenta, in which the epithelium of the maternal tissues is eroded to facilitate intercommunication. This is an advance over the epitheliochorial placenta, but the artiodactyls are not particularly advanced, when compared with other mammals, in which there may be still closer association of maternal and fetal blood vessels (endothelial and hemochorial placentas). Even in many syndesmochorial placentas the uterus lining may be wholly or partly restored before the end of pregnancy. Although there is no erosion of maternal tissues in the epitheliochorial placenta, the capillaries beneath the fetal and maternal surface layers may pass just beneath the surface layers, making them thin. The actual fingerlike processes (villi), through which the placenta contacts the uterus, are evenly distributed ("diffuse" placentas) in hippopotamuses, pigs, camels, and tragulids. In higher artiodactyls they are in pockets or groups called cotyledons ("cotyledonary" placentas). It is interesting that there are few of these cotyledons in deer—for instance only five in Père David's deer—but many in giraffes and bovids (up to 160 or 180 in giraffes and goats). The musk deer (*Moschus moschiferus*) is exceptional among deer in retaining a diffuse placenta.

CHAPTER 2
DEER

A deer is any of 43 species of hoofed ruminants that make up the family Cervidae in the order Artiodactyla. Deer are notable for having two large and two small hooves on each foot and also for having antlers in the males of most species and in the females of one species. Deer are native to all continents except Australia and Antarctica, and many species have been widely introduced beyond their original habitats as game animals. One species, the reindeer (also known as the caribou), has been domesticated. Some swamp and island species are endangered, but most continental species are flourishing under protection and good management. Deer, when granted some protection, readily exploit human-made disturbances caused by agriculture, forestry, and urbanization. White-tailed deer, normally a cherished North American game animal, have even become pests in suburbs and cities in the United States and Canada.

The word *deer* has been applied at times to species that are not cervids, such as the musk deer (*Moschus*) and the chevrotain, or mouse deer (*Tragulus*). However, the former is now placed in a separate family (Moschidae), while chevrotains are actually primitive ruminants of the family Tragulidae. With these exclusions, Cervidae becomes the deer family, a consistent, natural grouping of species.

MORPHOLOGY AND BEHAVIOUR

In all but one species of deer, males carry antlers; in the reindeer (*Rangifer tarandus*), both sexes carry antlers. The single antlerless form, the Chinese water deer (*Hydropotes inermis*), reflects an earlier pre-antler condition, as is shown by the fossil record. In this primitive condition males have long, sharp upper canines, called tusks, that are used for slashing and stabbing in territorial contests. Some species carry both antlers and tusks and show a progression of increased antler size and complexity with decreased size and functional structure of the tusks. (Musk deer resemble primitive deer in that males are armed with tusks.)

Male roe deer (Capreolus capreolus) *in velvet.* Hans Reinhard/Bruce Coleman Ltd.

Deer have several other distinguishing characteristics. All deer lack the gall bladder. Females have four teats. Deer may have scent glands on their legs (metatarsal, tarsal, and pedal glands), but they do not have rectal, vulval, or preputal glands.

Deer are specialized herbivores, as is reflected in their large and anatomically complex digestive organs, their mobile lips, and the size and complexity of their teeth. However, deer rely little on coarse-fibred grasses, and they have not evolved grazing specializations comparable to those found in bovids. Instead, they are highly selective feeders on young grasses, herbs, lichens, foliage, buds, aquatic plants, woody shoots, fruit, and natural ensilage — that is, plant food characterized by low fibre but high protein content, toxicity, and digestibility.

The bias of deer toward high-quality food has its origin in the exceptionally high demands of antler growth for minerals, protein, and energy. Antlers are "bone horns" that are grown and shed annually. The growing antlers are encased in "velvet," a highly vascularized, nerve-filled skin covered by short, soft hairs. The blood-engorged, growing antlers are warm to the touch and quite sensitive. Depending on the species, they take up to 150 days to grow, after which the velvet dies and is forcefully removed by rubbing the antlers against branches and small trees. Along with some blood residue, this imparts a brownish colour to the otherwise white antler bone. Antlers finish growing before the mating season and are used as weapons and shields in combat or as display organs in courtship. Normally shed after the mating season, antlers may be retained in some territorial tropical deer for more than a year. The relative demand for energy and nutrients declines with body size but increases exponentially for antler growth. Therefore, large-bodied species require more nutrients and energy to grow antlers than do small-bodied species. These requirements cannot be obtained from grasses but only from nutrient-rich dicotyledonous plants.

The requirement for nutrients and energy has critical repercussions on the ecology of deer. It confines deer to relatively productive habitats, excluding them from deserts, dry grasslands, and geologically old landscapes leached of nutrients. Moreover, it severely limits the abundance of Cervidae in mature, species-rich faunas in which many herbivore species compete for food. To meet their high nutrient demands, deer are specialized to exploit disturbed ecosystems. For instance, after a forest fire, an area normally passes through several ecological plant successions within a few decades before the original conditions are restored. Early plant successions normally contain an abundance of the type of plant food required by deer. Some disturbances, such as river flooding and the rise and fall of lake levels, occur annually and create local, perpetually immature, nutrient-rich ecosystems. Since disturbances such as wildfires, storm floods, avalanches, or wind-felled trees are unpredictable, deer have evolved great abilities to quickly find and colonize such transient habitats. For example, the severe ecological upheaval caused by the extreme climatic oscillations of the Ice Ages greatly favoured deer. Glaciers ground rock into highly fertile waterborne silt and wind-borne loess that refertilized landscapes and rejuvenated the soil. Extinctions swept away warm-climate competitors. From the tropics deer spread to colder and more seasonal landscapes, including the Alps and the Arctic. Like other families of large mammals that colonized extreme Ice Age environments, deer diversified and evolved into grotesque giants that had ornate coat patterns and large, bizarre antlers, which could grow only from nutrient-rich soils.

While deer tend to have broad, somewhat similar food habits, they are highly divergent in their antipredator

Elk (Cervus elaphus canadensis) *shedding velvet.* Wayne Lankinen/
Bruce Coleman Inc.

strategies. This divergence segregates species ecologically and thus minimizes potential food competition between species sharing the same space. A deer species that hides and, if discovered, departs in rapid jumps to hide again requires forests and thickets, while a highly specialized runner needs flat, unobstructed terrain to outrun predators. Specialized jumpers may choose to stay close to steep slopes and rugged terrain and thus avoid areas frequented by species that run and jump, while cliff climbers may exploit gradients and altitudes closed to others.

OLD AND NEW WORLD DEER

The family Cervidae divides into two fairly distinct groups, the Old World deer (subfamily Cervinae) and the New World deer (subfamily Capreolinae). This division reflects where the deer originally evolved, but now it is not a geographical distinction but instead derives from their different foot structures. In the Old World deer the second and fifth hand bones (metapodia) have almost completely disappeared except for proximal, terminal remnants. In the New World deer the remnants are distal.

OLD WORLD DEER

The Old World deer include the 11 species of tropical Asian muntjacs (genus *Muntiacus*), the most primitive deer. Males bear tusks and antlers on tall antler pedicles. The next evolutionary step is represented by tropical and subtropical deer that have a basic three-pronged antler plan. They include giants such as the sambar of India (*Cervus unicolor*); three species of large swamp deer of India and Southeast Asia, namely the barasingha (*C. duvaucelii*), Eld's deer (*C. eldii*), and the now-extinct Schomburgk's deer (*C. schomburgki*); the gregarious chital (*Axis axis*) of India and Sri Lanka and Timor deer (*C. timorensis*) of Indonesia; the small hog deer (*A. porcinus*) of India; and a plethora of small island species, including the Bawean deer (*A. kuhlii*) of Indonesia and the Calamian deer (*A. calamianensis*), Visayan deer (*C. alfredi*), and Philippine brown deer (*C. mariannus*), all three of the Philippines. In these species one sees the same basic "deer design" diversified into a large number of ecological niches.

Old World deer with a basic four-pronged antler structure occupy temperate zones. These include the sika (*C. nippon*) of Japan and the fallow deer (*Dama dama*) of Asia Minor. The sika stands at the base of a great radiation of species that led to the red deer (*C. elaphus*) and elk (*C. elaphus canadensis*), the great cold-adapted deer of Eurasia and North America sporting five- and six-pronged antlers. The fallow deer is the last survivor of a radiation of giant Pleistocene deer, the most spectacular of which was the Irish elk (*Megaloceros*), which weighed 600 kg (1,300 pounds) and whose antlers spread up to 4 metres (14 feet) in width. The white-lipped deer (*C. albirostris*) of the Tibetan Plateau and Père David's deer (*Elaphurus davidianus*) of the swamps along China's major rivers complete the category of Old World deer.

Barasinghas

The barasingha, also called the swamp deer, is a species of graceful deer (*Cervus duvauceli*) belonging to the family Cervidae that is found in open forests and grasslands of India and Nepal. The barasingha stands about 1.1 m (45 inches) at the shoulder. In summer, its coat is reddish or yellowish brown with white spots. In winter, its coat is heavier, particularly on the neck—brown with faint spots or none. The male of the species has long antlers that branch into a number of tines. Formerly more widespread, the barasingha is now found only in scattered areas and in national parks and reserves. It is listed in the *Red Data Book* as an endangered species.

CHINESE WATER DEER

The Chinese water deer (*Hydropotes inermis*) is a diminutive Asian deer of the family Cervidae, native to fertile river bottoms in Korea and the Yangtze River (Chang Jiang) valley in China. It is the only species of deer in which males lack antlers. Instead, they are armed with long, curved, and sharp upper canine teeth that protrude from the mouth. These tusks may exceed 5 cm (2 inches) in length. The water deer is also the only deer with inguinal glands.

Although water deer resemble extinct primitive deer in lacking antlers, they evolved from ancestors with antlers that were subsequently lost. Their morphology indicates that they are New World deer. Males stand about 50 cm (20 inches) tall at the shoulder and weigh up to 13 kg (29 pounds), and females weigh up to 11 kg (24 pounds). They have a rather uniformly coloured coat, yellowish brown above and yellowish white below. The tail is quite short, and there is no rump patch. Their coarse, thick coat and fur-covered ears are adaptations to cold, snowy winters.

Generally, water deer are encountered alone. To evade predators, they rely on hiding and on bursts of quick, rabbitlike, bounding flight. Observations of captive animals suggest that males use their tusks to defend territories. Preferring the lush vegetation that grows along river bottoms, water deer eat a surprisingly large amount of coarse-fibred grasses that serve as both food and cover.

The breeding season extends from early November to February, and the fawning season lasts from late April to June. Water deer give birth to several young at a time. The fawns weigh less than 1 kg (2 pounds) at birth. They hide quickly and remain out of sight.

CHEVROTAINS

The chevrotain, also called the mouse deer, is any of several species of small, delicately built hoofed mammals that make up the family Tragulidae. Found in the warmer parts of Asia and in parts of Africa, chevrotains are shy, solitary, evening- and night-active vegetarians. They stand about 30 cm (12 inches) at the shoulder and characteristically seem to walk on the hoof tips of their slender legs. The fur is reddish brown with spots and stripes of paler colour or white, while the underside is pale. The males have small, curved tusks protruding downward out of the mouth from the upper jaw.

The Asiatic chevrotains are placed in the genus *Tragulus*, which includes about three species found in forests from India to the Philippines. The water chevrotain (*Hyemoschus aquaticus*), larger than the Asiatic forms, is found in western equatorial Africa. It inhabits thick cover on the banks of rivers and, when disturbed, seeks escape in the water.

CHITALS

The chital (*Cervus axis,* sometimes *Axis axis*) is an Asiatic deer belonging to the family Cervidae. It lives in grasslands and forests in India and Sri Lanka in herds of up to one hundred or more. It stands 90–95 cm (35–37 inches) at the shoulder. Its spotted coat is reddish brown above and white below. The male chital has branching, usually three-tined antlers up to 100 cm (40 inches) long. The chital is also called the spotted deer or axis deer.

FALLOW DEER

The fallow deer (*Dama dama*) is a medium-sized deer of the family Cervidae that is frequently kept on estates, in parks, and in zoos. The common fallow deer (*D. dama dama*) is native to the eastern Mediterranean. A second, larger, more brightly coloured, short-antlered form, the Mesopotamian fallow deer (*D. dama mesopotamica*), is native to Iran. The common fallow deer has been introduced in many areas ever since the Neolithic Period (New Stone Age), and it now occurs wild in Europe and elsewhere and in captivity on deer farms around the world.

The common fallow deer stands about 90 cm (3 feet) at the shoulder. A buck generally weighs up to 100 kg (220 pounds) and the female 45 kg (100 pounds). It prefers open woods where it feeds mainly on herbs and foliage and sometimes on woody browse and grasses. Its coat is usually yellowish brown with white spots in summer and is more uniformly grayish brown in winter. Fallow deer flee from predators by using a form of stiff-legged jumping and running called stotting.

Fallow deer are the sole survivors of the Megacerines, a diverse deer lineage that was widespread and abundant early in the Ice Ages. (Their most famous member was the extinct Irish elk.) Fallow bucks carry flat antlers that are the largest among Old World deer and are the largest relative to their body size. The antlers (about 60 cm [2 feet] long) are broad, are flattened at the ends, and have a number of short tines. The fallow buck is the only Old World deer with flat antlers.

The rutting buck waves its antlers conspicuously toward the female that it follows in courtship, and it vocalizes loudly with each dip of the antlers. The buck's conspicuous Adam's apple slides up and down the throat with each bark. Rutting bucks form small breeding territories on female ranges and may unite these territories into conspicuous territory clusters called leks. Dominant males tend to use the scent of their urine to attract females during the mating season. The end of the bucks' penis sheath becomes swollen, which straightens a circle of urine-stained hair. Although bucks scrape the soil with their hooves and urinate into these scrapes, as many Old

World deer do, they do not roll or rub their bodies in the urine-soaked earth. Females trying to leave a buck's territory may be blocked by the buck, who moves with exaggerated, dancelike steps. If this conspicuous behaviour is ignored by the female, the buck may attack the female and drive her back. The rut peaks in October. A single fawn is born after about 235 days gestation. The females and young live in groups, while the males remain apart except in the breeding season.

Mesopotamian fallow deer live along rivers that traverse deserts. Few Mesopotamian fallow deer remain in the wild state, and they are extremely endangered.

MUNTJACS

Muntjacs, also called barking deer, are about seven species of small- to medium-sized Asiatic deer that make up the genus *Muntiacus* in the family Cervidae. Called barking deer because of their cry, muntjacs are solitary and nocturnal, and they usually live in areas of thick vegetation. They are native to India, Southeast Asia, and southern China, and some have become established in parts of England and France. Fea's muntjac (*M. feae*), of Myanmar (Burma) and Thailand, is an endangered species.

Most species of muntjacs stand 40–65 cm (15–25 inches) high at the shoulder and weigh 15–35 kg (33–77 pounds). Depending on the species, they range from grayish brown or reddish to dark brown. Males have tusklike upper canine teeth that project from the mouth and can be used to inflict severe injuries. The short antlers have one branch and are borne on long bases from which bony ridges extend onto the face (hence another common name, rib-faced deer). Females have small knobs in place of antlers.

In the 1990s two previously unknown species of muntjacs were discovered. One was found in the Vu Quang

*Chinese muntjac (*Muntiacus reevesi*)*. Kenneth W. Fink/Root Resources

Nature Reserve of northern Vietnam in 1994. It was named the giant, or large-antlered, muntjac (*M. vuquangensis*) because it appears to be larger than other muntjacs, with an estimated weight of 40–50 kg (88–110 pounds). The second species, which has the distinction of being the smallest deer in the world, was discovered near the town of Putao in

MUSK DEER

The musk deer (species *Moschus moschiferus*) is a small, compact, solitary, shy deerlike mammal that lives in mountainous regions from Siberia to the Himalayas. Grayish brown, with long, coarse, brittle hair, the musk deer stands 50–60 cm (20–24 inches) at the shoulder, slightly higher at the rump. It has large ears and a very short tail. Unlike true deer, musk deer have a gall bladder, and neither sex bears antlers. Instead, the male has long upper canine teeth that project downward from the mouth as tusks. Because of these differences, musk deer are frequently classified in their own family, Moschidae, separate from the deer family, Cervidae.

The male musk deer also has a musk-producing organ, the musk pod, on its abdomen. The musk from this organ is valued for use in perfumes and soaps. Musk deer are raised commercially in China specifically for the valuable musk.

northern Myanmar in 1999. Named the miniature muntjac (*M. putaoensis*), or leaf deer, it weighs only 11 kg (about 24 pounds). Although *M. putaoensis* was catalogued on the basis of one specimen, others have been found in the rainforests of Arunachal Pradesh in far northeastern India.

Père David's Deer

A large, rare Asian deer in the family Cervidae, Père David's deer (*Elaphurus davidianus*) is unknown in nature within historical times. Presumably native to northern China, it is now found only in zoos, private animal collections, and game reserves.

The deer is about 1.1 metres (43 inches) tall at the shoulder and is characterized by heavy legs, broad hooves, relatively small ears, and a long, bushy tail. The coat is reddish brown in summer and uniformly grayish brown in winter. The male has long antlers that fork shortly above the base, the front prong branching once and the rear prong extending backward, unbranched.

The only known population of this deer in the 19th century was the herd kept for the emperor of China in a game park near Beijing. Observations of the deer were made in 1865 by a French missionary, Armand David, and specimens were classified the following year by the French naturalist Henri Milne-Edwards. From 1869 to 1890 several Père David's deer were brought to European zoos. Most of the Chinese herd died in a flood in 1895, and the remaining deer were killed during the Boxer Rebellion (1900). A breeding population was then established at Woburn Abbey in England under the care of the duke of Bedford. The deer bred well in captivity and now survive in zoos and game parks around the world. For example, 20 animals were reintroduced to China in 1985, and after some two decades the population had grown to two thousand.

RED DEER

The red deer (*Cervus elaphus*) is a well-known deer that is native to Europe, Asia, and northwestern Africa and has been introduced into New Zealand. It has long been hunted both for sport and food. Found primarily in woodlands, the red deer lives in sexually segregated herds except during the breeding season, when the males (harts) fight for harems of females (hinds). A large animal, it stands about 1.2 m (4 feet) at the shoulder. Its coat is reddish brown, darkening to grayish brown in winter, with lighter underparts and a light rump. The hart has long, regularly branched antlers bearing a total of 10 or more tines. An animal with 12 tines is known as a "Royal," one with 14 tines is a "Wilson." The species *C. elaphus* includes a number of subspecies, one of which is the North American elk (*C. e. canadensis*).

REINDEER

Called caribou in North America, reindeer (*Rangifer tarandus*) are a species of deer (family Cervidae) found in the

Arctic tundra and adjacent boreal forests of Greenland, Scandinavia, Russia, Alaska, and Canada. Reindeer have been domesticated in Europe. There are two varieties, or ecotypes: tundra reindeer and forest (or woodland) reindeer. Tundra reindeer migrate between tundra and forest in huge herds numbering up to half a million in an annual cycle covering as much as 5,000 km (3,000 miles). Forest reindeer are much less numerous.

Large males can stand more than 1.2 metres (3.9 feet) tall at the shoulder and exceed 250 kg (550 pounds) in weight, whereas females are slightly smaller. Reindeer have deeply cloven hoofs so the feet can spread on snow or soft ground. They are also good swimmers. Colour varies from whitish in winter to brown in summer. Heavy guard hairs are hollow, which increases the coat's insulating properties. Reindeer are only deer species in which females also have antlers. Antlers with up to 44 points can grow to 1.4 metres (4.6 feet) long in males.

Reindeer mature as yearlings if their nutrition is good, though males cannot compete for females until their fourth autumn, when their antlers and body mass (which are correlated) have grown sufficiently large. The rut occurs in October and lasts only 11 days. Tundra males, aggregated with thousands of females for the fall migration, assess other males' antler size visually and thus generally avoid serious fights. Conversely, forest reindeer defend discrete harems and fight harder. In both varieties a single calf is born in May or June after a gestation of seven and a half months. The calf grows rapidly on its mother's milk, which is richer than that of any other ungulate. After one month it can eat fresh plant growth, and by three months it can survive if the mother dies, but normally weaning takes place at five to six months. Half of all calves born may be killed by wolves, bears, and lynx. Longevity is about 15 years in the wild, 20 in captivity.

Eurasian and American forest reindeer live in family groups of 6 to 13, with seasonal ranges of 500 square km (190 square miles) or less. Tundra reindeer spend winter dispersed in forests but aggregate in spring to migrate onto the tundra. In fall they mass again to return to the forest. Summer food includes grass, sedges, green leaves of shrubs and new growth of larch, willow, and birch; mushrooms are sought in late summer. In winter, metabolism slows, and reindeer rely on high-carbohydrate lichens called reindeer moss, which they reach by digging craters in the snow. The calf follows its mother and shares this food. The reindeer survive on this low-protein diet by recycling urea (normally a waste product) within the digestive system and making use of its nitrogen. Females keep their antlers all winter, which enables them to defend feeding craters from each other as well as males, which shed their antlers soon after the rut.

There are about 3.5 million caribou in North America and perhaps 1 million wild reindeer in Eurasia, mostly in Russia. Nearly 3 million domestic reindeer live in northern Europe. Traditional herders such as the Sami (Lapps) of Scandinavia and Russia find them quite valuable. They exploit reindeer as pack and draft animals and for meat, milk, and hides and carve the antlers into tools and totems. The herdsmen use boats to direct herds to offshore islands in summer. In the forests of the Da Hinggan region of China, the Evenk people use reindeer as pack animals and as mounts.

Of the nine subspecies recognized, two are forest ecotypes, one living in North America and the other in Eurasia. Fossil evidence from Alaska indicates that they evolved during the late Pliocene Epoch (3.6 million to 2.6 million years ago). During the last glaciation more than 11,700 years ago, they were hunted by the Clovis people of New Mexico and by many early Stone Age tribes in southern Europe.

Sambars

The sambar (*Cervus unicolor*) is a widely distributed deer found from India and Nepal eastward through Southeast Asia. The sambar live in forests, alone or in small groups. A large, relatively long-tailed deer, it stands 1.2–1.4 m (47–55 inches) at the shoulder. The coat forms a ruff around its neck and is an unspotted, dark brown in colour. The male sambar bears long, three-tined antlers. Several subspecies of sambar are recognized, among them the large Indian sambar (*C. u. niger*) and the smaller Malayan sambar (*C. u. equinus*).

Sikas

The sika (*Cervus nippon*) is a small, forest-dwelling deer of the family Cervidae that is native to China, Korea, and Japan, where it was long considered sacred. (*Sika* means "deer" in Japanese.) It is farmed in China for its antlers, which are used in traditional medicine.

Mature males of the smallest forms, the southern sikas, stand 80–86 cm (31–34 inches) at the shoulder and weigh about 80 kg (180 pounds). Males of the largest forms, the northern sikas, such as Dybowski's sika (*C. nippon hortulorum*), stand approximately 110 cm (40 inches) at the shoulder and weigh 110 kg (240 pounds). Females weigh about 60 percent as much as males. Their coats are reddish brown and spotted in summer and dark brown and sometimes without spots in winter. There is considerable geographic variation in size, coat characteristics, and colour. All have fairly long tails and a white rump patch rimmed by long white hair that can be flared wide in alarm. All mature stags grow a neck ruff in fall. The four-tined antlers of older stags may exceed 85 cm (33 inches) in length in the north and 70 cm (28 inches) in the south.

Males form territories during the mating season in September and October and advertise their position and social status with shrill rutting calls. Although more primitive than the closely related red deer and elk, sikas are quite similar in social behaviour to the elk. Males of both species advertise vocally during the rut, spray their bodies with urine in a similar manner, dig similar rutting pits, and court females in a similar fashion. Elk, however, are much more showy. Sikas are more sensitive to the cold than the red deer, which lives at higher latitudes and altitudes. Sikas are short-winded and run to hide in thickets, to which they are closely bound, despite being quite gregarious. Sikas compete aggressively for food and have broad eating habits. (They can subsist on fairly fibrous forages.) With their only ecological requirements being cover, plenty of forest edge, and rainy, short winters, sikas can occupy diverse habitats over a great range of altitudes and latitudes. Sikas are excellent swimmers. They are hardy and quite disease-resistant.

A review of sika taxonomy has revealed that many descriptions of these animals were based on skins bought in markets or on specimens from captive populations in China. In addition, domesticated sikas are widely distributed, which has led in mainland Asia to the blurring of geographic differences between subspecies. In Japan subspecific differences may be more meaningful, but even there sikas have been widely transplanted. Sikas have been introduced in many localities outside their native ranges, primarily in Europe, New Zealand, North America, and Europe, where they have hybridized with red deer.

NEW WORLD DEER

The New World deer came from a separate radiation that colonized North and South America and Eurasia. Among the grotesque giants that evolved in the Ice Age are the moose (*Alces alces*), the largest of all deer, standing 2 metres (7 feet) or more at the shoulder, and the reindeer, the most plains-adapted runner among deer with relatively large antlers. Also cold-adapted are the tiny Eurasian roe deer (*Capreolus* species) and the small, antlerless Chinese water deer of Korea and China. In the Americas the white-tailed deer (*Odocoileus virginianus*) colonized both continents. Its closest relative, the mule deer (*O. hemionus*), occupies western North America. Dwarf brocket deer (genus *Mazama*) are found southward from Mexico into Argentina. Two species of the tiniest deer, the pudu (genus *Pudu*), standing only 30 cm (12 inches) at the shoulder, live far apart in the central Andes and southern Chile, as do two species of the larger, rock-climbing Andean deer (genus *Hippocamelus*). The small pampas deer (*Ozotoceros bezoarticus*) and the

White-tailed deer fawn (Odocoileus virginianus), *four months old.* Encyclopædia Britannica, Inc.

red deer-sized marsh deer (*Blastocerus dichotomus*), both of South America, are endangered.

BROCKETS

Brockets are several species of small deer in the genus *Mazama*, family Cervidae, that are found from Mexico to South America. Timid browsers, brockets inhabit wooded areas and generally live alone or in pairs. There are about four species, among them the brown brocket (*M. gouazoubira*) and the red brocket (*M. americana*). Brockets are stout-bodied deer with arched backs and short tails, standing 43–69 cm (17–27 inches) high at the shoulder. The shade of the brown coat depends on the species. Males have short, unbranched antlers.

ELKS

The elk (*Cervus elaphus canadensis*), found in North America and in high mountains of Central Asia, is the largest and most advanced subspecies of red deer (*Cervus elaphus*). It is a member of the deer family, Cervidae. Recent genetic studies suggest that the "red deer" actually may be three species: the European red deer, the Tibetan–West Chinese red deer, and the elk.

The word *elk* is derived from the ancient Germanic root word meaning "stag" or "hart." In Europe, *elk* is the common name for the moose. In 16th-century Virginia the name was applied by English settlers to the native subspecies of the red deer, and that name also came into popular use in New England. An alternate name, wapiti ("white deer" in Shawnee), comes from the light-coloured coat of the bull elk. Although less ambiguous than *elk*, *wapiti* never became popular, and in North America today *elk* is the firmly established proper name. In Asia the elk, along with the red deer of Persia, is called by the Mongolian name *maral*.

Exceeded in size only by the moose, large male elk from Alberta average 380 kg (840 pounds) in early winter. Body mass varies considerably within and between populations and increases from south to north. Exceptional bulls exceed 500 kg (1,100 pounds) in weight, whereas bulls from southern California average about 110 kg (240 pounds). Compared with other red deer, female elk are more similar to bulls in external appearance and body mass. During winter all elk have well-developed, dark neck manes that contrast sharply with their tan or light brown body colour.

Elk are classic red deer in their biology. However, they are more highly adapted to life in open plains, grazing, and cold, long winters. They evolved as fast endurance runners that are very difficult to catch even with the best of horses, particularly in broken terrain. Nevertheless, they get their chief protection from predators by forming large groups.

Compared with European red deer, elk have longer gestation periods (255 days, versus 235 days in the European red deer), and the bulls retain their antlers longer (about 185 days, versus 150 or less in European red deer). In Asia elk are confined to cold grasslands found on the high plateaus of Outer Mongolia, southern Siberia, and the Altai and Tien Shan mountains, while more primitive red deer subspecies occupy the valley bottoms and upland forests. In North America, free of competing red deer, elk are found in diverse habitats from the Yukon to northern Mexico and from Vancouver Island to Pennsylvania. They thrive in coniferous rain forests along the Pacific coast, prairies, aspen parklands, sagebrush flats, eastern deciduous forests, the Rocky Mountains, and the once swampy valleys of California. Elk shun deserts, boreal forests, and tundra. Because of their wide distribution, elk from different regions in North America can differ considerably in size and antler growth. However, elk are remarkably

*Male elk (*Cervus elaphus canadensis*).* Alan Carey

homogeneous genetically throughout their range, even in their Asian populations.

While North American elk are uniform in coat markings and voice and thus cannot be differentiated by these features from some of their Asian counterparts, they are quite different from other subspecies of Asian elk, such as the Manchurian red deer (*C. elaphus xanthopygos*) and the small Alashan wapiti (*C. elaphus alashanicus*) of Inner Mongolia. These primitive elk have smaller bodies and antlers, less striking coat patterns, and a deeper voice than the North American elk. However, all male elk, American and Asian, have a high-pitched bugling call used during the rut. This call is a vocal adaptation designed to carry sound across long distances in open landscapes. On rare occasions, females bugle.

Elk are part of the old Siberian Ice Age fauna that crossed the Bering land bridge into Alaska. There they appeared along with caribou over one million years ago, but they were unable to establish themselves in the southern half of the continent, because of the presence of the native large fauna. Elk entered lower North America from Alaska, along with the grizzly bear, moose, and humans, only after the glaciers had retreated and most of America's old megafauna was extinct. Elk then spread into some of the empty ecological niches, and about 12,000 years ago their southward spread was halted by deserts.

The archaeological record suggests that elk became especially abundant after European diseases decimated Native American populations in the 16th century, thus greatly reducing human predation. Elk were valued by native peoples more for their hide and ceremonial value than for their meat. Although they were nearly exterminated by market hunting in the 19th century, elk have been widely reintroduced throughout North America and are now thriving.

Elk were introduced into New Zealand in 1909 in Fiordland, but they have been outcompeted by European red deer. Unlike the latter, the elk did not disperse, choosing to occupy higher elevations. They have also been introduced to Europe in the vain hope of creating larger antlered red deer. Although this effort failed and the elk went extinct, a parasite they brought along, the giant liver fluke (*Fascioloides magna*), has established itself in European deer and livestock.

Elk have been traditionally used on Asian deer farms dedicated to the production of velvet antlers, and this practice has spread globally. (Growing antlers are covered with velvet.) The velvet antlers are cut off bulls' heads and ultimately processed into folk medicines.

MOOSE

The moose (*Alces alces*) is the largest member of the deer family Cervidae. Moose are striking in their towering size, black colour, tall legs, pendulous muzzle, and dangling hairy dewlap (called a bell) and the immense, wide, flat antlers of old bulls. The name *moose* is common in North America derived from the word *moosh* ("stripper and eater of bark") in the Algonquian language of the Montagnais (Innu) Indians of Quebec, Can. In Europe, moose are called elk.

Moose inhabit the northern parts of North America and Eurasia. A European and west Siberian form and an American and east Siberian form can be distinguished by pelage and antler characteristics. The differences in regional body sizes reflect adjustment to local conditions and not the existence of genetically distinct subspecies. The largest moose specimens are found in Alaska and eastern Siberia where bulls weigh 600 kg (1,300 pounds) and stand 2 metres (7 feet) at the shoulder. The smallest moose are found in its southernmost populations in

Wyoming and Manchuria, where large bulls weigh 300–350 kg (660–770 pounds).

Moose primarily exploit plant communities of deciduous shrubs that have been disturbed by flooding, avalanches, or forest fires. They are avid visitors to mineral licks. In winter they may also avidly consume conifers such as fir and yew. In areas of particularly deep snow, moose may tramp a system of trails called a "moose yard." In summer they may also consume large amounts of aquatic vegetation. The large, mobile, sensitive muzzle appears to be a specialized feeding organ that allows moose to exploit the large stocks of submerged aquatic vegetation in shallow lakes and streams. Moose may dive and stay underwater for up to 50 seconds while feeding. Even calves are excellent swimmers.

Moose are bold and readily defend themselves against large carnivores. During calving season, moose cows face grizzly and black bears. In late winter when the snow is deep and moose cannot flee, they defend themselves against wolf packs. They choose hard, level ground with little snow for maneuverability, such as ridges blown free of snow or frozen lakes with a thin cover of snow. When hindered by deep snow, they back into dense conifers to protect their vulnerable inguinal region and lower haunches from attacks by wolves. They may then charge the wolves and attack them by slapping them with their front legs and kicking them with their hind legs. These blows are powerful enough to kill wolves.

Moose have killed humans. In Siberia, hunters armed with muzzle-loading guns feared wounded moose far more than they feared the large brown bear. With the thick skin on its head and neck and its dense skull, an attacking moose could not be readily stopped with a small, round rifle ball of soft lead.

A moose (Alces alces) browsing on deciduous willow (Salix) in winter. © Michael Giannechini—The National Audubon Society Collection/ Photo Researchers

Moose normally escape predators by trotting at high speed, which forces the pursuing smaller predators into expensive and tiring jumping but costs a moose relatively little energy. It readily comes to bay but on its terms: it chooses low water where wolves are hampered in their movements. Although moose are excellent swimmers, it does not choose deeper water, because northern wolves have relatively large paws and so are also excellent swimmers. Predation by wolves and bears removes the infirm but may also severely deplete healthy calves, despite the spirited defense of their mothers.

Moose mate in September so that the calves may be born in June to take advantage of spring vegetation. The antlers are shed of the blood-engorged skin called velvet in late August, and the bulls are in rut by the first week of September. Rutting bulls search widely for females, but the bulls may also attract females with the smell of their urine. They paw rutting pits with their forelegs, urinate into them, and splash the urine-soaked muck onto their hairy bells. Cows in turn may call to attract bulls. Actively rutting bulls appear to receive more than 50 punctures per mating season, but they are protected by a thick skin on the front and the neck. Rutting is expensive, as bulls lose virtually all of their body fat and their festering wounds must heal.

Because of their large body size, moose have a long gestation period of about 230 days. The young, commonly twins, are born tan in colour, which contrasts sharply with the dark colour of adults. They grow quickly but still require maternal protection against wolves in winter. They are driven off by their mother shortly before she gives birth again. The dispersed yearlings roam in search of new living space.

Young calf moose tame readily under human care and emerge as surprisingly intelligent, mischievous, but utterly loyal creatures. As mounts and beasts of burden, moose are superior to horses in muskeg and taiga. In the late 19th and early 20th centuries, moose became scarce owing to severe exploitation in unsettled times in Eurasia and to uncontrolled market hunting in North America. However, they responded readily to protection and management. Today moose are abundant in Eurasia and North America and are a cherished game animal. (The muzzle of the moose is considered a delicacy.) However, with the restoration of a predator fauna in North America, moose are again declining.

MULE DEER

The mule deer (*Odocoileus hemionus*) is a medium-sized, gregarious deer of western North America that derives its name from its large ears. Mule deer also have striking pelage markings, large antlers, and scent glands. Large bucks rarely exceed 95 kg (210 pounds), and does weigh about a third less. Mule deer belong to Capreolinae, the New World subfamily of the deer family, Cervidae. They are found from the Arctic Circle in the Yukon to northern Mexico. The smaller coast, or black-tailed, deer (*O. hemionus columbianus*) is found along the Pacific coast from Alaska to northern California. Although mule deer and black-tailed deer are the same species, the mule deer's mitochondrial DNA, which is passed down through the maternal line, is quite close to that of the white-tailed deer and not of the more primitive and ancestral black-tailed deer. Consequently, the mule deer is apparently a rather recent form that arose from hybridization of female white-tailed and male black-tailed deer.

Calm and inquisitive, these pretty deer readily seek out human habitations where predators are unlikely to venture. They are drawn to lush lawns, parks, and gardens and even readily integrate into city life. In the wild they

Mule deer buck (Odocoileus hemionus). Harry Engels—The National Audubon Society Collection/Photo Researchers

frequent forests, though they prefer open, rugged land-scapes. They flee with high jumps, leaping and landing on all four legs at once. Although this slows them down, it allows them to leave predators behind by quickly ascending steep slopes or jumping unpredictably over large obstacles. Their large, keen eyes and ears allow them to locate distant predators. Nevertheless, they are vulnerable to pack-hunting predators, such as wolves and coyotes.

Males and females sometimes form common herds in winter, but they segregate in spring. Mule deer are concentrate feeders; that is, they carefully select highly nutritious bits of forage. They may also consume partially rotted plants, as well as dry leaves, buds, fruit, flowers, sprouting grasses and herbs, the tips of some coniferous boughs, small twigs, and lichens that fall from trees. To foster body and antler growth, males seek out habitats rich in food even though these same habitats also attract predators. Females select secure habitats to save themselves and their vulnerable young.

Some populations undertake long migrations between winter and summer ranges. Mule deer bucks gather in fall and, irrespective of rank, frequently engage in friendly antler wrestling. Soon they join the females for the rut (early November to December). The courting male's face resembles that of a fawn, and he even bleats softly like a fawn. He detects estrus from the female's urine and may rush and gore a female that refuses to urinate. In each rutting season, males may be wounded over 30 times and females up to half a dozen times. Keeping rivals at bay, large males consort with one estrous female at a time. After the rut, males go into hiding to recover from exhaustion and injury. Births occur between April and September. Twins are common. The spotted fawns hide for over a month.

Mule deer populations have been restored since severe depletion by market hunting took place at the end of the 19th century. However, they are currently losing ground to the white-tailed deer (*Odocoileus virginianus*). White-tailed bucks breed with mule deer does and produce hybrids with damaged antipredator behaviour. Because such hybrids can neither run nor jump properly, they fail to fight off small predators and flee in a timely fashion when predators appear. Although elsewhere mule deer have declined because of forestry, drought, and growing predator populations, they have expanded in the Yukon.

ROE DEER

The roe deer, also called the roebuck, is a small, graceful Eurasian deer of the genus *Capreolus*, family Cervidae. There are two species of roe deer: the European, or western, roe deer (*Capreolus capreolus*) and the larger Siberian roe deer (*C. pygargus*). Despite their Old World distribution, roe deer are more closely related to New World deer than to Old World deer. They are well adapted to cold environments, and they range from northern Europe and Asia into the high mountains of Central Asia, and south to Spain.

The roe deer's coat is reddish brown in summer and grayish brown with a conspicuous white rump patch in winter. The male has short, usually three-tined antlers that are roughened and enlarged at the base, apparently to protect the skull against antler punctures. An almost tailless deer, the European roe deer stands 66–86 cm (26–34 inches) at the shoulder and rarely exceeds 30 kg (66 pounds) in weight. Siberian roebucks weigh about 50 kg (110 pounds).

Roe deer are adapted to the forest edge and are masters at exploiting the ecological opportunities caused by wildfires and floods. They also take advantage of human landscape disturbances and thrive when given a modicum of care and management. They are a popular game animal and are prized for their tasty venison. Roe deer are short-winded runners and expert hiders in thickets. When alarmed, the roe deer barks.

Roe deer have a very unusual reproduction biology, based on using the vegetation pulse of summer to pay directly for the high cost of rutting. Other northern deer, such as the red deer, use the summer's vegetation to store fat, which is used up later during the fall rutting period. The roe buck, however, foregoes costly fattening, forms a territory that overlaps the ranges of two or more females, and breeds these in late July or early August. For such a small-bodied deer, however, this poses a dilemma, because small deer have short gestation periods. If gestation commenced right after breeding, fawns would be born about 150 days later, in December, in the midst of winter. For fawns to survive and for females to support lactation, fawns must be born in late May, shortly after spring vegetation begins to grow. The roe deer solves this problem through delayed implantation, in which the fertilized egg, after forming a blastocyst, remains inactive in the uterus until the beginning of January. At that time the egg implants in the uterus and develops into a fawn, which is born in late May to early June, some 276–295 days after mating.

To breed in late summer, roe bucks become territorial in March, at which time they shed the velvet from their newly grown antlers and are ready to do battle. Consequently, roe bucks, unlike other deer, grow antlers in winter and not in summer. A small amount of fattening does occur in bucks just prior to becoming territorial and again before courting does. The buck concentrates on courting yearling females, apparently to bond them to his territory.

Roe deer have a high birth rate and often bear two (sometimes three) spotted fawns. Young roe deer are dispersed by adults, and yearlings look for living space on their own.

WHITE-TAILED DEER

White-tailed deer (*Odocoileus virginianus*), also called Virginia deer, are common American deer of the family Cervidae that cover a huge range from the Arctic Circle in western Canada to 18 degrees south of the Equator in Peru and Bolivia. The white-tailed deer gets its name from the long white hair on the underside of the tail and rump. During flight the hair is flared, and the tail is held aloft like a signaling flag. It belongs to the subfamily of New World deer. Although the white-tailed deer of North and South America are currently recognized as one species, genetically these deer are farther apart than are white-tailed and black-tailed deer in North America.

While this deer varies greatly in size, it changes little in its external appearance over its huge range. Its body and antlers are largest in cold temperate climates and on productive agricultural soils but are small in the tropics, in deserts, and on small islands. Large males can stand as high as 106 cm (42 inches) at the shoulder and can weigh up to 180 kg (400 pounds). The smallest variety, the Key deer of Florida, stands 76 cm (30 inches) at the shoulder and weighs 23 kg (50 pounds). The adult white-tailed deer has a bright reddish summer coat and a duller grayish brown winter coat with white underparts. The male has forward curved antlers that bear a number of unbranched tines.

The white-tailed deer is a specialist in exploiting disrupted forest ecosystems, but it is a poor competitor when faced with other species. For example, it has not held its own against European deer after its introduction to New Zealand and Europe. It has been locally outcompeted in North America by sika and chital.

The white-tailed deer predates the Ice Ages and is the oldest extant deer species. It became abundant only after the last glaciation when the indigenous Ice Age fauna of the Americas became extinct and competitive and predation pressures were lifted. Its high speed in running, its legendary skills at hiding, and its ability to move silently reflect severe pressure from extinct American Ice Age predators.

During the mating season in November and December, much of the courtship is carried on at a run as many males try to keep up with the speedy female. Mating is quick and unceremonious: the buck guards and mates with the female for a day before searching for another female in heat. After a gestation period of about 202 days, females become territorial before giving birth, often to twins.

Male white-tailed deer (Odocoileus virginianus). © Photos.com/ Jupiterimages Corporation

In the tropics reproduction may take place year-round. Mothers sometimes raise daughters to adulthood and then depart, leaving their home range to the daughters.

White-tailed deer may live apart from each other in summer but may form big herds in winter on open prairies or in forests. They trample down the snow in an area that is then known as a "deer yard." Food includes leaves, twigs, fruits, and nuts, as well as lichens and fungi. White-tailed deer readily turn to orchards and other cultivated vegetation when available. In urban areas these deer may become dangerous pests.

The white-tailed deer was formerly greatly reduced in its range and abundance by unrestricted hunting. By the mid-20th century, however, it had been restored to great abundance by game-management measures throughout North America. Today the white-tailed deer is a popular game animal. However, its overabundance where protected from predation and from adequate hunting has led to severe damage to forestry and agriculture, to high levels of collisions with cars and trucks and resulting injuries and fatalities among motorists, as well as to an upswing in dangerous transmissible diseases such as Lyme disease. The white-tailed deer carries parasites that have seriously depleted populations of woodland caribou, moose, and elk and have significantly affected livestock.

CHAPTER 3

ANTELOPES

An antelope is any of numerous Old World grazing and browsing hoofed mammals belonging to the family Bovidae (order Artiodactyla). Antelopes account for over two-thirds of the approximately 135 species of hollow-horned ruminants (cud chewers) in the family Bovidae, which also includes cattle, sheep, and goats. One antelope, the Indian blackbuck, bears the Latin name *Antilope cervicapra*. Nevertheless, *antelope* is not a taxonomic name but a catchall term for an astonishing variety of ruminating ungulates ranging in size from the diminutive royal antelope (2 kg [4 pounds]) to the giant eland (800 kg [1,800 pounds]). (The North American pronghorn antelope looks and acts much like a gazelle but belongs in a separate family, the Antilocapridae.) Africa, with some 71 species, is the continent of antelopes. Only 14 species inhabit the entire continent of Asia, and all but three of them are members of the gazelle tribe (Antilopini).

APPEARANCE AND BEHAVIOUR

As in all of Bovidae, all male antelopes have horns, which range from the short spikes of duikers to the corkscrew horns (more than 160 cm [63 inches] long) of the greater kudu. Two-thirds of female antelopes bear horns, and they are invariably thinner and usually shorter than those of the male. In gregarious species in which both sexes regularly associate in mixed herds, the horns are similarly shaped, and in female oryxes and elands they are often longer.

Antelopes have adapted to many different ecological niches and so vary in their size, shape, locomotion, diet,

Seven different kinds of antelopes: the gerenuk (Litocranius walleri), *the impala* (Aepyceros melampus), *Thomson's gazelle* (Gazella thomsonii), *the common eland* (Taurotragus oryx), *the saiga* (Saiga tatarica), *the suni* (Neotragus moschatus), *and the blackbuck* (Antilope cervicapra). Encyclopædia Britannica, Inc.

social organization, and antipredator strategy. Despite the diversity of adaptations, one important generalization can be made: there is a marked difference between antelopes of closed habitats and those of open habitats. The former (e.g., duikers, reedbucks, and bushbucks) are mostly small to medium-sized animals adapted for movement through undergrowth, with overdeveloped hindquarters, a rounded back, and short legs. This conformation is adapted to quick starts and a bounding, dodging run, which is how cover-dependent antelopes whose first line of defense is concealment try to escape predators that chance to find them. Their coloration is camouflaging. They are solitary, living alone or in mated pairs on home ranges defended as territories, and they are browsers of foliage rather than grazers of grass. By contrast, antelopes of open habitats are mostly medium to large grass eaters.

They are built for speed, having level backs with long, equally developed limbs (or with higher shoulders, as in the hartebeest tribe). Their coloration is revealing. They have a gregarious social organization and a mating system based on male territoriality (except in the kudu tribe).

ANTELOPE TYPES

Taxonomists assign antelopes to three subfamilies and 10 tribes that differ from one another as much as cattle (tribe Bovini) differ from sheep and goats (tribe Caprini). Yet antelopes are linked to both cattle and goats: the spiral-horned antelopes (tribe Tragelaphini, which includes the oxlike eland) are placed in the subfamily Bovinae together with cattle and the tribe Boselaphini, which includes the big nilgai and the little four-horned antelope. Although gazelles and their allies (including the blackbuck) are placed in a different subfamily (Antilopinae) from sheep and goats (Caprinae), several Asian bovids that look and behave like antelopes have been shown by DNA evidence to be caprines, notably the chiru, or Tibetan antelope (*Pantholops hodgsoni*), while three species—the Mongolian gazelle, the Tibetan gazelle, and Przewalski's gazelle—were placed in the genus *Procapra* for their caprine affinities.

IMPALAS (TRIBE AEPYCEROTINI)

Impalas (*Aepyceros melampus*) are swift-running antelopes, the most abundant ruminants in the savannas of eastern and southern Africa. Impalas are often seen in large breeding herds closely shepherded by a territorial male. The impala can be described as perfection in an antelope. It is both beautiful and athletic—a world-class high jumper. Having no close relatives, it is placed in its own tribe, Aepycerotini, of the family Bovidae.

Medium-sized with slender, evenly developed legs and a long neck, the impala stands 70–92 cm (28–36 inches) and weighs 40–76 kg (88–167 pounds). Males are about 20 percent heavier than females and have wide, lyrate horns 45–91 cm (18–36 inches) or longer, the largest antelope horns in East Africa. The sexes are coloured alike with a sleek, two-toned coat that is tan with a red-brown saddle. White markings include the eye line, the inside of the ears, a throat patch, the underside of the torso, and a bushy tail. Black markings include the crown between the ears, the ear tips, vertical stripes down the highs and tail, and prominent tufts on the back feet, which overlie scent glands of unknown function. The black-faced impala (*A. m. petersi*) of southwest Africa is a comparatively rare subspecies coveted by trophy hunters.

An "edge" species that prefers the ecotone between woodland and grassland, the impala is a mixed feeder that eats grass during the rainy season and switches to browse during the dry season. Despite habitat restrictions, its catholic diet makes the impala unusually adaptable, and it can even subsist in areas stripped of grass by livestock and located far from water.

The impala is a seasonal breeder that mates during the rains and births six months later, near the end of the dry season. During the rut, breeding males are highly vociferous: both territorial bulls and bachelors puff and grunt furiously as they run about flagging their white tails. The territorial proprietors try to keep bachelors separate from the herds of females and young. Large herds of up to 100 impalas enhance male sexual competition, and exhaustion causes rapid territorial turnovers. In southern Africa, territorial behaviour nearly ceases after the annual rut, though the maintenance of roadside dung middens attests to continuing space claims. Populations near the Equator have two mating and birth peaks, and males remain territorial the whole year. More sustained sexual competition could explain the bigger horns of East African impalas.

Young impalas hide in woodland or bush often for only a few days before joining a crèche of same-aged fawns that associate and socialize with one another more than with their own mothers. Large herds, tolerance of close packing by females, and tit-for-tat social grooming of both sexes and all ages distinguish the impala as one of the most gregarious antelopes. Where it is abundant, it is a preferred prey of carnivores that range in size from eagles (which prey on fawns) to lions, and its habit of feeding in bushed areas makes it unusually vulnerable to ambush and surprise. However, impalas compensate by being exceptionally vigilant, and they confuse attackers by running in all directions as they soar over bushes with jumps up to 3 metres (10 feet) high and 10 metres (33 feet) long.

TRAGELAPHINI: THE SPIRAL-HORNED ANTELOPE TRIBE

The tribe Tragelaphini, made up of antelopes with keeled, spiral horns, includes the eland (the largest of all antelopes) as well as such powerful animals as the bongo and kudu, among others.

BONGOS

Bongos (*Tragelaphus eurycerus*) are the largest, most colourful, and most sociable of the African forest antelopes, belonging to the spiral-horned antelope tribe, Tragelaphini, family Bovidae. The bongo is also the third heaviest antelope, after the related giant eland and common eland.

The bongo has short, sturdy legs and hindquarters that are higher and more developed than the forequarters. The bongo and eland are the only tragelaphines in which both sexes have horns. Male bongo horns are massive and make one tight spiral. The average length is 75 cm (30 inches; the maximum recorded length is 99 cm [39 inches]). Females have thinner and more parallel but equally long horns. Though short in stature (122–128 cm [48–50 inches] shoulder height), males weigh on average 300 kg (660 pounds) and up to 400 kg (880 pounds), whereas females weigh about 240 kg (530 pounds). The bright, glossy chestnut of the back and flanks turns a darker colour on the underside and legs. Males become darker with age. Indeed, male bongos in the Kenya highlands are nearly black. In both sexes, the reddish coat is vividly contrasted by white or yellow markings, which include 12 to 14 vertical stripes on the torso, bands on the edges of the huge, rounded ears, large chest and nose chevrons, cheek blotches, and banded legs. The bongo's striking coloration is actually concealing in the forest, where the markings serve to disrupt its outline. Bongos are primarily browsers, consuming the foliage of up to 80 different kinds of trees, bushes, forbs, and vines.

Two widely separated bongo subspecies exist in increasingly fragmented populations. The larger mountain bongo (*T. eurycerus isaaci*) is a relict of interglacial epochs when rainforest extended to the Indian Ocean; it occurs in pockets of protected mountain forest between 2,000 and 3,000 metres (7,000 and 10,000 feet) above sea level in the Kenya highlands. Mountain bongos frequent the bamboo and mountain heath zone in the dry season and then descend to the cloud forest, where they disperse, during the rains. Home ranges may exceed 100 square km (40 square miles). Herds of a dozen are considered large. They always include young calves and are trailed or accompanied by a bull during the mating season (October–January). Increasing human population, deforestation, poaching, ecological changes, disease, and predation by lions, hyenas, and leopards threaten the survival of the mountain bongo.

The lowland bongo (*T. eurycerus eurycerus*) inhabits lowland rainforests from western Africa and the Congo basin to southwestern Sudan. The lowland bongo's habitat could be more accurately described as a forest-savanna mosaic, as it depends on openings where sunlight penetrates to the forest floor. Two herds of 10–20 animals tracked in the Central African Republic's Dzanga-Ndoki National Park had home ranges of at least 49 and 19 square km (19 and 7 square miles). The focal points of these ranges were clearings around water holes and mineral licks created by elephants. By day the herds, composed of females and young, congregated in dense forest within a few kilometres of a lick. Before dusk they often moved directly to a clearing, where they spent hours eating clay soil, drinking clayish water, foraging on lush herbs and grass, and socializing. This and other studies suggest that bongos are much rarer than previously estimated, with a mean density in good habitat of only one animal per 4 square km (2 square miles). Adult males are usually solitary and, like other tragelaphine antelopes, nonterritorial. A single calf, born after a nine-month gestation, remains hidden for the first week or more.

BUSHBUCKS

The bushbuck (*Tragelaphus scriptus*), also called the harnessed antelope, is an African antelope of the family Bovidae, found in sub-Saharan forests and brush. It is nocturnal, shy, and usually solitary. The bushbuck stands about 1 m (39 inches) at the shoulder and ranges in colour from reddish brown to almost black, depending on the subspecies. Its markings vary but include white patches on the neck and throat and vertical stripes or rows of spots on the sides. Horns, present in males, are spirally twisted and relatively straight. The bushback inhabits areas of dense vegetation near bodies of water and feeds mainly on the leaves of shrubs and small trees.

ELANDS

Elands (genus *Taurotragus*) are two very large, oxlike African antelopes of the spiral-horned antelope tribe, Tragelaphini, family Bovidae. The giant, or Derby, eland (*T. derbianus*) inhabits woodlands filled with the broad-leaved doka tree in the northern savanna from Senegal to the Nile River. The common, or Cape, eland (*T. oryx*) ranges over the woodlands, plains, mountains, and subdeserts of eastern and southern Africa. The eland is the largest of all antelopes.

Bulls of both species attain shoulder heights of 150–180 cm (59–71 inches) and weigh nearly one ton. Males mature at seven years and continue to add bulk with age, whereas females are mature by four years and remain much slimmer, with a shoulder height of 120–150 cm (47–59 inches) and a weight of 317–470 kg (699–1,036 pounds).

The common eland is tawny with up to 12 white torso stripes and dark markings, which include foreleg garters, a short dorsal crest and neck mane, and the tuft of the hock-length tail. Colour is paler with indistinct markings in the southern subspecies (*T. oryx oryx*). A dewlap, present in both sexes, grows long and pendulous in bulls, which also turn darker and develop a thick, black forehead tuft. The horns are straight with one or two screwlike spirals and are usually longer and thinner in females.

The giant eland is reddish brown with a blackish neck and vertical white striping. It has large, rounded ears. Its horns are heavier and more widely divergent than those of the common eland. An eland's horns can stretch up to 123 cm (48 inches) long in bulls.

The giant eland is known to form herds of up to 60 animals, but it is more elusive and less sociable than the common eland, which sometimes aggregates in herds of hundreds on open plains (up to five hundred in Serengeti National Park). The average, however, is a dozen or less, and herd membership is quite fluid. Large herds invariably include numerous calves, whose strong mutual attraction forces mothers to remain in attendance. Though bulls often accompany female herds, they commonly associate in separate bachelor herds, which occupy smaller home ranges (50 square km [19 square miles], compared with 400 square km [154 square miles] for females in one Kenyan study) and denser woodland. Senior bulls often wander alone seeking mating opportunities, announcing themselves by the loud clicking of their forelegs as they walk.

Elands are both browsers and grazers. They feed mainly on green grass during the rains and then switch to the foliage of dicots during the dry season. Both sexes use their horns to break off branches too high to grasp with their lips and tongue.

The common eland has been domesticated in South Africa and Russia. In parks where they are well protected, bulls become quite tame. Paradoxically, the eland is usually the shyest of all African antelopes, possibly because bulk makes it short-winded: elands can trot for hours and are prodigious high jumpers (they spring over one another and 2-metre [7-foot] fences effortlessly), but they cannot sustain a gallop. Their size offers protection from other predators, and females with calves mount a group defense against lions, unlike most other antelopes.

The highly endangered western giant eland (*T. derbianus derbianus*) has been reduced to at most a few hundred animals. Without effective protection in its last refuges in Senegal's Niokolo-Koba National Park and an adjacent game reserve, the only hope for this subspecies' survival is a captive breeding program.

KUDUS

Kudus are two species of antelopes in the genus *Tragelaphus* of the spiral-horned antelope tribe, Tragelaphini, family

Bovidae. The very large greater kudu (*T. strepsiceros*) is common in southern African wildlife reserves. The svelte lesser kudu (*T. imberbis*) is an elusive dweller in the arid lowland thornbush of northeast and East Africa. Both species have corkscrew horns (in males only), depend on cover for food and concealment, and form small herds.

The greater kudu is the tallest antelope after the eland. Males stand 130–150 cm (51–59 inches) but are narrow-bodied, weighing on average 257 kg (567 pounds), with a maximum of 315 kg (694 pounds). Females average 120 cm (47 inches) and 170 kg (370 pounds). Colour varies from reddish brown to blue-gray with white markings, an adaptation for concealment that includes 6–10 vertical torso stripes, a short spinal crest, a nose chevron, and small cheek patches. The greater kudu also has white forelegs with dark garters and a black-tipped tail. Males have a beard, turn darker with age, and possess the longest horns of any antelope: 120–180 cm (47–71 inches) along the curve. These horns take six years of growth to complete two full turns. The horn's size and shape keep pace with and advertise the dominance status of the bearer.

The lesser kudu stands only about 100 cm (39 inches) high and weighs 92–108 kg (202–238 pounds). Females and young have a bright rufous coat, which darkens to slate-gray in males. The lesser kudu is vividly marked with 11–15 vertical white stripes, broad chest and throat patches, a nose chevron, and cheek patches. The legs are tawny and decorated with black and white patches, the tail is bushy with a white underside and a black tip, and there is a short, erectile dorsal crest but no beard. The horns of mature males make two and a half (rarely three) turns and measure 60–90 cm (24–35 inches) along the outer curve.

Both kudus are cover-dependent browsers that feed on more than one hundred different trees, shrubs, vines, herbs, seedpods, and fruits, as well as a little new grass.

Eating greens enables them to inhabit waterless country, yet greater kudus regularly drink at water holes. Both species depend on the green growth along watercourses in the dry season and disperse through deciduous woodlands in the rains. Home ranges may be as small as 55 hectares (136 acres) or as large as 600 hectares (1,500 acres), and bulls studied in South Africa covered 11 square km (4 square miles) in migrating between wet- and dry-season ranges. Both sexes of lesser kudu studied in Kenya's Tsavo National Park had ranges averaging 230 hectares (570 acres), at an average density of only one kudu per square km (three kudus per square mile).

The greater kudu is still widely distributed in the lowland Bushveld of southern Africa. However, in northeastern and East Africa, humans have crowded it out of the lowlands, and it is largely confined to mountains with dense woodland and thickets. Yet its secretiveness and nocturnal activity enable it to persist unusually close to civilization. The lesser kudu inhabits dense thornbush below 1,200 metres (3,900 feet) above sea level inside and outside East African parks.

In the baking heat of midday, kudus habitually stand motionless and are beautifully camouflaged in thickets. If hiding fails, kudus take abrupt flight with soaring bounds and often utter loud, hoarse barks. Both species occasionally form transitory herds of up to 25 animals, but the typical group consists of two to three females with their offspring. The kudus have stronger social (possibly kinship) bonds than other tragelaphine antelopes (e.g., the eland and nyala). The sexes segregate except for mating. Males leave female herds at age one and a half years, when their horns grow past their ears and thus advertise their gender, after which they associate in loose bachelor herds. Up to 10 greater kudu bulls sometimes get together—a grand sight—but males become increasingly solitary with age. Kudus are particularly vulnerable to cattle-borne diseases such as rinderpest, which decimated their populations in the 1890s.

NYALAS

The nyala (*Tragelaphus angasii*) is a slender antelope of southeastern Africa, a member of the spiral-horned antelope tribe, Tragelaphini, family Bovidae. The nyala is notable for its extreme gender differences (sexual dimorphism) and specialized habitat preferences that limit its distribution to the Lowveld of southern Africa.

Females and young sport short, bright chestnut coats with 8–13 white stripes on the torso, spots and bands on the legs, chest, and cheeks, and a bushy tail with a white underside. Females weigh about 58 kg (128 pounds) and have a shoulder height of 92 cm (36 inches). Males are much larger, standing 106 cm (42 inches) tall and weighing 98–125 kg (216–275 pounds), and carry horns 60–83 cm (24–33 inches) long with 1.5–2.5 twists. They gradually turn dark charcoal gray and shaggy as they mature and have a long fringe from throat to hindquarters and an erectile spinal crest from head to tail. Their stripes and spots mostly disappear under the long hair, but the tan lower legs, ears, and forehead persist. Males resemble a dryland version of the male sitatunga, whereas females could pass for lesser kudus.

The nyala is a cover-dependent browser and grazer that occupies the densest woodlands close to water on the coastal plain and in major river valleys of eastern Africa from southern Malawi to Natal. The habitat has to include high-quality grassland next to the cover where nyalas spend daytimes and from which they emerge to graze green grass at night during the rainy season. Browse, including the foliage of various dicotyledons as well as forbs, seeds, and fruits, dominates the dry-season diet.

Females and young form loose herds of five or six animals with home ranges of 50–100 hectares (120–250 acres). Males are nonterritorial, share overlapping ranges of about 80 hectares (200 acres), associate in fluid bachelor herds as subadults, and compete for dominance with a spectacular lateral display that gives the shaggiest seniors with the longest horns the advantage. Mating peaks occur during the summer in the southernmost populations, but births occur year-round, after a seven-month gestation. Calves lie out for 10–18 days before accompanying and foraging with their mothers.

The related mountain nyala (*T. buxtoni*), endemic to the Ethiopian highlands east of the Rift Valley and discovered only in 1908, is much more like a greater kudu than another nyala in size, proportions, and social organization. Both sexes are gray-brown with faded stripes but have two conspicuous white throat patches, nose chevron, cheek spots, and underside of the bushy tail and a brown-and-white spinal crest. Coat length varies seasonally. Senior males are sepia-coloured, with open spiral horns up to 120 cm (47 inches) along the curve. Males, nearly as big as the greater kudu, stand up to 130 cm (51 inches) and weigh up to 300 kg (660 pounds); females weigh 150–200 kg (330–440 pounds).

Specialized for montane habitats between 3,000 and 4,500 metres (10,000 and 15,000 feet) and having a limited geographic range, the mountain nyala is a particularly vulnerable species. Increasing human population and susceptibility to livestock diseases had already reduced the species to remnant groups outside of Ethiopia's Bale Mountains National Park. There, beginning in the 1970s, they increased to at least 1,700 over 15 years of effective protection. However, after the Ethiopian revolution of 1991, the park was overrun, and the mountain nyala population was reduced to an estimated 150 animals. After protection was restored, the population quickly increased to more than 2,500 by the end of the century. The mountain nyala is now classified as an endangered species.

NILGAIS (TRIBE BOSELAPHINI)

The nilgai (*Boselaphus tragocamelus*), also called the blue-buck, is the largest Asian antelope, a member of the tribe Boselaphini, family Bovidae. The nilgai is indigenous to the Indian subcontinent, and Hindus accord it the same sacred status as cattle (both belong to the subfamily Bovinae). Accordingly, the nilgai is the only one of the four Indian antelopes that is still abundant.

Nilgai is the Hindustani word for "blue cow," which describes the blue-gray of adult bulls. (Cows are orange-brown.) The nilgai's conformation, however, is more horselike than cowlike: it has a long neck with a short upright mane, a bony narrow head, a barrel-like chest, strong legs, and high withers sloping back to the croup. Conversely, it has a hock-length cow's tail that ends in a black tuft. Both sexes have similar markings: white areas include the cheek spots, ear tips, large throat bib, brisket, belly, rump patch, and underside of the tail. Its lower legs are banded black and white. Maximum contrast is achieved in prime males, which turn nearly black. They grow much bigger than cows, up to 1.5 metres (5 feet) tall and 300 kg (660 pounds), compared with 214 kg (471 pounds) for cows. They also have a thicker neck and a tassel of black hair bordering the white bib. But the male's cow-like horns are quite small, being 15–18 cm (6–7 inches) long.

Nilgais inhabit flat and rolling dry savanna covered by thin woodland and scrub. Requiring minimal cover, they avoid dense woods and are most abundant in central and northwest India. (However, Texas has more than 36,000 descendants of nilgais that were introduced in the 1930s, most of which are feral.) Mixed feeders, they prefer grass but also browse acacias and other trees and like flowers and fruits. They will stand on their hind legs to browse as high as possible. Overgrazing by cattle often leaves little food for the nilgais, which compensate by raiding crops. They are active during the day and even in the hottest weather seek shade only for midday siestas. Extending the usual morning and late-afternoon feeding peaks, nilgais often begin eating before dawn and keep feeding after dark. They drink regularly during the hot season but can go two to three days without water in cool weather.

The nilgai is only moderately gregarious. Herds of 10 or fewer are usual, and groups of 20 or more are exceptional. The sexes remain separate most of the time, and only one mature bull in either a bachelor or female herd is the rule. Herd membership is fluid, and the only lasting association is between mothers and calves. Adult males are often seen alone and wander widely. Whether the mating system is based on male territoriality or a male rank hierarchy remains unclear. Presence of dung middens suggests territorial demarcation, but these are used by all nilgais, even calves. There is a mating peak in November and December, but calves are born in almost every month, after a gestation of more than eight months. Cows breed again soon after calving and may be followed by calves of different ages. Over half of nilgai births are of single calves, but triplets are not uncommon. Calves spend a month in hiding before beginning to accompany their mothers.

DUIKERS (TRIBE CEPHALOPHINI)

Duikers are 17 or 18 species of forest-dwelling antelopes making up their own tribe, Cephalophini, and subfamily, Cephalophinae, in family Bovidae. They are found only in Africa. *Duiker* derives from the Afrikaans *duikerbok* ("diving buck"), which describes the sudden headlong flight of duikers flushed from hiding.

No other tribe of African antelopes contains so many species, yet duikers are so similar except in size that 16

Zebra duiker (Cephalophus zebra). Kenneth W. Fink—The National Audubon Society Collection/Photo Researchers

species are placed in the same genus, *Cephalophus*. Only the bush, or gray, duiker (*Sylvicapra grimmia*), which is adapted to the savanna biome, is placed in a separate genus.

Like most antelopes that live in closed habitats and rely on concealment to evade predators, duikers are compact and short-necked. Their hindquarters are more developed and higher than their forequarters. Duikers have sturdy, short legs, short tails, and fairly uniform, cryptic coloration. Most have grizzled (banded) hair. They move stealthily, lifting each leg high, and often "freeze" in mid-stride. The head is proportionally large with small ears, a wide mouth, and a bare, moist muffle. Two distinctive duiker traits are the erectile tuft of hair on the crown (*Cephalophus* means "head crest") and preorbital (cheek) glands that open into a horizontal slit and are present in both sexes. Gender differences are minimal: both sexes possess short, straight, back-slanting horns (absent in female bush duikers and some blue duikers), and females are often a bit larger than males.

Size ranges from that of the blue duiker (*C. monticola*), one of the smallest antelopes, only 36 cm (14 inches) high at the shoulder and weighing about 5 kg (11 pounds), to that of the yellow-backed duiker (*C. silvicultor*), up to 87 cm (34 inches) high at the shoulder and weighing 80 kg (180 pounds). It appears that the structure of the forest undergrowth selects for shoulder heights that enable duikers and other forest ungulates to move through or beneath the vegetation with minimal interference. When a number of different species share the same forest, those of similar size minimize competition by occupying different micro-habitats or being active at different times. For example, in the primary rainforest of Gabon, there are four duikers of similar size: the black-fronted duiker (*C. nigrifons*), Peters' duiker (*C. callipygus*), bay duiker (*C. dorsalis*), and white-bellied duiker (*C. leucogaster*). The white-bellied duiker prefers broken-canopy and secondary forest with dense undergrowth, the black-fronted duiker has elongated hooves adapted to the swampy forest it prefers, and the bay duiker is nocturnal, lying low during the day while the Peters' duiker is active. (Most duikers are active during the day.)

In closed-canopy forest, growth is sparse on the floor except where sunlight penetrates through gaps in the canopy. It is the duikers' ability to utilize the fruits, flowers, and leaves that rain down from the canopy that has enabled this tribe to exploit African forests by evolving different species that are specialized to subsist in virtually every type of wooded habitat. Fruit is a major component of every species' diet, although larger duikers eat more foliage. Duikers also eat flowers, roots, fungi, rotten wood, insects, and even birds and other small vertebrates.

Duikers live in monogamous pairs that jointly mark and defend their home range as a territory. Some duikers have a gestation of about five months, so they could produce two young a year. Some forest duikers may only reproduce annually.

NEOTRAGINI: THE DWARF ANTELOPE TRIBE

Tribe Neotragini includes some small African antelopes, such as the dik-dik, the klipspringer, and the royal antelope (the smallest of all the antelopes).

DIK-DIKS

Dik-diks (genus *Madoqua*) are four species of the dwarf antelope tribe, Neotragini, family Bovidae, that are adapted for life in the arid zones of eastern Africa. Three species inhabit the Horn of Africa: Guenther's dik-dik (*M. guentheri*), Salt's dik-dik (*M. saltiana*), and the silver dik-dik (*M. piacentinii*). Kirk's dik-dik (*M. kirkii*), the best-known dik-dik, is a common resident of acacia savannas in Kenya and Tanzania. Guenther's and Kirk's dik-diks overlap in Kenya. An isolated population of Kirk's dik-dik, different enough genetically to be considered a different species, inhabits Namibia.

Dik-diks are among the smallest antelopes. Kirk's dik-dik, the largest, stands only 35–45 cm (14–18 inches) tall and weighs 3.8–7.2 kg (8.4–15.8 pounds). Females are 0.5–1 kg (1–2 pounds) heavier than males. Dik-diks look delicate, with a pointed, mobile snout, large eyes and ears, prominent preorbital glands, pipestem legs, harelike hind limbs much longer than their forelimbs, and a vestigial tail. The coat is grizzled gray to gray-brown with tan flanks, limbs, and erectile head crest and whitish eye ring, ear lining, underparts, and rump. Only the males have horns, which are corrugated, backward-slanted spikes 7.5 cm (3 inches) long. A hairy proboscis with tiny slit-like nostrils is a dik-dik specialization most developed in

Guenther's dik-dik. In this proboscis, an enlarged nasal chamber richly supplied with blood is efficiently cooled by rapid nasal panting, with minimal loss of water in the exhaled air. With other water- and energy-conserving measures (fluctuating body temperature, lowered metabolic rate, concentrated urine, dry feces, resting in shade at the hottest hours, and nocturnal activity) as well as highly selective browsing on foliage, forbs, herbs, and succulents, dik-diks are superbly equipped to subsist in waterless bush country.

Like other dwarf antelopes, dik-diks live in monogamous pairs on territories of 1–35 hectares (2–86 acres), depending on cover and food resources. The best habitat supports up to 20 dik-diks per square km (52 dik-diks per square mile). Territories are demarcated with dung and urine, which are deposited in a ritual that also serves to maintain the pair bond. The female excretes first, followed by the male, who samples the female's urine stream (thereby monitoring her reproductive condition), paws over, and then marks his dung and urine over her deposit. Afterward the couple anoints nearby twigs with the tarlike secretions of their preorbital glands. Older offspring also participate in the dunging ceremony. Neighbouring pairs maintain and frequently add to adjacent borderline middens. Competition for suitable locations for territories is severe. Dik-diks have a gestation of five to six months and so can produce two young a year. Offspring leave as yearlings to seek mates and territories, but they have to find vacancies caused by the death of one or both members of a pair. As both sexes face the same risks, an equal adult sex ratio arises, thus supporting a monogamous system.

Vulnerable to a number of predators, ranging from eagles and cats to human beings, dik-diks use tactics typical of small cover-dependent antelopes. They lie low until detected and then take sudden zigzag flight into the nearest thicket. Breathy, toy-trumpet "zik-zik" calls (from which their common name derives) raise the alarm and, when sustained (often in duet), serve to harass predators and advertise the presence of a mated pair.

KLIPSPRINGERS

The klipspringer (*Oreotragus oreotragus*) is a rock-climbing antelope, resident in mountains of eastern and southern Africa. Its Kiswahili name "goat of the rocks" is apt, although it more closely resembles Eurasian goat antelopes such as the chamois and is radically different from other dwarf antelopes of its tribe, Neotragini, of the family Bovidae.

Adaptations for its specialized niche include a stocky build with massive hindquarters, a short neck, a vestigial tail, a dense undercoat with brittle, air-filled guard hairs, and the ability to stand on tiptoes of its truncated hoofs. Its colouring—shades of grizzled tan, gray, and brown, which vary with location—conceals the klipspringer from predators. It has no contrasting markings except its large, rounded ears, which are white inside and have black margins. Horns are straight spikes 10 cm (4 inches) long and are frequently present in both sexes in East African and Ethiopian populations. Its bounding gait and sure-footedness enable the klipspringer to outrun predators on precipitous slopes and rocky terrain—even on level, jagged lava fields—making such places sanctuaries. Insulation enables it to survive climatic extremes from sea level up to 4,500 metres (14,800 feet).

Klipspringers are equally adaptable in diet. They eat a wide variety of evergreen shrubs, succulents, vines, seeds, flowers, forbs, and herbs, including green grass. If necessary, they leave their rocky sanctuaries to feed, even at times of day when they are normally inactive. The plants they eat supply all the water they need.

Klipspringers inhabit mountain ranges of eastern Africa from the Red Sea Hills to the Cape and north to Angola along coastal ranges and river gorges. The Ethiopian highlands are the centre of their distribution. Isolated populations in Nigeria and the Central African Republic indicate a wider range in former epochs.

Like most dwarf antelopes (e.g., the dik-dik), klipspringers live in monogamous pairs and jointly defend their territories. These can be as small as 8 hectares (20 acres) in high-rainfall locations such as escarpments of the Ethiopian highlands, where up to 47 klipspringers per square km (122 per square mile) will compete for resources, or as large as 50 hectares (124 acres) in desert areas. Pairs associate closely, and a young of the year often accompanies the female. Offspring leave home as yearlings, by which time they are adult in size. Both sexes spend much time posting territorial boundaries with dung middens and tar-like globules of preorbital gland secretion daubed on twigs. The male is particularly vigilant and, in addition to marking, spends hours standing sentinel on promontories where he can see and be seen to advantage. He thus visually advertises territorial occupancy while guarding his property and family from intrusions by rivals and predators. The nursing female is thereby freed to spend extra time feeding. If her mate sounds the whistling alarm snort, she immediately bounds uphill to sanctuary. Disturbed pairs often call in duet, which can serve to discourage a predator, advertise the presence of a pair to homesteading individuals, and reinforce the pair bond.

After a gestation period of seven months, a single young is born. Births occur at any time of the year, with peaks during the rainy season. The hiding stage lasts two to three months, perhaps because of predation by eagles that regularly hunt hyraxes that share the klipspringer's habitat.

ORIBIS

Oribis (*Ourebia ourebi*) are small, swift African antelope, the most gazelle-like of the dwarf antelopes, tribe Neotragini, family Bovidae. They inhabit Africa's northern and southern savannas, living in pairs or small herds.

The oribi has a slender build and is long-limbed and long-necked. It stands 51–76 cm (20–30 inches) high and weighs about 14 kg (31 pounds). Females are slightly larger than males. The oribi has prominent ears, and the males have erect, spikelike horns 8–19 cm (3–7 inches) long. The coat is short, sleek, and tan to bright reddish brown. It has white underparts, rump, throat, and ear insides, as well as a white line over its eye. It has a bare black glandular spot below each ear and a stubby black tail. The oribi's colour varies with its location.

The oribi is dependent on tall grass for cover and food, in effect limiting its geographic range to higher-rainfall zones. It occurs in the northern savanna from Senegal to Ethiopia, in the coastal hinterland of East Africa into Tanzania, and as isolated populations in south-central and southeastern Africa southward to Cape Province.

The oribi is the only dwarf antelope and perhaps the smallest ruminant—that is, a grazer, or rather a grazer and a browser, as it eats foliage, herbs, and forbs when palatable green grass is unavailable. It derives sufficient water from its food to be water-independent. Oribis leave their territories to visit mineral licks, lawns of short grass created by larger ruminants, and postburn flushes of vegetation during the dry season. A number of oribis may thus gather on neutral ground. When annual fires remove all cover, loose herds of up to a dozen form, but, lacking the cohesion of sociable species, the members scatter in all directions when put to flight.

Both members of a pair defend territories of 30–100 hectares (75–250 acres) against same-gender intruders and demarcate property with dung middens in a ritual initiated by the female, whose elimination posture featuring the upraised black tail pompon attracts her mate and other family members. The male marks over the others' deposits. He also spends much of his time patrolling and marking the territory's boundaries by daubing the tarlike secretions of his large preorbital glands on grass stems, which are often prepared by biting off seed heads. Family members communicate with softer versions of the whistling alarm snort and with the odours from their battery of scent glands (inguinal, hoof, shin, and preorbital).

Although oribis are typically found in conventional mated pairs, novel polygamous variations on the monogamous and territorial theme have been observed. Up to half of oribi territories in an area may include two or more resident females, while the other females are often, but not always, stay-at-home daughters. Much more unusual, and unknown in other dwarf antelopes, in Tanzania's Serengeti National Park two or three adult males may jointly defend a territory. They do not do so as equals: the arrangement involves a territory owner who tolerates subordinate males. He does not gain extra females and is sometimes cuckolded by the subordinates, but cooperative defense does extend territorial tenure.

Oribis have an extended breeding season with birth peaks in the rains. Gestation is about seven months; newborns are dark brown, remain hidden for a month, and develop very rapidly, reaching adult size by one year. Adults too hide from predators. When flushed, they dash away in a zigzag, bounding run at 40–50 km (25–30 miles) per hour.

ROYAL ANTELOPES

The royal antelope (*Neotragus pygmaeus*) is a hare-sized denizen of West Africa's lowland rainforest. It is the world's smallest antelope. The similar dwarf antelope (*Neotragus batesi*) is only slightly bigger. Both belong to the Neotragini tribe of dwarf antelopes.

The royal antelope has many physical similarities to the hare: it has overdeveloped hindquarters and hind legs nearly twice as long as its forelimbs, a short tail, big eyes, and transparent but small ears. It stands about 25 cm (10 inches) and weighs 2.5–3 kg (5.5–7 pounds). Females are slightly larger than males, which have short (2.5–3 cm [1–1.2 inch]) but sharp back-slanted spikes for horns. The coat colour is red- or golden-brown with a rufous collar and white underparts, chin, and undertail.

Confined to the rainforest and adjacent forest-savanna mosaic that stretches from Ghana to Sierra Leone, the royal antelope inhabits dense vegetation that grows where sunlight penetrates to the forest floor, as well as secondary growth that succeeds clearing and cultivation. Although in some places it is common and even abundant, it is secretive, largely nocturnal, and seldom seen. Consequently, little is known about its ecology and behaviour, although presumably it fills the same niche as the dwarf antelope, which has been studied in Gabon. Its narrow muzzle and long tongue are adapted for browsing very selectively on leaves, forbs, vines, and the like, including cultivated plants.

Unlike most other members of the tribe, which live in monogamous pairs (e.g., the dik-dik), the royal antelope is apparently solitary and polygynous: females live singly in home ranges as small as 2 hectares (5 acres), several of which may be included in the territory of a male. The dwarf antelope breeds year-round, with seasonal peaks

and produces a single offspring after an estimated gestation of six months (maybe less).

ANTILOPINI: THE GAZELLE TRIBE

Tribe Antilopini includes graceful, long-legged antelopes
of arid, open country, notably the numerous gazelles and
the springbok.

BLACKBUCKS

The blackbuck (*Antilope cervicapra*) is an antelope (family Bovidae) indigenous to the plains of India. The
blackbuck is an antelope of the same tribe (Antilopini)
that includes gazelles, the springbok, and the gerenuk.
What sets the blackbuck apart from the rest is the adult
male's horns, which are long (50–61 cm [20–24 inches],
the record being 71.5 cm [28.1 inches]), spirally twisted,
V-shaped, and covered with pronounced ridges nearly to
the tips. In addition, there is a striking contrast between
the black-and-white coloration of mature male blackbucks and the reddish yellow coloration of females and
immature males—a much greater contrast than is found
in any of the blackbuck's tribal relatives.

Male blackbucks weigh 34–45 kg (75–100 pounds) and
stand 74–88 cm (29–35 inches) at the shoulder. Females are
not much smaller, weighing 31–39 kg (68–86 pounds) and
having shoulder heights only a few centimetres shorter
than the males. Females also have the same white markings as males, including circular eye patches, mouth,
underside, inner legs, and rump patch. The only obvious difference between females and immature males is
the presence of horns. Even black males, which are most
colourful at the end of the monsoon season, begin to fade
in midwinter after the annual molt and turn quite brown
by early April when hot weather returns. In fact there is

one southern Indian population in which the males never turn black. Nevertheless, male blackbucks are still darker than females and immature males.

Blackbucks are primarily grazers and frequent open short grassland, but they can survive in semidesert where there is sufficient vegetation and often frequent nearly barren salt pans. However, they avoid woodland and shrubland. They prefer green grass but browse when grass is sparse. Blackbucks in the semidesert of Rajasthan have been observed to drink twice a day. They are active in daytime, tolerate the hottest sun, and seek shade for only two to three hours at midday.

Blackbuck once lived on open plains over the whole Indian subcontinent, but their numbers and range have been drastically reduced as the human population has grown. The total blackbuck population, estimated at 80,000 in 1947, was down to eight thousand by 1964, but it has since recovered to 25,000 in protected areas. Late in the 19th century, in relatively well-watered savannas of East Punjab, aggregations of 8,000–10,000 were reported. Now groups larger than 30–50 are uncommon, consisting of bachelor males, females and young with or without a territorial male, and maternity herds of females guarding concealed young.

With a six-month gestation period, blackbucks can produce two young a year. Breeding occurs year-round, but the main birth and rutting peaks occur in February and March, with a secondary peak at the end of the monsoon in August and September. Only territorial males breed. They defend properties as small as 8 hectares (20 acres), but they do this for only a few weeks. Rutting bucks pursue and herd females, approaching with prancing steps, a curled tail, and their swollen preorbital glands everted while emitting throaty grunts. Territories are demarcated with dung middens and sticky black preorbital secretions deposited on grass stems and bushes.

Blackbucks rely mainly on eyesight to avoid capture. Fast as any antelope, the only predator they cannot outrun is the cheetah, which was once used by the Mughals for the sport of coursing blackbucks and gazelles. The main predators now—pariah dogs and jackals—feed mainly on fawns.

DIBATAGS

The dibatag (*Ammodorcas clarkei*), also called Clark's gazelle, is a rare member of the gazelle tribe, Antilopini, family Bovidae, indigenous to the Horn of Africa. The dibatag is sometimes mistaken for the related gerenuk.

A selective browser with a narrow, pointed snout, the dibatag is long-legged and long-necked. It stands 80–88 cm (31–35 inches) tall and weighs 22–29 kg (48–64 pounds). It is grayish brown in colour with ochre limbs and white cheek stripe, underparts, and rump. It also has a conspicuous black tail that is held erect during flight. Only males have horns, which are short (25 cm [10 inches]) and curved forward.

The dibatag's preferred habitat is waterless thornbush dominated by the genera *Acacia* and *Commiphora*, but it avoids thickets and very stony ground. It browses very selectively on green foliage, buds, and shoots of evergreen trees and shrubs, which are supplemented by herbs and sprouting grass during the rains. Like the gerenuk, it stands on its hind legs to reach higher foliage. Although the dibatag bears a striking resemblance to the gerenuk in conformation and shared gazelline traits, the two are different enough to be classified in different genera, and the fact that their distributions overlap indicates separation in habitat preferences and diet.

Formerly widespread in the semiarid and arid lowland plains of Ethiopia's Ogaden region, the dibatag was virtually eliminated from the northern Ogaden during 20 years of political unrest in the late 20th century, though it is still fairly common at places in the less-populated southern part. In Somalia, drought, overhunting, and habitat degradation caused by excessive numbers of livestock have eliminated the dibatag from most of its former range except for the central coastal hinterland. It is considered by local hunters to be more alert and elusive than any other antelope, but it is unprotected in any reserve and vulnerable to extinction through the attrition of its habitat. There are no dibatags in captivity. Its population density of 0.1–0.3 per square km (0.3–0.8 per square mile) is very low, and its former range, estimated at 200,000 square km (77,000 square miles), has been reduced to perhaps 10,000 square km (4,000 square miles).

As with the gerenuk, dibatag herds are very small. Singles and doubles are most common, although groups of up to five females and young have been recorded. Males patrol and mark their territories with dung middens and preorbital gland secretions that they deposit on twigs. Most births occur during the short rains of October and November, six months after mating peaks during the short rains of April and May.

GAZELLES

A gazelle is any of several fleet, medium-sized antelopes with slender, evenly developed limbs, level backs, and long necks. Most gazelles are tan-coloured, with white underparts and rump patch, a dark side stripe, and contrasting facial markings. They inhabit the arid lands of Asia from China to the Arabian Peninsula, North Africa from the Saharan deserts to the sub-Saharan Sahel, and northeast Africa from the Horn of Africa to Tanzania. Most gazelles are placed in the genus *Gazella*, family Bovidae.

Gazelles have adapted to inhabit waterless steppe, subdesert, and even desert. They can extract water from the plants they browse without having to drink. They have narrow jaws and incisor rows for highly selective feeding on the most nutritious growth. Their urine is concentrated, and, before excretion, moisture is extracted from their fecal pellets. Their coats are light-coloured and reflective. They can tolerate an increase in their core temperature by as much as 5 °C (9 °F). Gazelles seek shade and avoid activity in the hottest weather by feeding at night and early morning when plants contain the most moisture. If all else fails, they can cool down by rapid nasal panting.

The genus *Gazella* has traditionally been considered to contain 14 species. However, specialists in the taxonomy of the gazelle tribe (Antilopini), using genetic techniques for studying phylogenetic relationships, now believe that gazelles stem from not one but several different ancestors. Accordingly, five species, all African, have been removed from *Gazella* by some authorities and placed in two different genera. The three largest species—the dama gazelle, Grant's gazelle, and Soemmering's gazelle—are placed in the genus *Nanger* (formerly considered a subgenus), and two of the smaller species—Thomson's gazelle and the red-fronted gazelle, which are closely related enough to be considered sibling, or even the same, species—have become the genus *Eudorcas*. The *Gazella* genus as traditionally defined includes eight species that occur only in Africa, five that occur only in Asia, and one species that occurs both in Africa and Asia. In the revised classification, *Gazella* contains nine species—three exclusively African, five exclusively Asian, and one shared by both continents.

Asian Gazelles

The Arabian Peninsula is the centre of diversity of the revised genus *Gazella*, with five species: the mountain gazelle (*G. gazella*), the goitred, or sand, gazelle (*G. subgutturosa*), the Arabian gazelle (*G. arabica*; now extinct), the Saudi gazelle (*G. saudiya*; now extinct in the wild), and the dorcas gazelle (*Gazella dorcas*). The dorcas gazelle also ranges into North Africa. The range of the goitred gazelle extends across the Asian deserts to China, though its population is greatly reduced in numbers. A sixth Asian gazelle, the Indian gazelle or chinkara (*G. bennetti*), survives in the deserts of India and Pakistan.

Tribe Antilopini includes several Asian species of the genus *Procapra* that are also called gazelles: the Tibetan gazelle (*P. picticaudata*), Przewalski's gazelle (*P. przewalskii*), and the Mongolian gazelle (*P. gutturosa*). The last, with a population estimated at well over one million, may be the most numerous of all hoofed mammals.

African Gazelles

Of the three exclusively African *Gazella* species, two range north of the Sahara (along with the dorcas gazelle). The Atlas gazelle, also called Cuvier's, or the edmi, gazelle (*G. cuvieri*), is found in the Atlas Mountains. The rhim, or slender-horned, gazelle (*G. leptoceros*) is the most desert-adapted African gazelle and lives in the Sahara's great sand deserts (ergs) from Algeria to Egypt. The third indigenous species, Speke's gazelle (*G. spekei*), inhabits the coastal plain of Somalia.

The dorcas gazelle, though still the most abundant and widespread of the Saharan antelopes, has been eliminated from most of its North African range. However, sizable populations survive in the Sahel from Mauritania to the Nile and in the lowlands of countries bordering the Red Sea.

Thomson's gazelle (*Eudorcas* [*Gazella*] *thomsonii*) is still common in East Africa and abundant in the Serengeti ecosystem of Tanzania. An isolated subspecies, the Mongalla gazelle (*E. thomsonii albonotata*), occurs in southeastern Sudan. The red-fronted gazelle (*E.* [*G.*] *rufifrons*) is a Sahel version of Thomson's gazelle but is distinguished by a more rufous colour and a reddish border between the narrow black flank stripe and white underparts.

The dama gazelle (*Nanger* [*Gazella*] *dama*) is the largest gazelle, weighing up to 75 kg (165 pounds) and standing up to 120 cm (47 inches) at the shoulder. Formerly common in the grasslands and subdesert of the Sahel from Mauritania to Sudan, it now exists only in endangered remnant populations. This gazelle is unusual both for its form and for geographic variations in its colour pattern, which range from predominately rufous with extensive white underparts, rump, legs, and head in the west (*N. dama mhorr*) to nearly white in the east (*N. dama ruficollis*).

Grant's gazelle (*N.* [*G.*] *granti*) has the largest horns (up to 80 cm [31 inches]) and is still widespread both in and outside protected areas through most of its range from southern Sudan to central Tanzania. Soemmering's gazelle (*N.* [*G.*] *soemmeringii*) inhabits the arid savanna country of northeast Africa, where it is the ecological equivalent of Grant's gazelle. Clark's gazelle (*Ammordorcas clarkei*) of northeast Africa is also known as the dibatag.

Ecology and Behaviour

Like most antelopes of arid regions, gazelles are nomadic, migratory, or both. All gazelles are gregarious. Females and young band together, as do bachelor males. During migration, the sexes associate in mixed herds, but they are segregated by territorial males whenever breeding opportunities arise. Gazelles are unusually endowed with glands, which are located between the hooves, in the groin (inguinal glands), on the front of the forelegs, and ahead of the eyes (preorbital glands). In males of some species (Thomson's, red-fronted, Speke's, and goitred) the preorbitals produce a sticky black secretion that is daubed on twigs and grass stems to demarcate territories. However, the main way of posting territories, in all members of the gazelle tribe, is with urine and feces, which males deposit on dung middens in a linked, highly ritualized performance.

Because antelopes living in open plains can be run down by motorized vehicles, all gazelles (with few exceptions) have been decimated over most of their range by relentless hunting. Habitat degradation and competition with livestock have also harmed gazelle populations.

GERENUKS

Gerenuks (*Litocranius walleri*), also called Waller's gazelles, are the longest-necked members of the gazelle tribe, Antilopini, family Bovidae. They are a browsing antelope of the lowland arid thornbush of the Horn of Africa.

The gerenuk's shoulder height is 80–105 cm (31–41 inches), and the animal weighs 28–52 kg (62–114 pounds). It has a two-tone coloration, buff with a reddish brown saddle. Its underparts, rump patch, tail, throat patch, chin, eye rings, and lips are all white, as are the insides of its very large ears. Only the males have horns, which are S-shaped, heavily annulated, and 32–44 cm (13–17 inches) long. The elongated limbs and neck (*gerenuk* means "giraffe-necked" in Somali) and the pointed snout are adapted to selective nibbling of small leaves on thorny shrubs and trees—including foliage too high for other antelopes, which the gerenuk reaches by standing on its hind legs. Modified lumbar vertebrae, powerful hind legs, and wedge-shaped hooves make the gerenuk the only antelope that can stand unsupported in this manner. Its diet thus enriched with moisture, the gerenuk is able to exploit resources inaccessible to water-dependent herbivores. Indeed, its population density can actually increase with distance from permanent water. Degradation of grassland due to drought and overgrazing by domestic livestock has caused the thornbush to expand, which creates more habitat for the gerenuk and compensates to some extent for clearing, cultivation, and overhunting in other parts of its range.

It prefers well-spaced bushes and trees and avoids dense bush with restricted passage.

The gerenuk is less sociable than most other gazelles, a behaviour consistent with its semiclosed habitat preference and low population density—overall average of 0.05 per square km (0.13 per square mile) but 0.5 per square km (1.3 per square mile) where common, as in the drier bush country of northern Kenya and Somalia. Sightings of single animals, not only males but also adult females, are typical. Herds of two to eight are considered normal at relatively high densities, while herds of more than a dozen are unusual.

The gerenuk is a shy animal whose first line of defense when disturbed is to avoid detection by standing motionless under cover. Females have even been known to act like young in the hiding stage. When alarmed to the point of taking flight, a gerenuk trots more often than gallops away, and sometimes it even stots (that is, bounds with legs held stiff).

Two or three females, with or without offspring, may be found together, but groupings are fluid, the only constant association being between mother and dependent offspring. Before becoming territorial as adults, males associate in twos and threes and, given the opportunity, will attach to adult females. Large territories of about 2 square km (0.7 square mile) are typical and may not have common boundaries with their nearest neighbours; males cordon off a smaller activity area with tarlike secretions from their preorbital glands that they deposit on twigs at frequent intervals. Female home ranges are of comparable extent. Though gerenuks have been known to shift their home range, territorial males rarely venture off their property.

Though most births occur during the rainy season, the gerenuk breeds year-round, as mothers typically conceive again within weeks of giving birth. Gestation is about seven months, and the young remain hidden for several weeks.

The springbok (*Antidorcas marsupialis*), also called the springbuck, is a graceful, strikingly marked antelope of the gazelle tribe, Antilopini, family Bovidae. The springbok is native to the open, treeless plains of southern Africa. It once roamed in enormous herds but is now much reduced in numbers. It is the national and sporting emblem of South Africa.

Although closely related to true gazelles (genus *Gazella*), the springbok is placed in a separate genus because of a unique structure on its back that it displays when excited, consisting of a patch of white hair that is normally hidden beneath a skin fold but is erected during a special form of jumping known as pronking. The species name *marsupialis* refers to this concealed organ, which also happens to be lined with sebaceous scent glands.

Native to southwest Africa, where it is the most abundant plains antelope, the springbok was once a dominant migrating species, along with the black wildebeest and the blesbok, in South Africa's vast Highveld and Karoo regions, where it is still common on the farms and ranches that have subdivided and transformed this vast ecosystem. Migratory populations of springbok still exist in Botswana's Kalahari and in the subdesert and desert of Namibia and southwestern Angola. Of the several recognized subspecies, which are adapted to different climatic and ecological conditions, the Highveld-Karoo variety (*Antidorcas marsupialis marsupialis*) is the smallest, and the variety of Namibia's Kaokoveld (*A. marsupialis hofmeyri*) is the largest. Its shoulder height is 69–87 cm (27–34 inches), and its weight is 27–48 kg (59–106 pounds). The heavily ringed horns are 35–49 cm (14–19 inches) in length (smaller and thinner in females) and have an unusual stethoscope shape with hooked tips pointing inward. The coat is pale to rich cinnamon brown with extensive areas of white including the head, ears, underparts, backs of legs, rump, and tail. A heavy black side stripe, narrow cheek stripe, and tail tip contrast with the white markings.

A mixed feeder comparable to Thomson's gazelle, the springbok grazes during the rainy season and browses on foliage, forbs, and tsama melons during the dry season. It drinks when water is available but can subsist indefinitely on browse with a water content of at least 10 percent.

Springboks have an annual rut that commences at the end of the rainy season when the animals are in peak condition. Most young are born six months later in the spring, October and November, shortly before the rainy season begins. However, the timing may vary by as much as two months, reflecting the springbok's adaptive response to the variability of arid climates. Females conceive as early as six to seven months of age, whereas males take two years to mature. Rutting males defend territories of 25–70 hectares (62–173 acres) with loud grunts, attacking vegetation with their horns and depositing middens of urine and dung in a ritualized display. Outside of the mating season, females and males often occur in mixed herds, which aggregate at water holes and at bursts of vegetation created by local thunderstorms.

Although the spinal crest of white hair can be erected independently and pronking can be performed without unfolding the crest, the full display combines high, stiff-legged bounds with bowed back and lowered neck, during which the hair of the rump patch and spinal crest merge to form a big white patch. Springboks have been clocked at 88 km (55 miles) per hour, as fast as any gazelle, but they can be outrun by cheetahs over a short distance and by wild dogs over a long distance.

HIPPOTRAGINI: THE HORSE ANTELOPE TRIBE

Tribe Hippotragini, so-called because of the powerful build, erect mane, and thick neck of many of its members, includes the roan, sable, oryx, and addax antelopes.

ADDAXES

The addax (*Addax nasomaculatus*) is the most desert-adapted African antelope, formerly found throughout most of the Sahara but nearly exterminated in the wild in the last quarter of the 20th century by poaching from motorized vehicles. The addax's most striking feature is its long spiral horns.

Male addaxes weigh 100–135 kg (220–300 pounds) and have a shoulder height of 95–115 cm (37–45 inches). Their horns are 76–109 cm (30–43 inches) long. Females are nearly as tall as males and only 10–20 percent lighter; their horns are thinner than the male's but just as long. A stocky build and sturdy, rather short legs give the addax endurance but not speed. It was easily run down on the gravel plains and plateaus that were once part of its natural habitat. The addax's coat is lightest-coloured in summer and smoky gray in winter. The hindquarters, tail, underparts, and legs are white, as are a conspicuous face mask and mouth that contrast with a dark brown forehead tuft and gray muzzle. The throat is covered with a short brownish beard.

While other antelopes of North Africa—gazelles and the related scimitar-horned oryx—penetrate the central Sahara after rainfall has made the desert bloom, only the addax and the slender-horned, or Rhim, gazelle (*Gazella leptoceros*) live there in all seasons. Both are equipped with broad hooves that are adapted for traveling efficiently on sand, enabling them to inhabit the extensive accumulations of sand called ergs that serve as refuges from poachers.

Other adaptations for desert life are developed to a high degree in the addax, including a highly reflective coat, an ability to extract all the water it needs from plants and to conserve that water by excreting dry feces and concentrated urine, and an ability to tolerate a rise of daytime body temperature by as much as 6 °C (11 °F) before resorting to nasal panting to cool down. In the hottest weather, addaxes rest by day and feed at night and early morning when food plants have absorbed the maximum moisture from the air. The addax employs its short, blunt muzzle to graze coarse desert grasses, and when these are unavailable it browses on acacias, leguminous herbs, and water-storing plants such as melons and tubers.

The addax once ranged from the Atlantic to the Nile, on both sides of the Sahara. Herds of 2–20 animals were typical, but sometimes the addax migrated and aggregated in herds of hundreds where rain had revived the vegetation. Uncontrolled hunting has reduced the species to ranging in only a few remote areas of sand dunes in the desert. The number of survivors in the wild is estimated at just a few hundred in Mauritania, Mali, Niger, Chad, and Sudan. However, more than two thousand addaxes are maintained in American and European zoos and on private ranches. The best hope for the species' survival as a wild animal is the breeding of captive animals and their reintroduction into securely protected areas within their old natural range. Efforts to restore populations in Tunisia and Morocco are presently under way.

ORYXES

An oryx is any of three large antelopes (genus *Oryx*, family Bovidae) living in herds on deserts and dry plains of Africa and the Arabian Peninsula. Oryxes are powerfully built and deep-chested with short necks, blunt muzzles, and long limbs. The sexes look alike, although females are less muscular. The gemsbok (*O. gazella gazella*) is the largest, standing up to 138 cm (54 inches) tall and weighing

Arabian oryx (Oryx leucoryx). Rod Moon—The National Audubon Society Collection/Photo Researchers

238 kg (524 pounds). It also has the most striking coloration: gray-brown with contrasting black and white body and facial markings. The Arabian, or white, oryx (*O. leucoryx*) is the smallest, 102 cm (40 inches) tall and weighing 75 kg (165 pounds), with only faint dark markings to offset its whitish coat. The scimitar-horned oryx (*O. dammah*), 120 cm (47 inches) tall and weighing 200 kg (440 pounds), is mostly white except for the reddish brown neck and chest. The horns are long and straight in the gemsbok and the Arabian oryx. Females' horns are thinner but as long as those of males. The Arabian and scimitar-horned oryxes are listed as endangered species.

The three subspecies of *O. gazella* live in eastern and southern Africa: the beisa (*O. gazella beisa*) and fringe-eared oryx (*O. gazella callotis*) from the Horn of Africa south to Tanzania and the gemsbok in the Karoo region of South Africa. The scimitar-horned oryx, once found throughout northern Africa, was restricted to the southern rim of the Sahara (the Sahel) by the early 1980s and was virtually extinct in the wild by the century's end. The Arabian oryx once lived in the deserts of the Sinai and Arabian peninsulas and adjacent areas to the north. The last survivors were captured in the early 1970s and bred in captivity. Efforts to reintroduce their descendents, beginning in Oman in 1982, have been partially successful but are dependent on effective protection from poaching.

Classified as coarse grazers, oryxes feed on grasses and energetically dig for water-storing roots and tubers. They can go without drinking except under the harshest conditions, but they drink regularly where water is available.

Oryxes have an unusual social organization that is adapted to a nomadic existence in desert conditions. Isolation and low population density select against the dispersal of adolescent males, as is usual in social antelopes. Accordingly, oryx herds, which may number up to three hundred for the fringe-eared oryx (e.g., in Kenya's Tsavo National Park), include adults of both sexes. Females and males have separate dominance hierarchies. The alpha bull (or bulls) commands herd movements and enforces the same submissive behaviour from both sexes. Where conditions permit (e.g., where there are permanent water holes and grazing) some oryx bulls maintain individual territories.

Roan Antelopes

The roan antelope (*Hippotragus equinus*) is one of the largest and most formidable African antelopes, a member of the tribe Hippotragini, the so-called horse antelopes, family Bovidae.

The roan is a powerfully built animal with long, sturdy limbs and a thick neck that looks thicker because of an upstanding mane and a beard. The head is long and narrow with a wide gape, framed by long, tasseled ears. Named for its colour, the roan is reddish gray to reddish brown, with a striking black-and-white facial mask. The sexes look much alike, standing 126–150 cm (50–59 inches), but males are heavier (280 kg [620 pounds] versus 260 kg [570 pounds] for females) and have thicker, sickle-shaped horns 55–99 cm (22–39 inches) long, 10–20 percent longer than those of females.

The geographical range of the roan extends across broad-leaved deciduous woodlands in the northern savanna and throughout most of the southern savanna. A grazer and browser whose preferred habitat includes lightly wooded savanna, it also frequents floodplains and montane grasslands. It is mysteriously absent from Africa's eastern miombo woodlands and has become scarce in its southernmost range (especially in South Africa). Formerly common in West Africa, it has been eliminated from many areas by settlement and poaching. Its preference for relatively open habitat, along with its size and sedentary (nonmigratory) habits, make this species especially vulnerable.

Like most antelopes, the roan is sociable and territorial. Females live in herds of 6–20 plus their offspring (herds of 35 or more are no longer common). The size of home ranges varies greatly, from as small as 239 hectares (590 acres) at normal density (4 roan per square km [10 per square mile]) to as large as 100 square km (39 square miles). Males defend territories as small as 100 hectares (247 acres) at normal density. Where roan are few and far between, bulls can accompany female herds that range widely, thereby enjoying a monopoly denied males with territorial neighbours. Herd composition changes from hour to hour as members come and go, but all who share the same home range belong to the same social unit, and perhaps most are related, as female offspring settle in the maternal home range. However, males are evicted and forced by territorial males to disperse as subadults, which associate together in small bachelor herds until mature at six years of age. Females breed at two years, calve at three years, and thereafter produce young at roughly 10.5-month intervals (gestation 9–9.5 months). After a two to three week hiding stage, calves join the maternal herd, where they associate with other juveniles in creches. Resting juvenile subgroups are often left behind when the rest of the herd moves, making them vulnerable prey for leopards. However, roan have been known to kill lions that failed to overpower them immediately. Their curved horns and a sideways stabbing technique, together with an aggressive temperament, make the roan antelope unusually formidable.

SABLE ANTELOPES

The sable antelope (*Hippotragus niger*) is one of Africa's most impressive antelopes and a member of the horse antelope tribe, Hippotragini, family Bovidae.

Sable bulls, with their glossy black (sable) coats set off by white underparts, rump, throat, and facial markings and their great scimitar-shaped horns, are a favorite quarry of trophy hunters. Females and young are chestnut to sorrel in colour. Such pronounced colour differences make the sable antelope one of the most sexually dimorphic species in the bovid family. However, south of the Zambezi River, females of the *H. niger niger* ("black black") subspecies also turn extremely dark. The sable is a large antelope, standing 117–140 cm (46–55 inches) tall. Bulls weigh about 235 kg (517 pounds) and females about 220 kg (480 pounds).

The sable's geographic range extends through the southern savanna from central Tanzania to South Africa. Closely associated with the broad-leaved deciduous woodlands called miombo, the sable is an "edge" species that favours the ecotone between wooded savanna and grassland. It is a grazer and a browser. During the rainy season (September to April), it forages the grasses, forbs, and foliage of woodlands, and in the dry season it emerges onto grasslands where it concentrates on flushes of green herbage after annual fires sweep the countryside. It is water-dependent and visits pools and pans daily in the dry season, as well as mineral licks to gain salt and trace elements that are in short supply in the ancient, leached granitic soils of the African inland plateau.

The sable is a sociable and territorial antelope. Herds of females and young numbering up to 70 animals (sometimes even in the hundreds in Zimbabwe) live in large home ranges of 10 to more than 50 square km (4 to more than 19 square miles). Among females, there is a dominance hierarchy based partly on seniority. Herds frequently break up into smaller units of variable composition and may remain separated for long intervals. Creches of young calves regularly lag behind adults and are often found alone. Females conceive as two-year-olds and calve after a nine-month gestation. Seasonal breeding comes at the beginning of the rainy season (September–October), calving at the end (May–June). Female offspring remain in the home range, but the darkening colour and large horns of subadult males cause territorial males to drive them out in their fourth year, if not sooner. Thereafter, the young males join a bachelor herd or live as lodgers on the property of territorial males until they mature at five and are ready to compete for a territory that may be as large as 10 square km (4 square miles).

Predators and prey both occur at relatively low density in miombo woodland. Apart from occasional lions, spotted hyenas, and wild dogs, the main predator of the sable is the leopard. Adult sable are generally too large and formidable for leopards, but calves and yearlings are vulnerable.

REDUNCINI: THE REEDBUCK AND WATERBUCK TRIBE

Tribe Reduncini includes antelopes of genus *Kobus* and *Redunca* that are native to Africa south of the Sahara. They usually live in herds and are generally found near water, in such places as plains, woodlands, swamps, and floodplains.

KOBS

Kobs (*Kobus kob*) are small, stocky African antelopes (tribe Reduncini, family Bovidae) that occur in large numbers on floodplains of the northern savanna. The kob ranges from Senegal in the west to the Ethiopian border in the east and southward into western Uganda and eastern Congo. There are three distinct subspecies: the western kob (*K. kob kob*), the Uganda kob (*K. kob thomasi*), and the white-eared kob (*K. kob leucotis*) of southeastern Sudan.

The kob resembles a heavier impala. Its stocky build with strong legs and overdeveloped hindquarters make for a powerful bounding gallop but not for the fleetness and endurance of slimmer plains antelopes. Females are slender compared with males, which have thick necks and bulging muscles. At 94 kg (207 pounds), bucks weigh one-third more than does and stand 8 cm (3 inches) taller (90–100 cm [35–39 inches]). Armed with heavily ridged lyre-shaped horns 40–69 cm (16–27 inches) long, males stand out in a crowd of hornless females. They also have darker coats that enhance the white throat patch, underparts, eye rings, and insides of ears. Sexual dimorphism reaches its extreme in the white-eared kob, with males the colour of ebony. Male Uganda kob are a rich reddish brown with bold black stripes fronting their legs.

The kob avoids wetlands while remaining dependent on floodplain grassland near water. It prefers open habitat with short, green pasture. Large numbers of kob permanently reside on extensive plains (e.g., in Uganda's Queen Elizabeth National Park). They congregate on the highest, driest ground with the shortest, greenest grass during the rains and move downslope into the greenbelts of tall perennial grasses as the dry season progresses. The white-eared kob, formerly numbering in the hundreds of thousands, migrates over a large portion of the Nile floodplain in southeastern Sudan.

Traditional breeding arenas, or leks, are found on floodplains where kob aggregate, reaching densities of 40–60 animals per square kilometre (100–160 animals per square mile). The kob is one of only three antelopes (along with the lechwe and topi) known to form high-population-density breeding arenas. Surrounded by conventional territories of about 50 hectares (124 acres), "permanently" occupied by males competing for herds of 5–40 females and young, an arena is a lawn of short grass or trampled bare ground where 30–40 territorial males crowd together in a space the size of a single conventional territory. Mixed herds including hundreds of females and young and bachelor males circulate around the arenas, and most females come to an arena to breed on their day of estrus. Males are attracted by the females to the arenas, but females are probably guided by the accumulation of estrogen-rich urine deposited by earlier visitors to run the gauntlet of eagerly displaying rams and to home in on just a few centrally located courts. Breeding is year-round in most kob populations, but white-eared kob breed during migration on temporary arenas.

Gestation is about eight months, and calves hide for up to six weeks. Living in herds on open plains, kob are hard for stalking predators (big cats) to approach. When pursued by hyenas or wild dogs, they seek refuge in the nearest body of water.

LECHWES

The lechwe is an antelope species of the genus *Kobus*. A member of the waterbuck and kob tribe, Reduncini, it ranks second only to the nyala among the most aquatic African antelopes. The lechwe is one of only three ante-lopes (including the closely related kob and the topi) known to form breeding arenas, or leks, with a high popu-lation density.

There are two species of lechwes: the common lechwe (*K. leche*) and the Nile lechwe (*K. megaceros*). The three sub-species of the common lechwe—the red lechwe (*K. leche leche*), the Kafue lechwe (*K. leche kafuensis*), and the black lechwe (*K. leche smithemani*)—inhabit floodplains bordering marshes and swamps of the southern savanna, from south-eastern Congo (Kinshasa) through Zambia and northern Botswana to Angola. The Nile lechwe lives on the Nile floodplain bordering Al-Sudd swamp in southern Sudan.

Lechwes are sizeable, long-horned (males only) ante-lopes with a sturdy build. Hindquarters are higher and more massive than forequarters, the neck is long, and the muzzle is short and rather blunt. Lechwes are unusual in having widely splayed, elongated hooves that support them on soft ground (e.g., sitatunga). Their shoulder height is 85–105 cm (33–41 inches), and their weight is 60–130 kg (130–290 pounds). Males are 20 percent larger than females. Their lyre-shaped, heavily ridged horns are 45–90 cm (18–35 inches) long.

The coat is greasy and water-repellent. Females have tawny to chestnut coats and look much alike, apart from minor differences in markings. Red lechwe females are the most colourful: they are bright chestnut with white underparts, throat patch, facial markings, and undertail and with black stripes down the front of their legs. The presence of mature males is advertised not only by the sweeping long horns and head-high proud posture but by darker coats and markings, which are most pronounced in the black lechwe of Zambia's Lake Bangweulu. However, the most extreme contrast is seen in Nile lechwe rams, which are dark chocolate brown with whitish markings that include a large patch on the neck and shoulders.

Lechwes enter water to feed on aquatic grasses, an abundant resource underused by most other herbivores, and graze the grasses that spring up as floodwaters recede. They are quite literally "edge" species. On the widest, flattest floodplains, thousands of lechwes migrate distances of up to 80 km (50 miles) as the water rises and falls with the rainy and dry seasons. Zambia's Kafue Flats support some 65,000 Kafue lechwes, down from the 100,000 counted in 1971 before the construction of hydroelectric dams that altered the natural flooding cycle. Inaccessibility may have saved many of the 30,000–40,000 Nile lechwes inhabiting Al-Sudd, mostly on the west side of the Nile, from civil war in Sudan dating from the 1980s.

Concentrations of up to one thousand lechwes per square km (2,590 per square mile) are common late in the dry season on shrinking greenbelts. Females and young stay closest to the water, upon which lechwes, clumsy runners on dry land, depend to escape predators. Bachelor males aggregate on drier ground farther from the water and are kept separate by the aggression of territorial males, some of which also occupy sizeable properties farther inland, where females come during the rains when the population is more dispersed. However, most males become territorial only during the annual mating peak, which occurs when lechwes are most concentrated (December to January in Zambia, early in the rains). This is when lekking occurs, typically in a roughly circular arena about 0.5 km (0.3 mile) across where 50–100 males display to approaching females—most of which come to the leks to mate, but with just a few centrally placed males. Because aggregations are continually on the move, the leks are only temporary.

REEDBUCKS

The reedbuck (genus *Redunca*) is any of three medium-sized antelopes (family Bovidae) that inhabit the grasslands and marshes of sub-Saharan Africa.

The reedbuck is distinguished by a round glandular spot below each ear and curved horns (on males only) that point forward. These horns are shortest (14–41 cm [6–16 inches]) and most hooked in the bohor reedbuck (*R. redunca*) and the mountain reedbuck (*R. fulvorufula*). They are 30–45 cm (12–18 inches) and less hooked in the southern, or common, reedbuck (*R. arundium*). The southern reedbuck is the largest species, standing 65–105 cm (26–41 inches) tall and weighing 50–95 kg (110–210 pounds), compared with 65–76 cm (26–30 inches) and 19–38 kg (42–84 pounds) for the mountain reedbuck, the smallest of the three. Males are 10–20 percent larger than females, with thicker necks and bolder markings—pale underparts and a large white throat patch and white underside of the bushy tail. The southern reedbuck has a black stripe down the front of each foreleg.

Bohor reedbucks (Redunca redunca). Norman Myers/Photo Researchers

Coat colour ranges from plain gray-brown in the mountain reedbuck to variable shades of tan in the southern reedbuck and yellow-brown in the bohor reedbuck.

Bohor reedbucks occur throughout the northern savanna in suitable habitats and reach high densities on major floodplains. Their range extends in eastern Africa from Ethiopia to central Tanzania, where it overlaps with that of the southern reedbuck, which inhabits tall grasslands bordering watercourses, swamps, and lakes of the southern savanna. Indeed, both the bohor reedbuck and the southern reedbuck are limited to habitats with concealing tall herbage near or in wetlands. The bohor reedbuck is also found in montane grassland, where its range overlaps in some places with that of the mountain reedbuck. The mountain reedbuck occupies grasslands at elevations up to 5,000 metres (16,000 feet) in widely separated mountains of eastern and southern Africa, with a relict population in Cameroon.

Mountain reedbucks can go without drinking as long as green herbage is available, whereas the other two species are water-dependent. All three reedbucks depend on cover to hide from danger. They emerge to graze in the open mainly at night, although with protection they become more active during the day. Their build, with over-developed hindquarters, is adapted for quick starts and high bounds but not for sustained rapid flight. Lacking cover, they are vulnerable to wild dogs and spotted hyenas. Alerted and fleeing reedbucks emit whistling alarm calls. Males also employ these calls, often in duet with their mates, to advertise territorial status.

Reedbucks represent a transition from a solitary or monogamous social system, as represented by antelopes that live in closed habitats such as forests, to a sociable, polygynous system typical of antelopes that live in open habitats such as savannas. The southern reedbuck lives mostly in territorial couples. The bohor reedbuck is polygynous: males defend territories that include the ranges of two or more females and their current offspring. Mountain reedbucks live in small herds of three to eight females and young within home ranges that are divided among several territorial males. When fires remove the hiding places of southern reedbucks and bohor reedbucks, these two species also show a herding tendency. Females and young then seek mutual security by forming temporary herds, which may number in the hundreds on broad floodplains where bohor reedbucks reach high densities. Male bohor reedbucks associate in small bachelor herds after separating from their mothers.

Reproduction peaks in the rainy season. Beginning at one year of age for the mountain reedbuck and two years for the larger species, females reproduce at intervals of 9–14 months, with a gestation of seven and a half months. Males mature at three to four years.

ALCELAPHINI: THE HARTEBEEST TRIBE

Tribe Alcelaphini includes long-faced, plains-living, graz-ing African antelopes such as the hartebeest, wildebeest, and topi.

BLESBOKS

The blesbok (*Damaliscus pygargus phillipsi*) is one of the gaudiest of the antelopes, a South African version of the closely related topi. The blesbok ranged the treeless Highveld in countless thousands throughout the mid-19th century but was hunted nearly to extinction. It has been reintroduced, mainly on private farms, throughout and beyond its former range and is again one of the most abundant antelopes in South Africa. An isolated related subspecies, the bontebok (*D. p. dorcas*), confined to the coastal plain of Western Cape province, came nearer to extinction and is still uncommon. The largest population, of 200–250, lives in Bontebok National Park.

The smallest member of the hartebeest tribe, Alcelaphini, the blesbok is only 85–100 cm (33–39 inches) tall and weighs 55–80 kg (120–175 pounds). The male has S-shaped horns that are 35–50 cm (14–20 inches) long, whereas the female's horns are somewhat shorter and thinner. The blesbok's coat is a glossy, dark reddish brown, which contrasts with the white of its belly, lower legs, and facial blaze. The bontebok is even mo re colour-ful and glossier, with purple-black blotches on upper limbs and flanks, a white rump patch and upper tail, and a facial blaze bisected by a brown band. Newborn calves of both subspecies are light tan with dark facial blazes.

The antelopes that once dominated the Highveld were all migratory, like their counterparts on the plains of Botswana, Namibia, and East Africa. Less adapted to arid conditions than the springbok, the blesbok spent the rainy season grazing the Highveld's medium-height sweetveld grasses and in the dry season went west into the poor-quality sourveld grasslands, where it was able to graze more selectively than other species.

Despite the recovery of the Highveld herbivores in recent years, free-ranging migratory populations no longer exist, as the Highveld has been settled and divided into fenced ranches. The blesbok exists in separate, often inbred, units. The social and mating systems are resident, with semi-exclusive herds of three to nine females contained within a permanent territorial network whose males may control properties of 10–40 hectares (20–100 acres) for years. Herds of bachelor males are limited to undefended areas. In former times, the migratory populations were organized quite differently. Evidence of this can be seen in one subpopulation of several hundred that lives on a large ranch and moves about in mobile aggregations, which include mature males that set up temporary territories averaging slightly more than 2 hectares (5 acres).

The blesbok is a seasonal breeder, calving early in the summer rainy season (November and December) after an eight-month gestation. Calves are not hidden but accompany their mothers from birth—an apparent adaptation to a former migratory existence. Along with the wildebeest, the blesbok is the only antelope with follower young.

HARTEBEESTS

Hartebeests (*Alcelaphus buselaphus*) are large African antelopes (family Bovidae) with an elongated head, unusual bracket-shaped horns, and high forequarters sloping to lower hindquarters—a trait of the tribe Alcelaphini, which also includes wildebeests, the topi, and the blesbok. DNA studies indicate that there are about 10 subspecies of *A. buselaphus*, including some that were formerly recognized as separate species of *Alcelaphus*.

Hartebeest are found in herds on open plains and scrublands of sub-Saharan Africa. Once the widest-ranging of African antelopes, they also once lived in North Africa. One well-known variety, Coke's hartebeest, or the kongoni (*A. buselaphus cokei*), of East Africa, is the plainest and smallest subspecies, measuring 117 cm (46 inches) high and weighing 142 kg (312 pounds). This subspecies is lion-coloured, with no conspicuous markings except a white rump patch. It has a moderately elongated head and comparatively uncomplicated horns. The red hartebeest (*A. buselaphus caama*) of southwest Africa is the most colourful, with extensive black markings setting off a white belly and rump. It has a more elongated head and high horns that curve in a complex pattern and are joined at the base. The largest hartebeest is the western hartebeest (*A. buselaphus tora*), which weighs 228 kg (502 pounds) and stands 143 cm (56 inches) tall. Females are 12 percent smaller than males, with smaller but similarly shaped horns.

Lichtenstein's hartebeest (*A. buselaphus lichtensteinii*), which inhabits the miombo woodland zone of eastern and southern Africa, has also been treated as a separate species (*Alcelaphus lichtensteinii*). The preferred habitat of the hartebeest is acacia savanna, though Lichtenstein's hartebeest lives on the grassland-woodland ecotone in the broad-leaved deciduous miombo woodland zone. The hartebeest's long, narrow muzzle enables it to be a highly selective grazer in medium to tall grass, thereby gaining an advantage during the dry season when less-selective grazers (e.g., wildebeest and topi) cannot feed efficiently on the nutritious leaves and shoots that make up a small part of the unpalatable old growth.

Hartebeests are sociable, and adult males are territorial. Small herds of 6–25 females and young are the rule. In preferred habitat at relatively high density, a herd's home range covers 370–550 hectares (910–1,360 acres) and may overlap as many as 20–30 territories, averaging 31 hectares (77 acres). The best territories include pastures preferred by females in different seasons, from short upland grass during the rains to tall grass on clay soils that stay green through part of the dry season. In most regions, males defend territories the year round, as females breed within weeks of calving. The red hartebeest, the southernmost variety, breeds annually, calving at the end of the dry season after an eight-month gestation. Mothers may be followed by up to three offspring, including males up to two and a half years old. Territorial bulls tolerate these young males because their mothers defend them and they perform an elaborate submissive display. However, the young males eventually leave, join a bachelor herd, and then compete for a territory and mating opportunities when mature at four years. Females first calve at three years.

TOPIS

The topi (*Damaliscus lunatus*), also called the tsessebe or sassaby, is one of Africa's most common and widespread antelopes. It is a member of the tribe Alcelaphini (family Bovidae), which also includes the blesbok, hartebeest, and wildebeest. *D. lunatus* is known as the topi in East Africa and as the sassaby or tsessebe in southern Africa.

A lean, sleek animal built for sustained speed, the topi looks like a smaller and darker hartebeest, with higher forequarters sloping to lower hindquarters, but it has a less-elongated head and ordinary-looking horns, which are similar in both sexes. The largest populations occur on the vast floodplains of the northern savanna and in adjacent arid zones, notably in southern Sudan where hundreds of thousands of the tiang subspecies (*D. l. tiang*) once migrated in search of green pastures and may still be numerous despite decades of war in that region. Females are about 20 percent smaller but otherwise are similar to males, which average 115 cm (45 inches) high and 130 kg (290 pounds), with horns 30–40 cm (12–16 inch) long. The tsessebe has weaker, crescent-moon-shaped horns (hence *lunatus* from the Latin for "moon") and is also the least colourful subspecies. The basic tan coloration with dark blotches on the upper limbs intensifies toward the north and east, with the most colourful coat being the reddish brown of the East African topi—made more conspicuous by reverse countershading (lighter above and darker below). Young calves of all varieties are a similar light tan without markings.

The topi has one of the most variable social and mating systems of all the antelopes. Social systems range from resident small herds to huge migratory aggregations and from large individual territories to breeding arenas, or leks, where males crowd together and compete to inseminate females. However, all the variations are on a territorial theme: males must own property in order to reproduce. In wooded savanna where the preferred open grassland is patchy, males may hold onto territories of 50–400 hectares (125–1,000 acres) year after year, leaving only to drink or commute to areas where the first vegetation has grown after fires in the dry season. Herds of 2–10 females and their offspring of the year live in traditional home ranges that may include only a few territories. On wide plains topi often aggregate in hundreds (formerly in thousands) and are mobile, becoming migratory where the distance between wet-season and dry-season feeding grounds is long. There males can only afford to hold temporary territories or risk being left behind; therefore, they join the migration but reestablish a territorial network as soon as the aggregation resettles. During a mating season of about three months, leks are established at high density on wide plains in certain spots regularly occupied or traversed by large aggregations.

(Only two other antelopes are known to form leks: the kob and the lechwe.) As many as one hundred males may crowd together in an arena, where the central males may be only 25 metres (80 feet) apart. A few of them monopolize matings with the females, which come specifically to mate and are possibly guided to the favoured spot by the scent of their predecessors. Topi females calve toward the end of the dry season. Gestation is eight months, and the single calf hides for up to three weeks.

WILDEBEESTS

A wildebeest is either of two species of large African antelopes of the genus *Connochaetes*, tribe Alcelaphini, family Bovidae. Wildebeests (also called gnus) are among the most specialized and successful of African herbivores and are dominant in plains ecosystems.

The common wildebeest (*C. taurinus*) is a keystone species in plains and acacia savanna ecosystems from southeastern Africa to central Kenya. It is highly gregarious and superbly adapted for a migratory existence. *C. taurinus* has high shoulders sloping to lower hindquarters, a deep chest, a short neck, and thin legs. It is conspicuously coloured, its coat being slate gray to dark brown and reverse counter-shaded (that is, lighter above and darker below), with black vertical stripes on the forequarters as well as black markings on the forehead, mane, beard (white in two subspecies), and long tail. The horns, similar in both sexes, are cowlike.

Five different subspecies are recognized. The blue wildebeest, or brindled gnu (*C. taurinus taurinus*), of southern Africa is the largest, weighing 230–275 kg (510–605 pounds) and standing 140–152 cm (55–60 inches) tall. The western white-bearded wildebeest (*C. taurinus mearnsi*) is the smallest, 50 kg (110 pounds) lighter and 10 cm (4 inches) shorter than *C. taurinus taurinus*. It is also the most

Eastern white-bearded wildebeest (Connochaetes taurinus albojubatus).
Leonard Lee Rue III

numerous. More than one million inhabit the Serengeti Plains and acacia savanna of northwestern Tanzania and adjacent Kenya, the only remaining intact ecosystem within the species' range.

The black wildebeest, or white-tailed gnu (*C. gnou*), is a much smaller animal (110–147 kg [240–323 pounds], 106–121 cm [42–48 inches]) and is dark brown to black with a conspicuous white tail, prominent beard, facial tufts, and upright mane. Its curved horns point forward, are 45–78 cm (18–31 inches) long, and are exceptionally dangerous. It was once one of the dominant herbivores of the South African Highveld and Karoo, along with the blesbok, springbok, and now-extinct quagga, but it was hunted nearly to extinction in the late 19th century. However, it slowly recovered, and at the end of the 20th century it numbered around 20,000, though nearly all of these were found on private ranches.

Common wildebeests, with their blunt muzzle and wide row of incisor teeth, are able to feed efficiently and in dense aggregations on the short grasses that carpet plains in the semi-arid zone during the rainy season. Being water-dependent and ever in search of green grass, they migrate when the rains end and spend the dry season roaming the acacia savanna, where there is water, taller grass that stays green longer, and flushes of new grass that come up after fires or local thunderstorms. The Serengeti wildebeest population usually has its annual rut in June, while migrating. Five hundred thousand females are bred within the space of a month by thousands of bulls that compete to hold as many cows as possible on small, temporary territories. The noise and confusion make for one of the world's most spectacular wildlife events.

Eight months later most of the year's crop of calves are born during a similarly short birth peak, between the short and long rains. Unlike all other antelopes (except the related blesbok), wildebeest calves accompany their mothers as soon as they can stand instead of hiding for days or weeks. This is an adaptation to migrating. The wildebeest is possibly the most precocious of all hoofed mammals.

CHAPTER 4

SHEEP, GOATS, AND THEIR RELATIVES

S heep, goats, goat antelopes, and related mammals are members of the subfamily Caprinae, family Bovidae, of order Artiodactyla. Mainly Eurasian but also containing members from Africa and North America, they are agile animals. Many species are found in mountains or on steep, rocky slopes.

SHEEP

Sheep are ruminant (cud-chewing) mammals of the genus *Ovis* in the sheep and goat subfamily Caprinae, family Bovidae. The sheep is usually stockier than its relative the goat; its horns, when present, are more divergent; it has scent glands in its face and hind feet; and the males lack the beards of goats. Sheep usually have short tails. In all wild species of sheep, the outer coat takes the form of hair, and beneath this lies a short undercoat of fine wool that has been developed into the fleece of domesticated sheep. Male sheep are called rams, the females ewes, and immature animals lambs. Mature sheep weigh from about 35 to as much as 180 kg (80 to 400 pounds).

A sheep regurgitates its food and chews the cud, thus enabling its four separate stomach compartments to thoroughly digest the grasses and other herbage that it eats. The animals prefer grazing on grass or legume vegetation that is short and fine, though they will also consume high, coarse, or brushy plants as well. They graze plants closer to the root than do cattle, and so care must be taken that sheep do not overgraze a particular range. Sheep are basically timid animals who tend to graze in flocks and are almost totally lacking in protection from predators. They mature at about one year of age, and many breed when they reach the age of about one and a half years. Most births are single, although sheep do have twins on occasion. The lambs stop suckling and begin to graze at about four or five months of age.

Sheep were first domesticated from wild species of sheep at least 5000 BCE, and their remains have been found at numerous sites of early human habitation in the Middle East, Europe, and Central Asia. Domesticated sheep are raised for their fleece (wool), for milk, and for meat. The flesh of mature sheep is called mutton, and that of immature animals is called lamb. There were estimated to be more than one billion sheep in the world in the early 21st century. The major national producers are Australia, New Zealand, China, India, the United States, South Africa, Argentina, and Turkey. Countries that have large areas of grassland are the major producers.

Domestic sheep differ from their wild progenitors and among themselves in conformation, quantity and quality of fleece, colour, size, milk production, and other characteristics. Most breeds of domesticated sheep produce wool, while a few produce only hair, and wild sheep grow a combination of wool and hair. Several hundred different breeds of sheep have been developed to meet environmental conditions influenced by latitudes and altitudes and to satisfy human needs for clothing and food. Breeds of sheep having fine wool are generally raised for wool production alone, while breeds with medium or long wool or with only hair are generally raised for meat production. Several crossbreeds have been developed that yield both wool and meat of high quality, however.

Flock of sheep, Dubois, Idaho. Agricultural Research Service/U.S. Department of Agriculture (Image Number: K4166-5)

Of the more than two hundred breeds of sheep in the world, most are of limited interest except in local areas.

ARGALIS

The largest living wild sheep, the argali (*Ovis ammon*) is native to the highlands of Central Asia. *Argali* is a Mongolian word for "ram." There are eight subspecies of argali. Mature rams of large-bodied subspecies stand 125 cm (49 inches) high at the shoulder and weigh more than 140 kg (300 pounds). Rams in small-bodied desert populations stand only about 90 cm (35 inches) high at the shoulder and weigh less than 80 kg (180 pounds). Horns are present in both sexes but are especially long in rams. Females weigh about one-third less than males.

The Pamir argali is also known as the Marco Polo sheep. Italian traveler Marco Polo, who crossed the Pamir highlands in the 13th century, was the first Westerner to describe the argali. Horns in Marco Polo sheep may reach up to 1.8 metres (6 feet) in length. The horns of the larger Siberian argali are somewhat shorter but much more massive.

The ram's nuptial coat grows in just before the rutting season in November and December and, in most subspecies, features conspicuous neck ruffs and rump patches. Nuptial coats differ between subspecies in the presence or length of the neck hair, the length of the tail, the size and shape of the rump patch, and the colour of the pelage. The nuptial coat changes with the ram's age, and summer and winter coats also differ greatly.

The argalis are long-legged runners that escape predators primarily by speedy flight. They have superlative vision. Females and young climb cliffs and steep ridges more than large males, which, trading off food against security, are found on productive lowland meadows. Males suffer high predation mortality and have an average life expectancy of only seven to eight years.

Like all sheep, argalis are highly gregarious. Adult rams and ewes live in separate herds except during the brief mating season. Argalis are adapted to great cold, aridity, and very high elevations, as well as sudden rain and snowfalls. They occupy the most extreme habitats among wild sheep.

Males herd small harems during the mating season. Otherwise their social behaviour is more similar to American bighorn sheep than to their closest, but more primitive, relatives, the urials of southwestern Asia. Depending on food resources, one or two young are born after a 160-day gestation period. Juvenile mortality tends to be high.

Argalis are found from Uzbekistan in the west to southern Siberia in the east and from Outer Mongolia and northern China in the north to the Tibetan Plateau and the mountains of northern India and Pakistan in the south. Argalis are in great danger of extinction, depleted virtually everywhere through uncontrolled killing and livestock herding.

BIGHORN SHEEP

Bighorn sheep (*Ovis canadensis*), also called mountain sheep or American bighorn sheep, are stocky, climbing hoofed mammals of western North America known for their massive curling horns. Bighorns are brown with a white rump patch. Horns are present in both sexes, but they are bigger in males (rams). Six living subspecies are recognized. Males of the Rocky Mountain subspecies have horns averaging more than 1 metre (3.3 feet) long as measured along the outer curvature. A record of 1.33 metres (4.36 feet) was reported in 1900. Males of this subspecies are nearly 2 metres (6.6 feet) long and weigh up to 137 kg (300 pounds), though the average is 95 kg (71 kg in females, or ewes). The California bighorn is nearly as large, but desert bighorns are smaller.

Bighorns prefer open terrain near rocky refuges to which they can escape when they see predators. Diet consists of grass, sedge, shrubs, and herbs. The sheep live in single-sex groups of 2–12, migrating seasonally 1–32 km (0.6–20 miles) to higher elevations in the spring and summer. In late fall they retreat from heavy snowpack to lower elevations. Each young sheep learns a migratory route by following an older group member. Home ranges are thus inherited.

Before the rutting season, males engage in dramatic battles for dominance. Two rams launch themselves at each other from a few metres' distance for a clash of horns. Sometimes they begin from a threat-jump, in which the ram rears up on its hind legs before colliding with the opponent. The shock of impact is absorbed by a double layer of bone in the skull. Exhaustion leaves breeding rams vulnerable to malnutrition and predators, but ewes prefer to mate with dominant rams. Young rams cannot compete until their horns have reached full curl at seven or eight years of age. Bighorns can live 20 years or more, but life expectancy may be only six or seven years in populations that are reproducing rapidly.

Ewes have their first lambs at the age of three or four years. The single offspring (rarely twins) weighs 3–5 kg (6.6–11 pounds) and is born in spring after a gestation of nearly six months. Lambs are weaned before winter, when four to six months old. Malnutrition rather than predation accounts for many lamb deaths, as lactating mothers may reduce milk production in order to store fat against the coming cold. Lambs that gain more weight survive winter better and have higher lifetime reproductive success.

As many as two million bighorn once lived from Canada to northern Mexico. In the 1800s overhunting, habitat loss, and livestock diseases nearly drove the species to extinction. Despite conservation measures, they have not significantly recovered. Of the seven modern subspecies, Audubon's (Badlands) bighorn is extinct, and the Peninsular bighorn of Baja California, Mexico, and the Mexican bighorn are threatened or endangered. Translocations in the western United States restored the bighorn to some of its former range, but most herds are dangerously small or live in small ranges with no protected corridors for migration, and die-offs from livestock diseases still occur.

Related to the bighorn are the thinhorn, or Dall's sheep (*O. dalli*), which live in alpine zones of Alaska and western Canada, and the snow sheep of Siberia (*O. nivicola*). All belong to the family Bovidae, subfamily Caprinae (sheep and goats).

MOUFLONS

The mouflon (*Ovis aries*) is a small feral sheep (family Bovidae) of Corsica and Sardinia (*O. a. musimon*) and of Cyprus (*O. a. ophion*). The mouflon stands about 70 cm (28 inches) at the shoulder and is brown with white underparts. The male has a light, saddle-shaped mark on its back and bears large, downward curving horns with the tips turned outward. The mouflon most likely derives from a domestic sheep of Asia Minor that was introduced to Mediterranean islands some thousands of years ago (perhaps in the Neolithic period), presumably for meat, fur, and milk. No fossil evidence exists of any previous presence of mouflons on these islands. The female is usually hornless (a sign of past domestication), but females from Corsica often bear small horns. In the last few centuries, the mouflon has been introduced for hunting purposes into parts of continental Europe. The rut falls in late September and early October, with one, sometimes two, lambs being born in March. Like the domestic sheep, mouflons mainly graze (eat grass), but they also occasionally browse (eat from shrubs or trees).

SNOW SHEEP

Snow sheep (*Ovis nivicola*) are wild sheep belonging to the subfamily Caprinae, family Bovidae, that are distributed throughout the mountain regions of eastern Siberia. They are closely related to North American species such as the bighorn sheep (*Ovis canadensis*).

As in all wild sheep, sexual dimorphism privileges males, which are about 25 percent bigger than females. The males' horns are much larger and similar to those of the bighorn sheep. The body weight of rams approaches 150 kg (330 pounds), and its height at the withers is about 1 metre (39 inches) in the largest subspecies. The diploid number of chromosomes is 52. The rutting season is December to January, and births occur about six months later, when the snow melts and green vegetation sprouts. The snow sheep habitat ranges from the upper line of the forested zone to the limits of vegetation, a maximum altitude of 2,000 metres (7,000 feet). Southern slopes are the preferred wintering areas. The living conditions for these sheep are particularly severe in winter, with temperatures falling down to -60 °C (-76 °F), abundant snowfalls, and strong winds. Because of that, in Sakha, snow sheep undertake seasonal movements of 80–120 km (50–70 miles) to winter on the southern or eastern slopes of mountains, while in Kamchatka migrations of over 50 km (30 miles) have been documented. Snow sheep feed on lichens, grass, sedges, shrubs, moss, and mushrooms. Their main predator is the wolf, but the wolverine occasionally preys on them. Because of such hard living conditions, the mortality rate of the lambs can be quite high—up to 50 percent in the first year of life.

The status of snow sheep appears to be satisfactory at present, with a population of about 90,000 head, although any increased level of hunting (such as intensive poaching) would quickly lead to a decline. A totally isolated subspecies, the Putoran sheep (*O. n. borealis*), which is separated from the nearest population by about 1,000 km (600 miles), is restricted to the Putoran Mountains on the northwestern edge of the Central Siberian Plateau in central Russia and numbers about 3,500 head. The other subspecies are thriving, with the Kamchatka sheep (*O. n. nivicola*) numbering 12,000 individuals, the Yakutian sheep (*O. n. lydekkeri*) over 55,000 individuals, and the Okhotsk sheep (*O. n. alleni*) 11,000 individuals. The remaining two subspecies, the Koryak sheep (*O. n. koriakorum*) and the Chukotsk sheep (*O. n. tschuktschorum*) have populations of around 3,000–3,500 head each.

URIAL

The urial (*Ovis orientalis*) is a medium-size, rather stout-bodied wild sheep, distributed from northwest India and Ladakh to southwest Russia, Afghanistan, Pakistan, and Iran. Six to nine subspecies are usually recognized. They differ in the colour and size of the winter neck-ruff of males, as well as in the colour of their saddle patches and in their horn shape. (Horn tips can converge to the back of the neck, point forward, or sometimes diverge.) Urials show such genetic variation, both within and between populations, that it is hard for taxonomists to agree on their classification. Some zoologists give these sheep the taxonomic name of *O. vignei,* and others suggest *O. gmelini.* Mouflons have also been classified as urials by some zoologists, but others have recently split them into separate species (*O. aries*). Western urials (mouflons) have 54 diploid chromosomes, while eastern ones have 56. Urials weigh about 50 kg (110 pounds).

Urials are generally found in arid country at relatively low altitudes, although they live more than 4,000 metres (13,000 feet) above sea level in Ladakh. Most urials live in open habitats, with few or no trees, but there are indications that this may be a recent adaptation to changing environmental conditions and that the urial was originally more of a woodland animal than at present. The mating season typically falls in the autumn, and one or, on rare occasions, two young are delivered about five months later. Urial ewes withdraw into the upper reaches of ravines and eroded gullies and give birth in these shady retreats. Urials graze mainly on grass, but they may also feed upon a variety of forbs and leaves from shrubs and trees.

The urial, as a species, is considered vulnerable to extinction, but most subspecies are actually endangered (*O. o. bocharensis*, *O. o. punjabiensis*, *O. o. severtzovi*, and *O. o. vignei*). These wild sheep are especially threatened for several reasons. They live at low altitudes in open terrain that is usually near inhabited areas heavily used by cattle, sheep, and goats, all of which are ecological competitors and may infect them with disease. The close presence of man also brings excessive hunting or poaching. By inhabiting arid and low-productivity habitats, urials occur naturally at low densities, often at less than one individual per 100 hectares (250 acres). Male urials are highly prized by trophy hunters. Mature rams are usually overhunted, and local populations are gravely damaged. As with argalis and several other Caprinae species, urgent conservation measures and sustainable management are necessary for the urial's preservation.

GOATS

A goat is any ruminant and hollow-horned mammal belonging to the genus *Capra* in the sheep and goat subfamily Caprinae, family Bovidae. Related to the sheep, the goat is lighter of build, has horns that arch backward, a short tail, and straighter hair. Male goats, called bucks or billys, usually have a beard. Females are called does or nannys, and immature goats are called kids. Wild goats include the ibex and markhor.

Domesticated goats are descended from the pasang (*C. aegagrus*), which is probably native to Asia, the earliest records being Persian. In China, Great Britain, Europe, and North America the domestic goat is primarily a milk producer, with a large portion of the milk being used to make cheese. One or two goats will supply sufficient milk for a family throughout the year and can be maintained in small quarters, where it would be uneconomical to keep a cow. For large-scale milk production, goats are inferior to cattle in the temperate zone but superior in the torrid and frigid zones. Goat flesh is edible, that from young kids being quite tender and more delicate in flavour than lamb,

Angora goat. © R.T. Willbie/Animal Photography

which it resembles. Some breeds, notably the Angora and Cashmere, are raised for their wool; young goats are the source of kid leather.

IBEXES

An ibex is any of several sure-footed, sturdy wild goats of the genus *Capra* in the family Bovidae that are found in the mountains of Europe, Asia, and northeastern Africa.

The European, or Alpine, ibex (*C. ibex ibex*) is typical. Adult males weigh around 100 kg (220 pounds), while females are about 50 kg (110 pounds). Males stand about 90 cm (3 feet) at the shoulder (females are about 10 cm [4 inches] shorter) and have brownish to gray fur, which is darker on the underparts. The male has a beard and large, semicircular horns with broad, transversely ridged front surfaces. The European ibex lives at altitudes close to the snow line and moves to lower altitudes in winter. It lives in exclusively male or female herds, but very old males are often solitary. Formerly common throughout the western and central Alps, *C. ibex ibex* is now greatly reduced in numbers. It is protected locally in the Italian Alps and has been reintroduced to France, Switzerland, Austria, Germany, and Slovenia.

Among the species closely related to the European ibex are the Siberian, or Asiatic, ibex (*C. sibirica*), which is larger and has a longer beard and horns, and the Nubian ibex (*C. nubiana*), which is smaller and has long, slender horns. Other ibexes include the Spanish ibex (*C. pyrenaica*) and the walia, or Abyssinian ibex (*C. walie*), which has been reduced to a single population of about four hundred individuals in Ethiopia and whose numbers are still declining. Two subspecies of Spanish ibex are now extinct (*C. pyrenaica pyrenaica*, which lived in the Pyrenees, and *C. pyrenaica lusitanica*, which was found in Portugal) and one is vulnerable (*C. pyrenaica victoriae*, which lives in the Sierra de Gredos), but another is fairly abundant, with a population of about 9,000 head (*C. pyrenaica hispanica*).

The rut occurs in early winter, and, after about five and a half months, one kid is produced. The ibex can crossbreed with domestic goats and with wild goats (*C. aegagrus*). It has excellent climbing skills but avoids deep snow. It can climb trees to browse foliage if the lower branches are sturdy enough to carry its weight.

MARKHORS

Markhors (*Capra falconeri*) are large wild goats of the subfamily Caprinae, family Bovidae, formerly found throughout the mountains from Kashmir and Turkistan to Afghanistan but now greatly reduced in population and range. The flare-horned markhor (*C. f. falconeri*) occurs in Afghanistan, Pakistan, and India; the straight-horned markhor (*C. f. megaceros*) lives in Afghanistan and Pakistan; and the Bukharan markhor (*C. f. heptneri*) is present in Afghanistan, Tajikistan, Uzbekistan, and Turkmenistan. All subspecies are considered endangered to critically endangered. Habitat loss, overhunting for meat and trophies, and competition from livestock are the main causes of its decline. The markhor stands about 95–102 cm (37–40 inches) at the shoulder and has long (up to 160 cm [63 inches]) corkscrew-shaped horns. Its coat is reddish brown in summer and long, gray, and silky in winter. The male has a long, heavy fringe on its throat and chest.

GOAT ANTELOPES

Goat antelopes, also called rupicaprins (*Tribe Rupicaprini*), are goatlike mammals of the genus *Rupicapra*, subfamily Caprinae, family Bovidae. Goat antelopes owe their name to their physical characteristics, which are intermediate between those of the stockily built goats (subfamily Caprinae) and the long-legged antelopes (subfamily Antilopinae). Some taxonomists split this tribe into Naemorhedini (serow, *Capricornis* species; goral, *Naemorhedus* species) and true Rupicaprini (chamois, *Rupicapra* species; mountain goat *Oreamnos* species).

Goat antelopes are well adapted to life in precipitous, rocky terrain and can stand the cold well. Males are the same size as or slightly larger than females. Both sexes have dark brown, short, backward-curving, stiletto-like horns. Such effective weapons are readily used in fights among themselves and against predators.

Goat antelopes vary in the location and use of scent glands. The goral has extremely small preorbital glands, the chamois and mountain goat have two large supraoccipital glands, and the serow bears large preorbital glands. Chamois and serow use their secretions from these glands to leave territorial olfactory signs and to scent-mark stems, bushes, and tree trunks as a dominance display during aggressive interactions with others of their species. The use of these glands in mountain goats is still unknown: they are rudimentary but become large in mature males during the rut. All goat antelopes have their mating periods in autumn and early winter, but tropical populations of serow and goral may rut at any time of the year. Normally, only one kid is delivered, after five to six months of gestation.

It has been suggested that goat antelopes are the living ancestors of sheep and goats, because they are much less differentiated in their morphology and behaviour than are species of *Ovis* and *Capra*. Such a view is not fully supported by genetic and paleontological data, however. Goat antelopes bear some common anatomical and behavioral traits, but they should certainly not be considered anything more than a loosely knit group, with only the serow and the goral being closely related to each other. The group probably originated five to seven million years ago in Central and East Asia. The Rupicaprini tribe must have split no less than four to five million years ago, with the chamois and some extinct forms reaching Europe one and a half to two and a half million years ago (most likely using mountain chains and steep river banks as corridors), the mountain goat passing to North America through the land bridge between Siberia and Alaska, and the goral and serow staying in Asia. Since then, epigenetic and genetic factors must have acted to differentiate the genera strongly, even if originally they all belonged to the same tribe. While chamois and mountain goats are abundant, most species of the serow and goral are presently declining or threatened with local extinction, mainly because of poaching and the destruction of their forested mountain habitats.

CHAMOIS

A chamois is either of two species of goatlike animal, belonging to the genus *Rupicapra*, family Bovidae, that are native to the mountains of Europe and the Middle East. The two species of chamois are the Pyrenean chamois (*R. pyrenaica*), which is found in the Cantabrian Mountains, Pyrenees, and central Apennines, and the chamois (*R. rupicapra*), which is distributed from the western Alps and the Tatra Mountains to the Caucasus and northern Turkey.

A chamois is about 80 cm (31 inches) tall at the shoulder and weighs 25–50 kg (55–110 pounds). Both sexes possess vertical horns that hook sharply backward at the ends. Males are slightly larger than females. Their colour is relatively variable, but all subspecies of chamois have black and white face markings and a black tail and legs. The chamois is chestnut brown to black in winter and pale brown in summer. In winter, the Pyrenean chamois has two large whitish shoulder patches and a large pale rump patch, and it is reddish brown in summer. A thick underfur develops in cold weather.

Chamois live in small herds. The older males join these only in November during the rutting season, when they engage in fierce battles for mates. The chamois's skull is fragile and not adapted for clashing head-on, as goats and sheep do; instead, chamois chase each other up and down steep cliffs and meadows, trying to gore the throat, abdomen, and groin of the chased individual. Before starting a fight, they usually engage in long sequences of dominance displays in which they present their sides, attack bushes with their horns, call threats at each other, and scent-mark grass blades or stems. Females fight more often than males, but they engage in nonlethal attacks on their opponents' shoulders and rump. Gestation lasts about 21 weeks, and the usual number of offspring is one. In summer the sure-footed chamois may ascend up to the snowline; in winter they often descend to wooded regions. The popular sport of chamois hunting reduced their populations in many areas, but improved management regimes in the 20th century rebuilt their numbers throughout most of their range. Agile and wary, chamois are difficult to approach where they are hunted. They feed in summer on herbs and flowers and in winter on young shoots, lichens, and grass dug out of snow.

The soft, pliant skin of the chamois is made into the original "chammy," or "shammy," leather. The flesh is prized as venison. In the 20th century chamois were introduced into New Zealand, where their numbers quickly increased up to almost 100,000 by the 1970s and where they threatened the local vegetation. The chamois population has since decreased by about 20,000. *Gemsbock*, a German name for the male chamois, is applied, as *gemsbok*, to a southern African oryx.

Mountain Goats

Mountain goats (*Oreamnos americanus*), also called Rocky Mountain goats, are stocky North American ruminants of the family Bovidae. Surefooted relatives of the chamois, mountain goats cling to steep cliffs in habitats ranging from ocean shores to glaciated mountain tops. They are agile, methodical climbers, adapted to the insecure footing of snow-covered and icy cliffs, where predators are loath to follow. On these cliffs, they readily turn on their pursuers, including humans.

Mountain goats belong to the goat antelope tribe, Rupicaprini, of the bovid family. Despite their unusual appearance and behaviour, they are close relatives of sheep and true goats. Mountain goats occur from the Yukon and Alaska to Utah, but most are found in British Columbia. They have been successfully restored to their former abundance in some areas and have also been introduced to some areas where they were never native, including Kodiak Island, the Olympic Peninsula of Washington, the Rocky Mountains of Colorado, and the Black Hills of South Dakota. They occurred in early postglacial times on Vancouver Island but became extinct. Unfortunately, restoration efforts there have failed. Mountain goat populations fluctuate and are sensitive to human impacts. Consequently, they are constantly being watched to ensure the timely application of corrective management.

Stocky climbers with muscular legs and broad hooves, mountain goats stand about 1 metre (39 inches) at the shoulder. Large males can weigh more than 120 kg (260 pounds), and females weigh about 60–90 kg (130–200 pounds). The hair is coarse, white, and shaggy over a thick, woolly underfur. A beard frames the slender muzzle. The sexes look alike and bear sharp, slightly backward-curving, black horns that are 5–25 cm (2–10 inches) long. Unlike

Mountain goats (Oreamnos americanus) *on the Mount Evans Highway, outside of Denver, Colo.* © Denver Metro Convention & Visitors Bureau

true goats, mountain goats do not butt heads but instead stab each other with their horns. Because the horns can cause severe injury, mountain goats are highly reluctant to fight. Nevertheless, males grow a thick skin as a body armour against attacks by rivals or females.

To compensate for their narrow preference for cliffs, mountain goats eat a great variety of plants: grasses, herbs, foliage, twigs, lichens, and, in particular, alpine firs and other conifers. They may excavate these plants at the timberline from beneath deep snow. In summer when lactating or growing new coats of hair, mountain goats may reluctantly leave the security of their cliffs to supplement their nutrient intake with visits to mineral licks. Among other minerals, inorganic sulfur is used by the goat's rumen flora to synthesize the rare amino acids cysteine and methionine, which are essential to the goat's hair growth at that time.

Mountain goats are unusual in that males readily defer to females. Females live in small bands but may become territorial in severe winters, whereas adult males are solitary. Courting males crawl to females and make sounds like those of baby goats. They mate in late November and December. After the mating season, females may drive the males off their wintering ranges. A single kid (rarely two) is born in late spring after about 180 days of gestation and joins a nursery group within a week after birth. Adult female mountain goats are very protective mothers. In winter females with young may become territorial and lay claim to an area of favourable cliff habitat. They then chase all other goats from their territories and readily attack hesitating males. Females are more likely to fight than males.

GORALS

Gorals are three species of small goatlike mammals (genus *Naemorhedus*, family Bovidae) that are native to highlands from India and Myanmar to the Russian Far East. Gorals weigh 22–32 kg (48–70 pounds) and stand 55–80 cm (22–31 inches) at the shoulder, depending on the sex and species. They have slightly backward-curving, cylindrical, sharply pointed horns and a brownish gray to bright red coat. The sexes are similar in appearance, with males slightly larger than females. The goral is a ruminant (cud chewer) closely related to the serow, but it is distinguished from the serow by peculiarities in its skull form as well as by its smaller size, shorter horns, and absence of conspicuous preorbital glands. Gorals are solitary (adult males) or live in small groups (females, subadults, and kids) either in mountain woods with glades or at forest edges, up to the timberline. The rut falls in the autumn, with some local variation. Gestation is six months, and normally only one offspring is delivered.

Modern taxonomy provisionally accepts three species of goral: the red goral (*N. baileyi*), which lives in a narrow area between Tibet, Myanmar, and India; the long-tailed goral (*N. caudatus*), which ranges from southeast Asia up to the Sikhote-Alin mountains of eastern Siberia; and the Himalayan goral (*N. goral*), which occurs over the entire Himalayan region. The first two species are vulnerable to extinction, whereas the third species is still fairly abundant. Habitat loss, as well as poaching for meat and medicinal use, are the major threats to goral survival.

SEROWS

Serows (genus *Capricornis*) are goatlike mammals that range from Japan and Taiwan to western India, through eastern China, Southeast Asia, and the Himalayan region. Serows belong either to the tribe Rupicaprini (goat antelopes) or, according to another view, to their own tribe (Naemorhedini), of the subfamily Caprinae (family Bovidae). There are at least three distinct species: the widespread mainland serow (*C. sumatraensis*), the Japanese serow (*C. crispus*), and the Formosan serow (*C. swinhoii*). Horns that are stout, sharp, and bent slightly backward are common to both sexes. The diploid number of chromosomes is 46 in the mainland serow, whereas it is 50 in the Formosan and Japanese species.

The coloration of the mainland serow is extremely variable. The head, neck, and long mane are grizzled black, and the fur may turn rusty red on the shoulders, flanks, and lower thighs. There is a varying amount of white on the muzzle, throat, chest, and mane. Weight is about 90 kg (40 pounds) and shoulder height 110 cm (40 inches). Both sexes are similar in size. Mainland serows are forest-dwelling, solitary, and territorial (i.e., each adult individual is intolerant of other individuals of the same sex within the area where it lives). They range from sea level in the Malayan peninsula to more than 4,000 metres (13,000 feet) above sea level in the Himalayan mountain range. Well adapted to climbing, they sometimes use large tree trunks overhanging cliffs as safe resting sites. Their nocturnal, elusive habits have made the collection of reliable information about their biology difficult. The red serow (*C. sumatraensis rubidus*) of Bangladesh, Myanmar, and India and the Sumatran serow (*C. sumatraensis sumatraensis*) of Malaysia and Sumatra are the most endangered subspecies. Where official protection is accorded, it is usually on paper only, as the serow is hunted for meat and its body parts, which are used in local medicine. (For example, it is believed that the broth obtained by boiling a serow head is a remedy for arthritis.)

The Formosan serow, a much smaller species (25–30 kg [55–66 pounds]), is from Taiwan and has woollier and softer pelage than the mainland serow. Its body coloration is brown to reddish and is yellowish on the chin, throat, and neck. Little is known about this species, and it is considered vulnerable to extinction.

The Japanese serow (36–38 kg [79–84 pounds] and about 75 cm [30 inches] at shoulder height) is the only species not threatened (about 100,000 head in existence). It is endemic to the Japanese islands of Honshu, Shikoku, and Kyushu. Once severely threatened because of overhunting and habitat loss, it was designated as a "special natural monument" in 1955. Since then the Japanese serow has steadily increased its numbers, because of both the virtual elimination of poaching and the creation of favourable habitats such as monoculture conifer plantations. Indeed, culling operations to limit serow numbers have been conducted every year since 1978. This species is covered with long soft hair, which forms a ruff on the neck. Its coloration varies from grizzled black to nearly white.

AOUDADS

The aoudad (*Ammotragus lervia*), also called the Barbary sheep, is a North African goatlike mammal of the family Bovidae. This species has been inappropriately called a sheep, although recent genetic information reveals that it is much more closely related to wild goats. The aoudad stands about 102 cm (40 inches) at the shoulder. It has a fringe of long, soft hair hanging from its throat and forequarters and has semicircular horns that curve outward, back, and then inward over the neck. Both fringe and horns are more pronounced in the male. The aoudad occurs in dry, mountainous, or rocky country and lives in small family groups. It can go without water for about five days. When threatened, the aoudad stands motionless and is concealed by its tawny brown coat, which blends in with the surrounding rocks. It is considered vulnerable to extinction in all its natural range, where only scattered, small populations survive. The aoudad is probably extinct in Egypt. Introduced to the southwestern United States and northern Mexico for hunting purposes, it has established thriving populations there, where it outcompetes indigenous ungulates such as desert bighorn sheep.

PRONGHORNS

Pronghorns (*Antilocapra americana*), also called American antelopes, are North American hoofed mammals, the sole living members of the old ruminant family Antilocapridae (order Artiodactyla). The pronghorn is the only animal that has branching horns and sheds them annually. This graceful denizen of open plains and semideserts is reddish brown and white in colour, with a short, dark brown mane, white underparts, two white bands on the throat, and a large circular white patch of long hair on the rump.

The rump patch can be suddenly erected to warn other pronghorns of danger; the flash of white from the rump patch can be seen by a human for 3–4 km (2–2.5 miles). Its common name to the contrary, it is not closely related to the antelopes.

Pronghorns stand about 80–100 cm (2.5–3.25 feet) at the shoulder. Large northern males weigh about 40 kg (90 pounds) and the females slightly less. They are highly evolved runners. Faster than any Old World antelope, they can attain a speed of 70 km (40 miles) per hour and leap 6 metres (20 feet) at a bound. With eyes as large as those of elephants, pronghorns have astonishingly acute vision and can readily identify predators at distances of up to 1 km (0.6 mile). Their extreme adaptations reflect the severe predation on pronghorns during the Ice Age.

Both sexes bear horns. Those of the male are longer and branch into two prongs. The longer prong curves backward and the shorter projects forward. Pronghorn

Pronghorn (Antilocapra americana). Leonard Lee Rue III

bucks shed their horns in October after the mating season. The horns grow during winter and are fully grown just before the territorial contests of the bucks in spring.

The short mating season is in late summer and early fall. Bucks on fertile pastures become territorial and mate in seclusion with females that have entered estrus. In dry areas bucks may form harems. Pronghorns use the summer's vegetation to replenish the energy lost by their mating activities, and consequently they have a lengthy gestation period (250 days) for their small body size. Females implant half a dozen or more embryos, but only two survive, one in each of the two uterine horns. Thus, twin births are normal. The extra embryos succumb to intrauterine competition, in which embryos kill off their neighbours using outgrowth from their fetal membranes that penetrates and dispatches the losers.

Pronghorns normally live in small bands in summer, but they may form large herds in winter. They are found from Alberta to northern Mexico. Nearly exterminated in the late 19th century, pronghorns have returned to great abundance with the help of dedicated conservation efforts. Today they are common game animals. Only the small desert-adapted Sonoran pronghorn of southern Arizona and northern Mexico and the peninsular pronghorn of Baja California remain endangered.

MUSK OXEN

The musk ox (*Ovibos moschatus*) is a shaggy-haired Arctic ruminant of the family Bovidae. Musk oxen are stocky mammals with large heads, short necks, and short, stout legs. Their name derives from their musky odour and from their superficial resemblance to the ox, though they are not closely related to cattle. Musk oxen are closely related to the mountain goat, chamois, and serow and are placed in the bovid subfamily Caprinae, along with the true goats and sheep.

Bulls from the southern Barren Grounds in Canada stand about 135 cm (53 inches) at the shoulder and weigh about 340 kg (750 pounds), whereas cows weigh about 250 kg (550 pounds). Northern musk oxen are smaller than those that live farther south. Horns are present in both sexes and are as much as 60 cm (24 inches) long in old males. The male's horns have a broad base and proceed sideways from the midline of the skull, dip downward at the sides of the head, and curve upward at the ends. Females and young have similar, but smaller, horns. The musk ox's coat is of long, dark brown hair that reaches nearly to the feet. Its hair conceals the short tail and nearly covers the small ears. Shorter hair covers the face. Underneath the shaggy coat is a thick wool, called qiviut (or qiveut), which is shed in summer and is used by Arctic craftsmen to make a fine yarn similar to cashmere or guanaco.

Musk oxen travel in herds, often of 20–30 individuals. They are not aggressive, but when attacked the adults encircle the young and present a formidable front of horns that is effective against Arctic wolves and dogs. However, this defensive formation makes musk oxen very vulnerable to human hunters. Musk oxen feed on grasses, sedges, and willows. In summer they store large amounts of fat, which they use to supplement the meagre forage in winter. They are highly adapted for conserving energy in cold weather. Musk oxen have a rutting season lasting two months in late summer, and a single calf is born after 244–252 days gestation. The female's fat may be used to support lactation for calves that are born before grass and low-growing plants are uncovered by the melting snow.

In the Pleistocene Epoch (which occurred from 2.6 million to 11,700 years ago), musk oxen were circumpolar in distribution. However, after the Ice Ages ended they were confined to parts of northern Canada, the high Arctic islands, and Greenland, and in the late 19th century they were severely depleted by hunting. The Thelon Game Sanctuary, established in 1927 in Canada's Northwest Territories, saved the musk ox on the North American mainland. In 1935 and 1936, musk oxen were successfully introduced on Nunivak Island, Alaska, and some of these musk oxen were subsequently transplanted to Siberia and Scandinavia.

BLUE SHEEP

The blue sheep, also called the bharal, is either of two species of sheeplike mammals (genus *Pseudois*, subfamily Caprinae, family Bovidae) that inhabit upland slopes in a wide range throughout China, from Inner Mongolia to the Himalayas. Despite their name, blue sheep (*P. nayaur*) are neither blue nor sheep. As morphological, behavioral, and molecular analyses have shown, these slate gray to pale brown sheep-looking caprines are actually more closely related to goats (genus *Capra*) than to sheep (genus *Ovis*).

Blue sheep are sexually dimorphic, with males larger (60–75 kg [130–165 pounds]) than females (35–45 kg [80–100 pounds]). Adult males have beautiful, rather large, backward-sweeping horns (more than 50 cm [20 inches] long and weighing 7–9 kg [15–20 pounds]), whereas females have rather small horns. Like sheep, males lack a beard and do not have calluses on their knees or a strong body odour. Like goats, they have a flat, broad tail with a bare ventral surface, conspicuous markings on their forelegs, and large dew claws. Chromosomal analyses have indicated that the ancestral caprine stock led first to the genus *Capra* (with 60 diploid chromosomes) and blue sheep (with 54 diploid chromosomes) and then to other genera of Caprinae. A more recent molecular analysis has shown that blue sheep are more closely related to goats than to sheep.

The behavioral repertoire of blue sheep shows a mixture of goatlike and sheeplike patterns. Blue sheep live in groups; in treeless slopes, alpine meadows, and shrub zones above the timberline; on relatively gentle hillsides with grasses and sedges; and near cliffs, which serve as useful routes of escape from predators. They seldom move farther than 200 metres (600 feet) from a rocky retreat. This is a sheeplike terrain preference, as goats tend to stay on steep slopes and rocky cliffs. *Pseudois* probably split early from the ancestral *Capra* stock and, because of having settled in a habitat usually occupied by sheep, has convergently evolved some *Ovis*-like anatomical and behavioral traits, thus obscuring its affinity with goats.

Blue sheep populations are heavily affected by hunting. Although even subsistence hunting by locals can prove destructive because of the use of modern firearms, it is hunting by and for foreigners that is particularly damaging to the survival of the species. From the 1960s to the '80s, blue sheep were killed commercially in the Chinese province of Qinghai. About 100,000–200,000 kg (200,000–400,000 pounds) of blue sheep meat from Qinghai were exported yearly to a luxury market in Europe, principally Germany. Hunts in which foreign tourists kill mature males have greatly affected the age structure of some populations. However, blue sheep are still widespread and are even abundant in some areas.

The dwarf blue sheep (*P. schaeferi*) inhabits the steep, arid, barren lower slopes of the Yangtze River gorge (2,600–3,200 metres [8,500–10,500 feet] above sea level). Above these slopes, a forest zone extends 1,000 metres (3,300 feet) upward to alpine meadows, where the larger *P. nayaur* occurs. In blue sheep, horn girth, rather than length, gives an indication of habitat quality, and

P. schaeferi has notably thinner horns than *P. nayaur*. This suggests that the former is only a low-quality population rather than a true species.

CHIRU

Also called Tibetan antelope, chiru (*Panthalops hodgsoni*) are small, gregarious, graceful antelope-like mammals of the family Bovidae that live on the high alpine steppes of the Tibetan Plateau. Males carry thin, long horns that curve slightly forward; females are hornless. On each side of the blunt muzzle are two small bulges that contain air sacs used in vocalization.

Adult males stand about 83 cm (33 inches) at the shoulder and weigh about 40 kg (88 pounds), whereas females stand about 74 cm (29 inches) at the shoulder and weigh about 25 kg (55 pounds). The stocky body stands on long, slim legs indicative of swift running and irregular, long-distance travels between seasonal ranges. The chiru has a modest rump patch, a short tail, and fairly small ears.

During the breeding season in December, the male's face and the fronts of its legs, which are those parts most visible to a challenging rival, are black and sharply contrasted by white fur, as well as by the yellowish gray-brown colour of the body. The winter coat is dense and woolly. This nuptial pelage is typical only of adult males over four years of age. Females lack the sharply contrasting coat patterns.

Sexes segregate into different herds in summer and travel apart, with females going on longer migrations of up to some 300 km (200 miles). During the rutting season large herds form in which males defend and herd harems. Single fawns are born in late June and early July. The fawns are suckled with a rich milk high in fat, and they grow rapidly. Adult size is reached in less than two years from birth.

Chiru feed on low alpine grasses, forbs, and shrubs. They may have to excavate these from below snow. Chiru are preyed upon by wolves, snow leopards, and lynxes. Many chiru starve to death after sudden high snowfalls and die from especially low temperatures. In both summer and winter, there is high mortality among the young and among males as compared with females. The maximum age reached by adults appears to be younger than 10 years.

The chiru is the only genus of large mammals endemic to the Tibetan Plateau. Despite its antelope-like appearance, the chiru is not related to antelopes or to gazelles but represents the last remnant of a group of ruminants that split off from the sheep, goat, and goat antelope lineages during the Neogene Period. It was extremely abundant on the Tibetan Plateau and surrounding high-elevation alpine steppes, but now it survives only in the extreme climate of the Tibetan Plateau.

Large numbers of chiru are poached for their fine wool, which is smuggled into India and then made into scarves and shawls that fetch exorbitant prices in affluent countries. Despite the enactment of protective measures, the future of this species is uncertain, as once-abundant herds have shrunk severely and rapidly.

CHAPTER 5

CATTLE AND SWINE

Cattle (tribe Bovini, family Bovidae) and swine (family Suidae) are two groups of artiodactyls whose domesticated members are of great economic importance, having provided milk, meat, and hide since prehistoric times. Though descended from a small number of wild bovids and suids, domestic cattle and domestic swine (or pigs) are related to a number of other species described in this chapter.

CATTLE

Cattle are members of the tribe Bovini, family Bovidae, a group that includes the familiar domestic cattle, oxen, yaks, and water buffaloes. Also included are wild bovines such as the bison, gaur, and Cape buffalo, and semidomesticated animals such as the gayal.

AUROCHS

The aurochs (also spelled auroch; *Bos primigenius*) is an extinct wild ox of Europe, family Bovidae, from which cattle are probably descended. The aurochs survived in central Poland until 1627. The aurochs was black, stood 1.8 metres (6 feet) high at the shoulder, and had spreading, forward-curving horns. Some German breeders claim that since 1945 they have re-created this race by crossing Spanish fighting cattle with longhorns and cattle of other breeds. Their animals, however, are smaller and, though they resemble the aurochs, probably do not have similar genetic constitutions. The name aurochs has sometimes been wrongly applied to the European bison, or wisent (*Bison bonasus*).

BANTENGS

The banteng (*Bos banteng*), also called the Bali cattle, is a species of wild Southeast Asian cattle, family Bovidae, found in hill forests. A shy animal resembling a domestic cow, the banteng attains a shoulder height of about 1.5–1.75 metres (60–69 inches). It has a slight ridge on the back, a white rump, white "stockings" on the legs, and slender, curving horns. Bulls are dark brown or black, and cows and young are reddish brown. The banteng is kept as a domestic animal in some areas.

BISON

Bison are two species of oxlike grazing mammals that constitute the genus *Bison* of the family Bovidae. The American bison (*B. bison*), commonly known as the buffalo or the plains buffalo, is native to North America, while the European bison (*B. bonasus*), or wisent, is native to Europe. Both species were drastically reduced in numbers by hunting and now occupy small, protected areas that are tiny fractions of their former ranges.

The American bison differs from domestic cattle or oxen in several respects. It is larger and has a broad, heavy head that is carried low and cannot be raised to shoulder level. The bison also has a pronounced hump at the shoulders, heavy forequarters, and 14 ribs instead of the 13 found in cattle. The coarse, shaggy fur is dark brown in colour. It grows especially long on the head, neck, and shoulders and usually forms a beard on the chin. On rare occasions a white bison is born. These unusual specimens were especially honoured—and even worshiped—by

American Indians. Both bison sexes bear short, upcurved horns, those of the cow being smaller. Bison are large, powerful animals. A mature bull stands about 2 metres (6.5 feet) at the shoulder and weighs more than 900 kg (1,980 pounds). The female is about 1.5 metres (5 feet) tall and weighs about 320 kg (700 pounds).

Bison live in small groups, or bands, whose basic unit is one or more females and several generations of their offspring. Adult males live on the band's periphery or form their own small groups. Large temporary herds of bison may arise from the congregation of dozens or even hundreds of individual bands. During the mating season, which reaches its height in August, bulls engage in head-butting

American bison, or plains buffalo (Bison bison). Alan G. Nelson/Root Resources

contests to determine their social dominance. The cow usually gives birth to a single calf in May after about nine months' gestation. All members of the band protect the young. Bison prefer grass and herbs, but they will also eat twigs and leaves. Bison herds undertake short seasonal migrations, moving a few hundred miles southward in winter and then moving back north when warmer weather returns. Their usual gait is a plodding walk, but they also trot, canter in a stiff-legged manner, or run with a rolling motion. In spite of their bulk, they are agile and fast, having been clocked at speeds of 65 km (40 miles) per hour. Bison are unpredictable animals. Sometimes they can be approached closely without evincing alarm, but at other times they stampede at the least provocation.

Some authorities distinguish two subspecies of American bison, the plains bison (*B.b. bison*) and the wood bison (*B.b. athabascae*), though the differences between them are minor. The plains bison formerly inhabited most of the United States east of the Rocky Mountains and the Great Plains provinces of Canada. It greatly outnumbered the wood bison, which lived in northwestern Canada and Alaska. The plains bison once roamed over North America in numbers estimated at approximately 50 million when Europeans arrived, in what was probably the largest aggregation of large animals known to recorded history. The bison formed the mainstay of the economy of the Plains Indians, providing them with meat for food, hides and fur for clothing and shelter, and sinew and horn for tools, yet the Indians' hunting activities had little impact on the bison population.

With the westward movement of white civilization in the 18th and 19th centuries, the bison were wantonly slaughtered in ever-growing numbers: they were hunted for subsistence, for the commercial sale of their meat and hides, or simply for sport. By the early 19th century the bison had been exterminated east of the Mississippi River. The extension of railroads across the Great Plains in the 1860s led to the decimation of the immense herds that foraged on the vast grasslands there. One hunter alone, William F. Cody ("Buffalo Bill"), killed 4,280 animals in 1867–68 while supplying buffalo meat for railroad construction crews. The white man's slaughter of the bison also had a conscious political objective— to deprive the Indians of their means of subsistence, thereby making it easier to drive them on to reservations or make them adopt settled agricultural pursuits. Much of the hostility between the Indians and the white men was caused by the whites' unremitting destruction of the bison herds. By 1870 the bison population on the Great Plains had been divided into two parts, lying north and south, respectively, of the Union Pacific railway line. The southern herd was completely destroyed by 1875, and the northern one by 1885. By 1889 there were fewer than one thousand bison left alive in all of North America.

About 1900, as the bison neared extinction, concerted action by American and Canadian cattlemen and conservationists resulted in the gathering of the remaining animals into government preserves, zoos, and commercial ranches on both sides of the border. The present commercial herds now total as many as 400,000 plains bison. Some 20,000 plains bison are protected in preserves in the United States and Canada, and more than 10,000 wood bison reside on preserves in Canada. This number is sufficient to ensure the survival of the species, though a major concern of conservationists is the maintenance of genetic diversity among protected bison herds. The wood bison is considered to be a threatened subspecies in Canada.

The European bison, or wisent, differs from the American bison in several respects. It lives in woodlands and is slightly larger and longer-legged than the American bison but is less heavily built. The European bison's range originally extended eastward across Europe to the Volga River and the Caucasus Mountains. It became extinct in the wild after World War I, but herds built from zoo-bred animals were subsequently reestablished, most notably in the Belovezhskaya (Polish: Białowieża) Forest in Belarus and Poland. Other countries that are home to the European bison include Lithuania, Russia, and Ukraine.

CAPE BUFFALO

Cape buffalo (*Syncerus caffer caffer*), also called African buffalo, are the largest and most formidable of Africa's wild bovids (family Bovidae) and a familiar sight to visitors of African parks and reserves. The Cape buffalo is the only member of the buffalo and cattle tribe (Bovini) that occurs naturally in Africa. (The forest, or red, buffalo, *S. caffer nanus*—a much smaller and less familiar subspecies—inhabits forests and swamps of Central and West Africa.)

The Cape buffalo is not very tall—it stands only 130–150 cm (51–59 inches) tall and has relatively short legs—but it is massive, weighing 425–870 kg (935–1,910 pounds). Bulls are about 100 kg (220 pounds) heavier than cows, and their horns are thicker and usually wider, up to 100 cm (40 inches) across, with a broad shield (only fully developed at seven years) covering the forehead. The coat is thin and black, except in young calves, whose coats may be either black or brown.

One of the most successful of Africa's wild ruminants, the Cape buffalo thrives in virtually all types of grassland habitat in sub-Saharan Africa, from dry savanna to swamp and from lowland floodplains to montane mixed forest and glades, as long as it is within commuting distance of water (up to 20 km [12 miles]). It is immune to some diseases that afflict domestic cattle in Africa—in particular, the bovine sleeping sickness (nagana) transmitted by tsetse flies. However, the Cape buffalo is susceptible to cattle-borne diseases. In the 1890s a rinderpest plague swept the African continent from Ethiopia to the Cape of Good Hope and killed up to 90 percent of the buffalo, as well as many antelopes. Although buffalo populations recovered over the next decades, they have continued to suffer from periodic outbreaks of rinderpest, foot-and-mouth, and other diseases to which both buffalo and cattle are susceptible, while at the same time they have had to compete with ever-increasing numbers of cattle for essentially the same feeding niche as bulk grazers.

To sustain its bulk, the Cape buffalo must eat a lot of grass, and therefore it depends more on quantity than quality. It is able to digest taller and coarser grass than most other ruminants, has a wide muzzle and a row of incisor teeth that enable it to take big bites, and can use the tongue to bundle grass before cropping it—all bovine traits. When grass is scarce or of too poor quality, buffaloes will browse woody vegetation. Their preferred habitat includes refuge from heat and danger in the form of woodland, thickets, or reeds, pastures with medium to tall grass (preferably but not necessarily green), and access to water, wallows, and mineral licks. The largest populations occur in well-watered savannas, notably on floodplains bordering major rivers and lakes, where herds of more than one thousand are common. On a floodplain in Zambia's Kafue National Park, the average herd was 450, with a range from 19 to 2,075.

Extremely gregarious, buffaloes are one of the few African ruminants that lie touching. Herds include both sexes and live in traditional, exclusive home ranges. Clans of related females and offspring associate in subgroups. A male dominance hierarchy determines which bulls breed. All-male herds are predominately old and sedentary, as are

RINDERPEST

Rinderpest is an acute, highly contagious viral disease of ruminant animals, primarily cattle, that is common in Africa, the Indian subcontinent, and the Middle East. It has occurred in Brazil and Australia but was quickly eradicated in those countries. Rinderpest has not been reported in the United States. Rinderpest is the most severe infectious disease of cattle and is characterized by its sudden development and high mortality. Besides cattle, it can seriously affect water buffalo, giraffes, some types of antelopes and wild pigs, and other cloven-hoofed ruminants. It is also called steppe murrain, cattle plague, or contagious bovine typhus.

Rinderpest is caused by a paramyxovirus (genus *Morbillivirus*) closely related to those that cause measles in humans and viral distemper in dogs. The virus is transmitted by close direct or indirect contact. After an incubation period of three to nine days, fever and loss of appetite occur in an infected animal. These symptoms are followed within a few more days by discharges from the eyes and nose, salivation, mouth ulcers, and a disagreeable, fetid odour. As the virus invades the internal organs, the animal exhibits laboured breathing, dehydration, diarrhea, often with abdominal pain, and eventually marked straining to evacuate. In many cases a skin eruption (streptothricosis) develops on the back and flanks. Prostration, coma, and death come about six to 12 days after the first symptoms appear. The actual cause of death is dehydration.

Modern cell-cultured vaccines are effective in preventing rinderpest. The eradication of the disease in a particular area or region depends on control of the disease in wild animals and the elimination of infected domestic animals. Immunization by vaccine combined with quarantine is the most effective method of control.

lone bulls. Calves are born year-round, after a nine-month gestation. Though weeks pass before calves can keep up with a fleeing herd, they do not go through a hiding stage but follow under their mothers' protection as soon as they can stand. Herds also cooperatively defend members. They put to flight and even kill lions when aroused by distress calls.

DOMESTIC CATTLE

Domestic cattle are bovine farm animals that are raised for their meat or milk, their hides, or draft purposes.

In the terminology used to describe the sex and age of cattle, the male is first a bull calf and if left intact becomes a bull. If castrated he becomes a steer and in about two or three years grows to an ox. The female is first a heifer calf, growing into a heifer and becoming a cow. Depending on the breed, mature bulls weigh 450–1,800 kg (1,000–4,000 pounds), and cows 360–1,090 kg (800–2,400 pounds). Males retained for beef production are usually castrated to make them more docile on the range or in feedlots. With males intended for use as working oxen or bullocks, castration is practiced to make them more tractable at work.

All modern domestic cattle are believed to belong to the species *Bos taurus* (European breeds such as Shorthorn and Jersey) or *Bos indicus* (zebu breeds such as Brahman) or to be crosses of these two (such as Santa Gertrudis). Many contemporary breeds are of recent origin. The definition of a breed is difficult and inexplicit, although the term is commonly used and, in practice, well understood. It may be used generally to connote animals that have been selectively bred for a long time so as to possess distinctive identity in colour, size, conformation, and function, and these or other distinguishing characteristics are perpetuated in their progeny.

GAURS

The gaur (*Bos gaurus*) is a species of wild cattle in family Bovidae. The gaur lives in small herds in the mountain forests of India, Southeast Asia, and the Malay Peninsula. Larger than any other wild cattle, it attains a shoulder height of 1.8 m (6 feet) or more. It is heavy-bodied and typically blue-eyed and has curving horns, a high ridge on the forepart of the back, and white "stockings" on the legs. Bulls are dark brown or blackish, cows and young reddish brown. Greatly reduced in numbers, gaurs survive only in scattered herds in India, Myanmar (Burma), West Malaysia, and Thailand.

GAYALS

The gayal (*Bos gaurus frontalis*), also called the mithan, is a subspecies of the gaur and the largest of the wild oxen, subfamily Bovinae (family Bovidae), which is kept and used by the hill tribes of Assam and Myanmar (Burma).

Smaller than the gaur and with shorter legs, the gayal stands 140–160 cm (55–63 inches) at the shoulder. Bulls weigh up to a ton, 20–25 percent more than cows. The gayal lacks the gaur's massive shoulder hump, and its skull is shorter, wider, and flatter. The horns of both sexes protrude from the sides of the head and are thicker, but shorter, than those of the gaur. A double dewlap at the chin and throat is well developed. Bulls are black and females brown-black. Both have white stockings. Some gayals are piebald, and even white, as the result of hybridizing with cattle.

Gayals are not tame enough to be herded like cattle. However, they live and forage in the vicinity of settlements, to which they come close to spend the night. They can be lured right up to a village with salt, an important element in the diet of all cattle. Gaurs are water-dependent grazers and browsers with a preference for green grass and other monocots that grow in forest clearings, which may explain the origins of the gayal. The clearings created by the hill tribes for growing crops provide food for gaurs also. The crops as well as the grass and forbs that colonize abandoned fields are undefended. When these factors are combined with the proximity of settlements to water and the protection from predators (primarily tigers) gained by sleeping close to people who tolerate, and even promote, the arrangement, all the conditions for self-domestication are met. The final stage of self-domestication is reached when animals have so lost their fear of humans that they can be used for food and trade. Such is the fate of the gayal.

The social organization and mating system of the gayal remains unchanged from its wild progenitors. The mating call of the bull gayal sounds like a gaur and unlike any other bovine. It is loud and as resonant as the base notes of an organ. Further proof of the relationship of the two animals is the mating of gayal cows with gaur bulls, which is promoted by gayal keepers to improve the breed.

KOUPREYS

The kouprey (*Bos sauveli*) is an elusive wild ox (tribe Bovini, family Bovidae) of Indochina and one of the world's most endangered large mammals, if it is not already extinct.

Unknown to science until 1937, the kouprey was rare even then: no more than an estimated 2,000 existed in eastern Thailand, southern Laos, westernmost Vietnam, and the northern plains of Cambodia; the last named is considered the centre of distribution, where it is the national symbol. The presence of the gaur and the banteng, two other common wild oxen, may also have delayed recognition of the kouprey, which could be mistaken for either species by casual observers. The kouprey is intermediate in size, standing 1.7–1.9 metres (5.6–6.2 feet) tall and weighing 700–900 kg (1,500–2,000 pounds). Old bulls are very dark brown with white stockings (like the banteng and the gaur) and have a very large dewlap (present, though smaller, in the other two). However, the kouprey's dorsal hump is less developed, and the tail is longer. Cows and young are a different colour from females of the banteng and gaur, being gray with a darker underside and darker forelegs. Kouprey horns, 80 cm (32 inches) long, are also thinner and differently shaped: horns of males grow sideways, then forward and upward, and finally inward. Frayed horn tips, a peculiarity of this species, develop in older bulls. Females have lyre-shaped horns half as long as those of males.

Koupreys are primarily grazers whose habitat is dry open forest and tree and orchard savanna, preferably adjacent to dense forest offering shelter during very hot weather. They leave the plains for the hills during the rainy season. Salt licks are important to koupreys. From the little that is known of kouprey social organization (there are none in captivity, and they are only fleetingly observed in the wild), it appears the same as in other *Bos* species. Males and females range in separate small herds most of the year but mix in the dry season. Bulls become increasingly solitary with age. They follow cow herds and seek out females in estrus during the April mating season. Having found a cow in heat, a bull forms a tending bond, in which the bull follows the cow closely until she is ready to mate—unless, that is, he is displaced by a bigger bull, as an established male dominance hierarchy determines which bulls have priority. Calves are born nine months later, before the hottest months of the dry season. Cows leave the herd to calve and rejoin a herd when the calf is about a month old.

By the late 1960s the number of surviving koupreys was estimated to be no more than on hundred. For the last half of the 20th century an almost continuous state of warfare and political unrest in the kouprey's range kept outsiders away. None has actually been seen by reliable observers for many years, though researchers remain optimistic that one hundred to three hundred still survive in Cambodia's northern plains. If well-managed protected areas were established that had the support of local people, the kouprey could possibly be saved.

OXEN

The ox (*Bos taurus,* or *B. taurus primigenius*), is a domesticated form of the large horned mammals that once moved in herds across North America and Europe (whence they have disappeared) and Asia and Africa, where some still exist in the wild state. South America and Australia have no wild oxen. Oxen are members of the Bovidae family.

The castrated male of *B. taurus* is a docile form especially useful as a draft animal in many less developed parts of the world. Oxen are also used for food in some areas.

WATER BUFFALO

The water buffalo (*Bubalus bubalis*), also called the arni, is either of two forms, wild and domestic, of Asian mammal similar to the ox. There are 74 breeds of domestic water buffalo numbering some 165 million animals, but only small numbers of wild water buffalo remain. Both forms are gray to black with off-white "socks" and one or two white chevrons on the neck. Domestic forms may have more white. Horns in both sexes curve backward in a crescent. The record horn length is just under 2 metres (6.6 feet)—the longest among cattle or any other bovid, although in domestic forms the horns are shorter or even absent. Single offspring are born after a gestation of 10 to 11 months. Longevity of the domesticated water buffalo can be 40 years, but the wild form is not as long-lived, even in captivity.

The domesticated water buffalo (*Bubalus bubalis*) is the "living tractor of the East" and has been introduced to Europe, Africa, the Americas, Australia, Japan, and Hawaii. There are two types, river and swamp, each considered a subspecies. The river buffalo was present by 2500 BCE in India and 1000 BCE in Mesopotamia. The breed was selected mainly for its milk, which contains 8 percent butterfat. Breeds include the Murrah with its curled horns, the Surati, and the Jafarabadi. Swamp buffalo more closely resemble wild water buffalo and are used as draft animals in rice paddies throughout Southeast Asia. Breeds range from the 900-kg (2,000-pound) Thai and haizi to the 400-kg (800-pound) wenzhou and carabao. Children ride them to their wallows after their labours and clean their faces and ears.

The wild water buffalo is sometimes referred to as a different species (*B. arnee*). It can interbreed with domestic water buffalo. This wild form is a huge animal, nearly 3 metres (10 feet) long and 2 metres (6.5 feet) tall and weighing up to 1,200 kg (2,600 pounds). Females are about two-thirds this size. The hooves are large and splayed, and two flexible joints (fetlock and pastern) near the hooves allow for easier walking through deep mud. Wild water buffalo live in Southeast Asian swamps and forests, where they feed on grass and sedges, mostly at night. By day they rest in water up to their nostrils, or they wallow and "shovel" mud onto themselves with their horns to keep cool and escape biting insects. Five to eight closely related cows and offspring live together, perhaps with a bull, while young males live in bachelor groups. Feral herds number up to 30 animals. Their sense of smell is quite acute, and if a predator is detected, the group will advance together with horns lowered. A few dozen herds possibly persist from east-central India to Thailand, but these will likely be lost as they interbreed with feral domestic forms.

Three other *Bubalus* species, two anoas (dwarf buffalos) and the tamarao, live in forests of Sulawesi and the Philippines. The wild water buffalo and all its Asian relatives are endangered by habitat loss and overhunting. Water buffalo and the African Cape buffalo (*Syncerus caffer caffer*) diverged from yaks and bison about three million years ago.

YAKS

Yaks (*Bos grunniens*) are long-haired, short-legged oxlike mammals that were probably domesticated in Tibet but have been introduced wherever there are people at elevations of 4,000–6,000 metres (14,000–20,000 feet), mainly in China but also in Central Asia, Mongolia, and Nepal.

Wild yaks are sometimes referred to as a separate species (*Bos mutus*) to differentiate them from domestic yaks, although they are freely interbred with various kinds of cattle. Wild yaks are larger, the bulls standing up to 2 metres (6.5 feet) tall at the shoulder and weighing over 800 kg (1,800 pounds). Cows weigh less than half as much. In China, where they are known as "hairy cattle," yaks are heavily fringed with long black hair over a shorter blackish or brown undercoat that can keep them warm to –40 °C (-40 °F). Colour in domesticated yaks is more variable, and white splotches are common. Like bison (genus *Bison*), the head droops before high massive shoulders. Horns are 80 cm (30 inches) long in the males, 50 cm (20 inches) in females.

It is not known with certainty when yaks were domesticated, although it is likely that they were first bred as beasts of burden for the caravans of Himalayan trade routes. Yaks' lung capacity is about three times that of cattle, and they have more and smaller red blood cells, improving the blood's ability to transport oxygen. Domesticated yaks number at least 12 million and were bred for tractability and high milk production. Yaks are also used for plowing and threshing, as well as for meat, hides, and fur. The dried dung of the yak is the only obtainable fuel on the treeless Tibetan plateau.

Ruminant grazers, wild yaks migrate seasonally to the lower plains to eat grasses and herbs. When it gets too warm, they retreat to higher plateaus to eat mosses and lichens, which they rasp off rocks with their rough tongues. Their dense fur and few sweat glands make life below 3,000 metres (10,000 feet) difficult, even in winter. Yaks obtain water by eating snow when necessary. In the wild, they live in mixed herds of about 25, though some males live in bachelor groups or alone. Yaks seasonally aggregate into larger groups. Breeding occurs in September–October. Calves are born about nine months later and nursed for a full year. The mother breeds again in the fall after the calf has been weaned.

Wild yaks once extended from the Himalayas to Lake Baikal in Siberia, and in the 1800s they were still numerous in Tibet. After 1900 they were hunted almost to extinction by Tibetan and Mongolian herders and military personnel. Small numbers survive in northern Tibet and the Ladakh steppe of India, but they are not effectively protected. They are also endangered because of interbreeding with domestic cattle.

In the family Bovidae, the yak belongs to the same genus as cattle as well as the banteng, gaur, and kouprey of Southeast Asia. More distantly related are the American and European bison. *Bos* and *Bison* diverged from water buffalo (genus *Bubalus*) and other wild bovines about three million years ago. Despite its ability to breed with cattle, it has been argued that the yak should be returned to its former genus, *Poephagus*.

SWINE

Swine are short-legged, hoofed omnivorous mammals belonging to the family Suidae, order Artiodactyla, that include the domestic pig and its wild relatives. They are stout animals with small eyes, a small tail, and coarse, sometimes sparse, hair. Their hooves have two functional and two nonfunctional digits. All have a long, mobile snout ending in a rounded cartilage disk used to dig for food. Some species have tusks. Females bear litters of two to 14 young; gestation is four to five months. Swine originated in the Old World, though domestic pigs are found worldwide. Wild pigs may live up to 25 years or more.

BABIRUSAS

The babirusa (*Babyrousa babyrussa*) is a wild East Indian swine, family Suidae, of Celebes and the Molucca islands.

The stout-bodied, short-tailed babirusa stands 65–80 cm (25–30 inches) at the shoulder. It has a rough, grayish hide and is almost hairless. Its most notable feature is the exaggerated development of the upper and lower canine teeth, or tusks, of the male. Those of the upper jaw grow upward from their bases so that they pierce the skin of the

Babirusa (Babirousa babyrussa). W. Suschitzky

muzzle and curve backward, eventually almost touching the forehead.

The babirusa is a docile, retiring, night-hunting animal of dense jungle. It is a fast runner and swims readily. When foraging, it roots in soft soil near rivers and in swamps. The babirusa is considered good to eat and is often hunted locally.

BOARS

Boars are wild members of the pig species *Sus scrofa,* family Suidae. The term *boar* is also used to designate the male of the domestic pig, guinea pig, and various other mammals. The terms *wild boar* and *wild pig* are sometimes used to refer to any wild member of the *Sus* genus.

The wild boar—which is sometimes called the European wild boar—is the largest of the wild pigs and is native to forests ranging from western and northern Europe and North Africa to India, the Andaman Islands, and China. It has been introduced to New Zealand and to the United States (where it mixed with native feral species). It is bristly haired, grizzled, blackish or brown in colour, and stands up to 90 cm (35 inches) tall at the shoulder. Except for old males, which are solitary, wild boars live in groups. The animals are swift, nocturnal, and omnivorous and are good swimmers. They possess sharp tusks, and, although they are normally unaggressive, they can be dangerous.

From earliest times, because of its great strength, speed, and ferocity, the wild boar has been one of the favourite beasts of the chase. In some parts of Europe and India it is still hunted with dogs, but the spear has mostly been replaced with the gun.

In Europe the boar is one of the four heraldic beasts of the chase and was the distinguishing mark of Richard III,

Bush pig (Potamochoerus porcus). Anthony Bannister/Animals Animals

king of England. As an article of food, the boar's head was long considered a special delicacy.

BUSH PIGS

The bush pig (*Potamochoerus porcus*) is an African member of the pig family, Suidae, resembling a boar but with long body hair and tassels of hair on its ears. The bush pig lives in groups, or sounders, of about four to 20 animals in forests and scrub regions south of the Sahara. It is omnivorous and roots for food with its snout. The adult bush pig stands 64–76 cm (25–30 inches) tall at the shoulder. Its coat colour ranges from reddish brown to blackish, with black-and-white face markings and a white crest on the back. There are several subspecies of bush pig, among them the reddish brown animal called the red river hog (*P. porcus porcus*).

DOMESTIC PIGS

In Britain, the term *pig* refers to all domestic swine. In the United States, *pig* is used to refer to younger swine not yet ready for market and weighing usually less than 82 kg (180 pounds), others being called hogs. Domestic North American pigs originated from wild stocks still found in European, Asian, and North African forests. Wild pigs are not truly native to North America but are believed to have been introduced on Christopher Columbus' second voyage in 1493 and brought to the mainland in the early 1500s. There is little difference between wild pigs, or boars, and domestic swine, though the tusklike teeth of domestic pigs are not as developed as the tusks of their wild kin, who use the sharp ends to forage for roots and as a defensive weapon.

Domestic pigs are categorized according to three basic types: large-framed lard types with a comparatively thick layer of fat and carcasses usually weighing at least 100 kg (220 pounds); smaller bacon types, with carcasses of about 70 kg (150 pounds); and pork types with carcasses averaging around 45 kg (100 pounds).

In the early 21th century, China had the largest hog population of any country in the world, but scientific breeding was concentrated in Europe and the United States. Denmark produced the Landrace breed, raised for its excellent bacon. The Yorkshire (Large White), the world's most popular breed, originated in Britain in the 18th century.

PECCARIES

Peccaries (family Tayassuidae) are three species of pig-like mammal found in the southern deserts of the United States southward through the Amazon Basin to Patagonian South America. Closely resembling the wild pig, or boar, the peccary has dark, coarse hair and a large head with a circular snout. The ears are small, as is the tail, which is generally not visible. Its spearlike canine teeth give the peccary its other common names, javelin and javelina. These teeth do not protrude but make notable lumps in the lips.

Peccaries are the New World counterparts of swine (family Suidae) and differ from true pigs in certain skeletal and dental features. They also have a scent gland under the skin that opens on the ridge of the back and gives off a strong, musky odour. This gland is the reason for the mistaken belief that peccaries have two navels, one above and one below. Peccaries are omnivorous, feeding on a variety of plants, small animals, and carrion. They have a barking alarm call and when disturbed make a rattling sound by chattering their teeth. Although ferocious when harassed, they are sometimes tamed by South American Indians. Peccaries are also hunted for their hides and meat. Litters usually consist of two young, born after a five-month gestation period.

There are three species. The collared peccary (*Pecari tajacu*) is the smallest and the most common, living throughout the entire tayassuid range in a variety of habitats. Distinguished by a pale stripe around the neck, collared peccaries are less than a metre (3.3 feet) long and weigh between 17 and 30 kg (37 and 66 pounds). They live in a variety of habitats, generally roving during the day in herds of about a dozen, although larger and smaller groups are also common.

The white-lipped peccary (*T. pecari*) is slightly darker and larger, weighing 25–40 kg (55–88 pounds). Named for the white area around the mouth, its range is limited to Central and South America, where forest and scrub are the primary habitats. These peccaries live in herds of 50 to over three hundred and are more severely impacted by habitat destruction.

The Chacoan peccary (*Catagonus wagneri*) is the largest, weighing over 40 kg. It is also the least common, living only in the dry Chacoan region of South America. About five thousand are estimated to remain and were thought to be extinct by the scientific community until 1972. These endangered peccaries usually form small herds of seven animals or less. The population has been affected by both hunting and the clearing of its habitat for cattle pastures, causing concern about the species' long-term survival.

WARTHOGS

The warthog (*Phacochoerus aethiopicus*), a member of the pig family Suidae, is found in open and lightly forested areas of Africa. The warthog is a sparsely haired, large-headed, blackish or brown animal standing about 76 cm (30 inches) at the shoulder. It has a coarse mane extending

Warthog (Phacochoerus aethiopicus). Karl H. Maslowski

from the neck to the middle of the back, and it has a long, thin, tufted tail that it carries high while it is running. The male has two pairs of bumps, or warts, on the face. Both sexes bear tusks. Those of the lower jaw form sharp weapons, and those of the upper jaw curve upward and inward in a semicircle, attaining a length of more than 60 cm (24 inches) in some males.

The warthog is a gregarious animal that feeds on grass and other vegetation. It often shelters in enlarged aardvark burrows, which it enters backward so as to be able to defend itself.

CHAPTER 6

CAMELIDS, GIRAFFIDS, AND HIPPOPOTAMUSES

C amels, giraffes, hippopotamuses, and their relatives are very well-known artiodactyls of both the Old World and the New World. The Asian camels and their South American relatives have long been important as pack animals and for producing milk, meat, and wool-like fibre. The giraffe and the hippopotamus are prominent natives of sub-Saharan Africa that can be seen in zoos around the world.

CAMELIDAE: CAMELS AND THEIR RELATIVES

Camelids, members of the family Camelidae, include the familiar single-humped Arabian camel and the double-humped Bactrian camel, species of genus *Camelus* descended from animals that first appeared in North America 40 million years ago. South American camelids are the llama, alpaca, guanaco, and vicuña. Collectively, these animals are known as lamoids and are frequently classified in a single genus, *Lama*. Unlike camels, lamoids do not have the characteristic humps. They are slender-bodied animals and have long legs and necks, short tails, small heads, and large, pointed ears.

The genera *Camelus* and *Lama* diverged 11 million years ago. By 2 million years ago (the early Pleistocene Epoch), *Camelus* representatives had crossed back to Asia and were present in Africa (Tanzania). During the Pleistocene

(2,600,000 to 11,700 years ago), camelids reached South America; North American camelid stock became extinct 10,000 years ago.

CAMELS

Camels (genus *Camelus*) are two species of large ruminating hoofed mammals of arid Africa and Asia known for their ability to go for long periods without drinking. The Arabian camel, or dromedary (*C. dromedarius*), has one back hump; the Bactrian camel (*C. bactrianus*) has two.

These "ships of the desert" have long been valued as pack or saddle animals, and they are also exploited for milk, meat, wool, and hides. The dromedary was domesticated about 2000–1300 BCE in Arabia, the Bactrian camel

*Bactrian camel (*Camelus bactrianus*). © George Holton—The National Audubon Society Collection/Photo Researchers*

by 2500 BCE in northern Iran and northeast Afghanistan. Most of today's 13 million domesticated dromedaries are in India and the Horn of Africa. Wild dromedaries are extinct, although there is a large feral population in interior Australia descended from pack animals imported in the 19th century. About one million domesticated Bactrian camels live from the Middle East to China and Mongolia. Wild Bactrian camels are endangered. The largest population—one thousand—lives in the Gobi Desert.

NATURAL HISTORY

Camels have an unmistakable silhouette, with their humped back, short tail, long slim legs, and long neck that dips downward and rises to a small narrow head. The upper lip is split into two sections that move independently. Both species are about 3 metres (10 feet) long and 2 metres (6.5 feet) high at the hump (itself 20 cm [8 inches]). Males weigh 400 to 650 kg (900 to 1,400 pounds), and the female is about 10 percent smaller. Colour is usually light brown but can be grayish. Domesticated Bactrian camels are darker, stockier, and woollier than the wild form. Heavy eyelashes protect eyes from blowing sand, and the nostrils can be squeezed shut. The dromedary has horny pads on the chest and knees that protect it from searing desert sand when it lies down, and the Bactrian camel lacks these callosities. Camels are generally docile, but they will bite or kick when annoyed. When excited, camels huff so sharply that spit is incidentally expelled.

Camels do not walk on their hoofs. Weight is borne on the conjoined pads of the third and fourth toes, and the other toes have been lost. Dromedaries have a soft, wide-spreading pad for walking on sand. Bactrian camels have a firmer foot. Like the giraffe's, the camel's gait is a pace, with both legs on a side moving together. Short bursts of 65 km (40 miles) per hour are possible, but camels are excellent plodders. Bactrian camels can carry more than 200 kg (450 pounds) for 50 km (30 miles) in a day, while the more lightly built dromedaries can carry up to 100 kg (220 pounds) for 60 km (37 miles) if they are worked in the coolness of night.

During catastrophic droughts, herdsmen may lose all of their cattle, sheep, and goats, while 80 percent of the camels will survive, owing to the camel's ability to conserve water and tolerate dehydration. In severe heat a camel survives four to seven days without drinking, but it can go 10 months without drinking at all if it is not working and the forage contains enough moisture. Even salty water can be tolerated, and between drinks it forages far from oases to find food unavailable to other livestock. The body rehydrates within minutes of a long drink, absorbing over 100 litres (25 gallons) in 5–10 minutes. Cattle could not tolerate such a sudden dilution of the blood because their red blood cells would burst under the osmotic stress. Camel erythrocyte membranes are viscous, which permits swelling. A thirsty camel can reduce urine output to one-fifth normal volume and produce feces dry enough that herders use it as fuel for fires. Another adaptation is minimization of sweating. The fine woolly coat insulates the body, reducing heat gain. The camel also can allow its body temperature to rise to 41 °C (106 °F) before sweating at all. This reduces the temperature difference between the camel and its environment and thereby reduces heat gain and water loss by as much as two-thirds. Only in the hottest weather must the camel sweat. It tolerates extreme dehydration and can lose up to 25–30 percent of its body weight—twice what would be fatal for most mammals.

Camels have also adapted to desert conditions by being able to endure protein deficiency and eat items other livestock avoid, such as thorns, dry leaves, and salt-bush. When food is plentiful, camels "overeat," storing fat in one area on the back and forming a hump. When the fat is depleted, the hump sags to the side or disappears. Storing fat in one place also increases the body's ability to dissipate heat everywhere else.

When not corralled, camels form stable groups of females accompanied by one mature male. Females breed by three to four years of age; males begin to manufacture sperm at age three but do not compete for females until they are six to eight years old. Males compete for dominance by circling each other with the head held low and biting the feet or head of the opponent and attempting to topple it. After one camel withdraws from the bout, the winner may roll and rub secretions onto the ground from a gland on the back of its head. The dominant male breeds with all the females in each stable group. After a gestation of 13 or 14 months, one calf weighing up to 37 kg (81 pounds) is born, usually during the rainy season. Milk yields of 35 kg (77 pounds) per day are achieved in some breeds (e.g., the "milch dromedary" of Pakistan), though normal yield is about 4 kg (9 pounds) per day. Pastoralists typically divert most milk to their own use during the calf's first nine to 11 months, then force weaning and take the rest. The calf is otherwise suckled 12 to 18 months. Females and males reproduce until about 20 years old. Longevity is 40 years.

Cultural Significance

Camels are among those few creatures with which humans have forged a special bond of dependence and affinity. Traditional lifestyles in many regions of the Middle East, North Africa, and Central Asia would never have developed without the camel, around which entire cultures have come into being. This camel-based culture is best exemplified by the Bedouin of the Arabian Peninsula—the native habitat of the dromedary—whose entire traditional economy depended on the produce of the camel. Camel's milk and flesh were staples of the Bedouin diet, and its hair yielded cloth for shelter and clothing. Its endurance as a beast of burden and as a mount enabled the Bedouin to range far into the desert. The mobility and freedom that the camel afforded to desert Arabs helped forge their independent culture and their strong sense of self-reliance, and they celebrated the camel in their native poetic verse, the *qaṣīdah*, in which the *nāqah* (female camel) was a faithful, unwavering mount. Among these nomadic people, a man's wealth was measured not only by the number of camels he possessed but also by their speed, stamina, and endurance.

Until modern times, the camel was the backbone of the caravan trade, a central pillar of the economy in large parts of Asia and Africa. In settled regions, the caravansary, located on the outskirts of most urban centres, served as a hub for business and as a source of information about the outside world for the city's residents. In the central Islamic lands, it likewise set the scene for many tales in the rich Arab-Persian oral tradition of storytelling, such as those found in *The Thousand and One Nights*. In Central Asia, vast and numerous camel caravans ensured the wealth and growth of the great trading cities of the Silk Road, upon which goods moved between Asia and Europe.

Today the camel remains an important part of some local economies, although it has been surpassed by automated forms of transportation for most tasks. Camels are still bred for their meat, milk, and hair. Also, beginning in the late 20th century, the age-old sport of camel racing was revived, particularly in the countries of the Arabian Peninsula but also as far afield as Australia and the United States.

ALPACAS

The alpaca (*Lama pacos*) is a South American member of the camel family, Camelidae. It is closely related to the llama, guanaco, and vicuña, which are known collectively as lamoids. The alpaca and the llama were both apparently domesticated several thousand years ago by the Indians of the Andes Mountains of South America. The other two lamoid species, the guanaco and vicuña, exist basically in the wild state.

Like other lamoids, alpacas are slender-bodied animals with a long neck and legs, a short tail, a small head, and large, pointed ears. Alpacas are readily distinguished from llamas by their smaller size. They stand approximately 90 cm (35 inches) high at the shoulder and weigh 55 to 65 kg (121 to 143 pounds). The alpaca also differs from the llama in having a rounded, rather than squarish, body and in its habit of pressing its tail close to the body rather than holding it erect, as does the llama. The alpaca's shaggy coat varies in colour from the usual black or brown through lighter shades of gray and tan to pale yellow and, occasionally, white. The present distribution of alpacas is limited to central and southern Peru and western Bolivia. Alpacas are the most limited in range and the most specialized of the four lamoids, being adapted to marshy ground at altitudes from 4,000 to 4,800 metres (13,000 to 15,700 feet). In adaptation to the reduced oxygen content of the air, their red blood corpuscles are exceptionally numerous.

Alpacas are the most important of the lamoids for wool production. During the period of Incan civilization, the wearing of robes made of alpaca and vicuña wools was reserved for the nobility and royalty. Two breeds of alpaca, the huacaya and the suri, were developed in pre-Columbian times. The wool of the suri is fine and silky and grows long enough to touch the ground if the animal is not sheared. The wool of the huacaya is shorter and coarser by comparison. The alpaca's wool is remarkably lightweight, strong, lustrous, high in insulation value, and resistant to rain and snow. It is used in parkas, sleeping bags, and fine coat linings. Alpaca fibre is sometimes

SPECIALTY HAIR FIBRES

Specialty hair fibres are textile fibres obtained from certain animals of the goat and camel families that are valued for such desirable properties as fine diameter, natural lustre, and ability to impart pleasing hand (characteristics perceived by handling) to fabrics. Specialty hair fibres obtained from the goat family include mohair, from the Angora goat, and cashmere, sometimes referred to as cashmere wool, from the Kashmir goat. Common goats yield the less-valuable goat hair that is used mainly in low-cost felts and carpets manufactured for the automobile industry. Fibres obtained from animals of the camel family include camel hair, mainly from the Bactrian camel, and guanaco, llama, alpaca, and vicuña fibres, all from members of the genus *Lama*.

Specialty hair fibres are gathered by hunting or domesticating the animals for their pelts or by periodic collecting of fleece from live animals. Most of the fibres are low in the crimp (waviness) and felting (tendency to mat together) properties associated with the sheep fibre normally called wool. In the United States, however, the Wool Products Labeling Act (1939) allows the designation of such fibres as "wool" in fibre-content labels.

Like wool and the finer, shorter fur fibres, hair fibres grow from the epidermis of the animal, forming the characteristic coat, and are composed chiefly of the protein substance keratin. Their chemical properties are similar to those of wool. The animal is usually covered with two types of fibre. An outer coat of shiny, stiff guard hairs affords protection from the elements. The undercoat, or down, composed of short, fine, soft fibre, provides insulation against heat and cold. Short, coarse, brittle hairs, called kemp, may be intermingled with both types of fibre. Separation of the downy fibre from other hair may be achieved by combing or by a blowing process that causes the heavier fibre to fall away. Such operations may be repeated several times to minimize coarse-fibre content.

Long fibres with fine diameter and light colour are usually the most desirable and expensive. An exception is vicuña, valued for its fairly dark cinnamon-brown colour. Specialty hair fibres, costly because of their rarity and the processing they require, may be used alone in luxury fabrics for fine garments. They may also be blended with wool or other fibres to enhance appearance or texture, imparting softness or special effects. The coarse guard hairs are frequently blended with wool to impart lustre.

combined with other fibres to make dress and lightweight suit fabrics and is also woven as a pile fabric used both for coating and as a lining for outerwear. Peru is the leading producer of the wool, with most of it being marketed in the city of Arequipa. The Peruvian government has established a breeding program to improve the quality of alpaca wool and increase its production.

Alpacas are normally sheared every two years, with the suris yielding fine fleeces of about 3 kg (6.5 pounds) per animal, and the huacayas giving coarser fleeces weighing about 2.5 kg (5.5 pounds). Hair growth in two years is about 30 cm (12 inches) in the huacaya and 60 cm (24 inches) in the suri. Individual fibres within the fleece range from about 20 to 40 cm (8 to 16 inches) in length at the time of shearing. Alpacas have a natural life span of 15–20 years.

GUANACOS

Guanacos (*Lama guanacoe*) are South American members of the camel family, Camelidae. They are closely related to lamoids: the alpaca, llama, and vicuña. Unlike camels, lamoids do not have the characteristic camel humps. They are slender-bodied animals with long legs and necks, short tails, small heads, and large, pointed ears. They graze on grass and other plants. When annoyed, they spit. Lamoids are able to interbreed and to produce fertile offspring.

The guanaco, like the vicuña, is a wild lamoid that lives in small bands of females, usually led by a male. The guanaco ranges from the snow line to sea level throughout the Andes from Peru and Bolivia southward to Tierra del Fuego and other islands. The adult stands about 110 cm (43 inches) at the shoulder. It is pale brown above and white below, with a grayish head.

The soft, downy fibre covering of the young, or guanaquito, comprises about 10 to 20 percent of the fleece and belongs to the group of textile fibres called speciality hair fibres. Guanaco fibre, introduced for textile use in the mid-1900s, is valued for its rarity and soft texture and is used for luxury fabrics. It is considered to be finer than alpaca but coarser than vicuña. The pelts, especially of the guanaquito, resemble those of the red fox and are used by the fur industry, which provides the textile industry with waste fibre remaining after processing.

Depending on the authority, the llama, alpaca, and guanaco may be classified as distinct species or as subspecies of llama (*Lama glama*). Certain structural features lead some experts to classify the vicuña as *Vicugna vicugna.*

LLAMAS

Llamas (*Lama glama*) are South American members of the camel family, Camelidae, that are closely related to the alpaca, guanaco, and vicuña. Most herds of llamas are maintained by the Indians of Bolivia, Peru, Ecuador, Chile, and Argentina. The llama is primarily a pack animal but is also used as a source of food, wool, hides, tallow for candles, and dried dung for fuel. The largest of the lamoids, it averages 120 cm (47 inches) at the shoulder. A 113-kg (250-pound) llama can carry a load of 45–60 kg (100–130 pounds) and average 25 to 30 km (15 to 20 miles) travel a day. The llama's high thirst tolerance, endurance, and ability to subsist on a wide variety of forage makes it an important transport animal on the bleak Andean plateaus and mountains. The llama is a gentle animal, but, when overloaded or maltreated, it will lie down, hiss, spit and kick, and refuse to move. Llamas breed in the (Southern Hemispheric) late summer and fall, from November to May. The gestation period lasts about 11 months, and the female gives birth to one young. Although usually white, the llama may be solid black or brown, or it may be white with black or brown markings.

The llama and the alpaca (*L. pacos*) are domestic animals not known to exist in the wild state. They appear to have been bred from guanacos during or before the Inca Indian civilization to be used as beasts of burden.

Depending on the authority, the llama, alpaca, and guanaco may be classified as distinct species or as subspecies of *Lama glama*. Because of certain structural features, the vicuña is sometimes classified into a separate genus from the other lamoids and is known as *Vicugna vicugna*.

Llamas are normally sheared every two years, each yielding about 3–3.5 kg (about 7–8 pounds) of fibre. Llama fleece consists of the coarse guard hairs of the protective outer coat (about 20 percent) and the short, crimped (wavy) fibre of the insulating undercoat. The coarse fleece is inferior to the wool of the alpaca. The hair's colour is usually variegated, generally in shades of brown, although there are some pure blacks and whites. Cleaning reduces the final yield of fleece to about 66–84 percent of the original weight. Individual locks of hair appear wavy. The fairly downy fibres have about two to four crimps per cm (three-fourths of a crimp to about one and a half crimps per inch), but the coarse hairs are fairly straight. The hair's length ranges from 8 to 25 cm 3.15 to 9.8 inches), the coarse hairs being longest. The difference in diameter between the guard hairs and the downy fibre is not so great as it is in cashmere. Diameter ranges from about 10 to 150 micrometres (millionths of a metre) with undercoat fibre usually from 10 to 20 micrometres.

The scales of the outer layer of the fibre are indistinct, and the cortical layer contains pigment, with variations in the amount and distribution, which produces the various colours and tones. All but the finest fibres are likely to possess a hollow central core, or medulla, resulting in low density, which makes the fibre fairly light in weight.

Llama fibre is used, alone or in blends, for knitwear and for woven fabrics made into outerwear. It is used locally for rugs, rope, and fabric.

VICUÑAS

Vicuñas (*Lama vicugna* or *Vicugna vicugna*) are South American members of the camel family, Camelidae, that are closely related to alpacas, guanacos, and llamas (all known as lamoids). Depending on the authority, the llama, alpaca, and guanaco may be classified as distinct species of llama (*Lama glama*). Because of differences in the incisor teeth, however, some authorities place the vicuña in a separate genus, *Vicugna*. Most vicuñas inhabit Peru, with smaller numbers found in Bolivia, Chile, and Argentina.

The vicuña is covered with a remarkably long, fine, soft, and lustrous coat that varies in colour from light cinnamon to a pale white, with long white fleece hanging from the lower flanks and the base of the neck. The annual yield of fleece sheared from domesticated vicuñas shows a wide range of from 85 to 550 g (3 to 20 ounces) per animal. Vicuña fibre is strong and resilient, but it is highly sensitive to chemicals and is generally used in its natural colour. The costly fibre is made into high-priced coats, dressing gowns, and shawls.

The dense, silky fleece of the vicuña, once reserved for the Incan nobility, provides excellent insulation against the temperature fluctuations the animal encounters in its natural habitat: semiarid grasslands in the central Andes at altitudes of 3,600–4,800 metres (12,000–16,000 feet).

A swift, graceful animal, the vicuña is the smallest of the camelids, with a shoulder height of about 90 cm (36 inches) and a weight of about 50 kg (110 pounds). When in danger, they emit a high, clear whistle. Vision and hearing are more highly developed than their sense of smell.

Like guanacos, vicuñas are wild, with temperaments that preclude domestication. The animals graze on low grasses and ruminate while resting. They travel in small bands of females, usually led by a male who acts as lookout and defends his territory against intruders. Vicuñas use communal dung heaps to mark their territorial boundaries. They spit frequently and noisily, like all lamoids. A single young, born in February about 11 months after the parents have mated, remains close to the mother for at least 10 months. The life expectancy is about 15 to 20 years.

Vicuñas have been hunted for centuries with a resulting decline in numbers. The Inca rounded the animals up, sheared their wool, and then released them. The vicuña are also killed for meat sometimes. In Spanish colonial times greater numbers of the animals were hunted and killed, and though protective legislation was introduced in the 19th century, poaching continued to reduce their total numbers, which declined from a million in Incan times to only about 10,000 by the late 1960s. Subsequent conservation efforts managed to increase the population to more than 80,000 by the late 20th century. The vicuña is listed as vulnerable in the *Red Data Book* and is now protected effectively in South American countries.

GIRAFFIDAE: GIRAFFES AND OKAPIS

Giraffes are long-necked, cud-chewing hoofed mammals of family Giraffidae that are native to Africa. In addition to their distinctive long necks, they have long legs and a coat pattern of irregular brown patches on a light background.

The only close relative of the giraffe (and the only other member of family Giraffidae) is the rainforest-dwelling okapi. Giraffes or something very similar lived in Tanzania two million years ago, but Giraffidae branched off from other members of the order Artiodactyla—cattle, antelope, and deer—about 34 million years ago.

GIRAFFES

Giraffes (*Giraffa camelopardalis*) are the tallest of all land animals. Males (bulls) may exceed 5.5 metres (18 feet) in height, and the tallest females (cows) are about 4.5 metres (about 15 feet). Using prehensile tongues almost half a metre long (about 20 inches), they are able to browse foliage almost 6 metres (20 feet) from the ground. Giraffes are a common sight in grasslands and open woodlands in East Africa, where they can be seen in reserves such as Tanzania's Serengeti National Park and Kenya's Amboseli National Park.

Giraffes grow to nearly their full height by four years of age but gain weight until they are seven or eight. Males weigh up to 1,930 kg (4,250 pounds), females up to 1,180 kg (2,600 pounds). The tail may be a metre (about a 3 feet) in length and has a long black tuft on the end. There is also a short black mane. Both sexes have a pair of horns, though males possess other bony protuberances on the skull. The back slopes downward to the hindquarters, a silhouette explained mainly by large muscles that support the neck. These muscles are attached to long spines on the vertebrae of the upper back. There are only seven neck (cervical) vertebrae, but they are elongated. Thick-walled arteries in the neck have extra valves to counteract gravity when the head is up. When the giraffe lowers its head to the ground,

Masai giraffe (Giraffa camelopardalis tippelskirchi). © Animals Animals

special vessels at the base of the brain control blood pressure. The gait of the giraffe is a pace (both legs on one side move together). In a gallop it pushes off with the hind legs and the front legs come down almost together, but no two hooves touch the ground at the same time. The neck flexes so that balance is maintained. Speeds of 50 km (31 miles) per hour can be maintained for several kilometres, but 60 km (37 miles) per hour can be attained over short distances. According to an Arabic saying, a good horse is one that can "outpace a giraffe."

Giraffes live in nonterritorial groups of up to 20. Home ranges are as small as 85 square km (33 square miles) in wetter areas but up to 1,500 square km (580 square miles) in dry regions. The animals are gregarious, a behaviour that apparently allows for increased vigilance against predators. They have excellent eyesight, and when one giraffe stares, for example, at a lion a kilometre (about half a mile) away, the others look in that direction too. Giraffes live up to 26 years in the wild and slightly longer in captivity.

Giraffes prefer to eat new shoots and leaves, mainly from the thorny acacia tree. Cows in particular select high-energy, low-fibre items. They are prodigious eaters, and a large male consumes about 65 kg (145 pounds) of food per day. The tongue and inside of the mouth are coated with tough tissue as protection. The giraffe grasps leaves with its prehensile lips or tongue and pulls them into the mouth. If the foliage is not thorny, the giraffe "combs" leaves from the stem by pulling it across the lower canine and incisor teeth. Giraffes obtain most water from their food, though in the dry season they drink at least every three days. They must spread the forelegs apart in order to reach the ground with the head.

Females first breed at four or five years of age. Gestation is 15 months, and, though most calves are born in dry months in some areas, births can take place in any month

Reticulated giraffe (Giraffa camelopardalis reticulata*), Kenya.* © Corbis

of the year. The single offspring is about 2 metres (6 feet) tall and weighs 100 kg (220 pounds). For a week the mother licks and nuzzles her calf in isolation while they learn each other's scent. Thereafter, the calf joins a "nursery group" of similar-aged youngsters, while mothers forage at variable distances. If lions or hyenas attack, a mother sometimes stands over her calf, kicking at the predators with front and back legs. Cows have food and water requirements that may keep them away from the nursery group for hours at a time, and about half of extremely young calves are killed by lions and hyenas. Calves sample vegetation at three weeks but suckle for 18–22 months. Males join other bachelors when one to two years old, whereas daughters are likely to stay near the mother.

Bulls eight years and older travel up to 20 km (12 miles) per day looking for cows in heat (estrus). Younger males spend years in bachelor groups, where they engage in "necking" bouts. These side-to-side clashes of heads cause mild damage, and bone deposits subsequently form around the horns, eyes, and back of the head. A single lump projects from between the eyes. Accumulation of bone deposits continues through life, resulting in skulls weighing 30 kg (66 pounds). Necking also establishes a social hierarchy. Violence sometimes occurs when two older bulls converge on an estrous cow. The advantage of a heavy, knobbed skull is soon apparent. With forelegs braced, bulls swing their necks and club each other with their skulls, aiming for the underbelly. There have been instances of bulls' being knocked off their feet or even rendered unconscious.

Paintings of giraffes appear on early Egyptian tombs. Just as today, giraffe tails were prized for the long wiry tuft hairs used to weave belts and jewelry. In the 13th century, East Africa supplied a trade in hides. During the 19th and 20th centuries, overhunting, habitat destruction, and rinderpest epidemics introduced by European livestock reduced giraffes to less than half their former range. Today giraffes are numerous in East African countries and also in certain reserves of Southern Africa, where they have enjoyed somewhat of a recovery. The West African sub-species is reduced to a small range in Niger.

Nine subspecies of giraffes are recognized on the basis of coat pattern. For example, the reticulated giraffe (*Giraffa camelopardalis reticulata*) of northeastern Africa has smooth-edged polygonal patches so closely spaced that the animal appears to be wearing a white net over a base colour of deep chestnut brown. Individual patterns, however, are unique.

OKAPIS

The okapi (species *Okapia johnstoni*) is a cud-chewing hoofed mammal that is placed along with the giraffe in

Okapi (Okapia johnstoni). Kenneth W. Fink/Root Resources

the family Giraffidae (order Artiodactyla). Found in the rainforests of the Congo region, the okapi was unknown to science until about 1900. Its neck and legs are shorter than those of the giraffe, and the shoulder height of females, which are larger than males, is about 1.5 m (5 feet). The coat is sleek and deep brown, almost purple, with the sides of the face dull reddish. The buttocks, thighs, and tops of the forelegs are horizontally striped with black and white, and the lower parts of the legs are white with black rings above the hooves. The eyes and ears are large, and the tongue is long and prehensile. The male has short horns covered with skin except at the tips.

The okapi is a shy, elusive animal that lives among dense cover and browses on leaves and fruit. It appears to be solitary. It has been exhibited in many zoological gardens and has been successfully bred in captivity. Gestation is about 14–15 months.

HIPPOPOTAMUSES

The hippopotamus (*Hippopotamus amphibius*) is an amphibious African ungulate mammal, the second largest land animal (after the elephant). *Hippopotamus* is Greek for "river horse," and the animal has been known since ancient times. Hippopotamuses are often seen basking on the banks or sleeping in the waters of rivers, lakes, and swamps next to grasslands. Because of their great size and aquatic habits, they are safe from most predators. They are not safe from humans, however, who have long valued their hide, meat, and ivory and at times have resented them for ruining crops. Once ranging over the entire continent and beyond, hippos now live in eastern, central, and parts of southern Africa.

The hippopotamus has a bulky body on stumpy legs, an enormous head, a short tail, and four toes on each foot. Each toe has a nail-like hoof. Males are usually 3.5 metres (11.5 feet) long, stand 1.5 metres (5 feet) tall, and weigh 3,200 kg (3.5 tons). The skin is 5 cm (2 inches) thick on the flanks but thinner elsewhere and nearly hairless. Colour is grayish brown, with pinkish underparts. The mouth is half a metre (20 inches) wide and can gape 150° to show the teeth. The lower canines are sharp and may exceed 30 cm (12 inches) long.

Hippos are well adapted to aquatic life. The ears, eyes, and nostrils are located high on the head so that the rest of the body may remain submerged. The ears and nostrils can be folded shut to keep out water. The body is so dense that they can walk underwater, where they can hold their breath for five minutes. Although often seen basking in the sun, hippos lose water rapidly through the skin and become dehydrated without periodic dips. They must also retreat to the water to keep cool, for they do not sweat. Numerous skin glands release a pinkish "lotion," which led to the ancient myth that hippos sweat blood; this pigment actually acts as a sunblock, filtering out ultraviolet radiation.

Hippos favour shallow areas where they can sleep half submerged ("rafting"). Their populations are limited by this "day living space," which may become quite crowded—as many as 150 hippos may use one pool in the dry season. In times of drought or famine, they may embark on overland migrations that often result in many deaths. By night, hippos walk along familiar paths as far as 10 km (6 miles) into surrounding grasslands to feed for five or six hours. The long canines and incisors are used strictly as weapons. Grazing is accomplished by grasping grass with the tough, wide lips and jerking the head. Near the river, where grazing and trampling are heaviest, large areas may be denuded of all grass, which results in erosion. Hippos, however, eat relatively little vegetation for their size (about 35 kg [80 pounds] per night), as their energy requirement is low because they are buoyed in warm water much of the time. Hippos do not chew cud but retain food for a long time in the stomach, where protein is extracted by fermentation digestion. Their digestive process is responsible for cycling tremendous quantities of nutrients into the African rivers and lakes and thereby supporting the fish that are so crucial as a protein source in the diet of the local people.

Females (cows) mature as early as three years of age in zoos, but maturity in the wild may not take place until past age 13. A single calf weighing about 45 kg (99 pounds) is born after a gestation of eight months. The calf can close its ears and nostrils to nurse underwater. It may climb onto its mother's back out of water to rest. It begins to eat grass by one month and is weaned at six to eight months of age. Cows produce a calf every two years. Young calves are vulnerable to crocodiles, lions, and hyenas. It is thought that attacks on small boats are antipredator behaviour, with the hippos mistaking them for crocodiles. As a result, hippos have long had a largely undeserved reputation as aggressive animals. Cows live in "schools," but they are not permanently associated with other cows, though sometimes they maintain bonds with offspring for some years. Longevity is up to 49 years in captivity but rarely more than 40 in the wild.

Males mature at about eight years of age, but dominant bulls more than 20 years old do most of the mating. Bulls monopolize areas in the river as "mating territories" for 12 years or more. Subordinate males are tolerated if they do not attempt to breed. Cows aggregate in these areas during the dry season, which is when most mating takes place. Rare battles may erupt when strange bulls invade territories in the mating season. Most aggression is noise, splash, bluff charges, and a yawning display of the teeth, but opponents may engage in combat by slashing upward at each other's flanks with the lower incisors. Wounds can be fatal despite the thick skin there. Adjacent territorial bulls will stare at each other, then turn and, with rear end out of the water, flip feces and urine in a wide arc by rapidly wagging the tail. This routine display indicates that the territory is occupied. Territorial and subordinate males alike make dung piles along pathways leading inland, which probably function as olfactory signposts at night. Hippos recognize individuals by scent and sometimes follow one another nose to tail on night treks.

Trampling and crop raiding by hippos led to early and determined efforts to exterminate them. Their hides and meat were also valued. Hippos were extinct in northern Africa by 1800 and south of Natal and the Transvaal by 1900. They are still fairly common in East Africa, but the Lake Chad race in west-central Africa is vulnerable. Populations continue to decrease continentwide. There remains a demand for hippo teeth as a fine-grained "ivory" that is easy to carve. It was once used to make false teeth.

The rare pygmy hippopotamus (*Hexaprotodon liberiensis*), the other living species of the family Hippopotamidae, is about the size of a domestic pig. The pygmy hippo is less aquatic than its larger relative, although when pursued it hides in water. Less gregarious, it is seen alone or with one or two others in the lowland tropical forests of Liberia, Côte d'Ivoire, Sierra Leone, and Guinea, along streams and in wet forests and swamps. Liberians call it a "water cow." It eats some grasses and also fresh leaves of trees and bushes, herbs, and fallen fruits. The Niger delta subspecies is critically endangered.

Hippopotamidae is related to pigs (family Suidae) and peccaries (family Tayassuidae). These groups diverged from other members of the order Artiodactyla about 45 million years ago, but molecular studies suggest that hippos and cetaceans (whales and dolphins) have an earlier common ancestor and may be more closely related. A fossil resembling today's pygmy hippo dates to the early Miocene Epoch (23 million to 16 million years ago). Hippos eventually reached Europe and Asia, though climate changes and overhunting by humans exterminated all species outside Africa by the end of the Pleistocene Epoch (11,700 years ago). Three species lived on Madagascar until recent times, and their extinction may have coincided with the arrival of humans about one thousand years ago.

CHAPTER 7

PERISSODACTYLS: ODD-TOED UNGULATES

A perissodactyl is by definition any member of the order Perissodactyla, a group of herbivorous mammals characterized by the possession of either one or three hoofed toes on each hindfoot. They include the horses, asses, and zebras, the tapirs, and the rhinoceroses. The name (Greek *perissos*, "odd," and *daktylos*, "finger") was introduced to separate the odd-toed ungulates from the even-toed ones (Artiodactyla), all of which had previously been classified as members of a single group.

GENERAL FEATURES

The Perissodactyla comprise three families of living mammals: six species of horses (Equidae), four species of tapirs (Tapiridae), and five species of rhinoceroses (Rhinocerotidae). These families are remnants of a group that flourished during the Paleogene and Neogene periods (from 65.5 to 2.6 million years ago), a time when it was much richer in species and in variety of form than at present and played a dominant role in the fauna of the world. Today, there are far fewer species of perissodactyls than artiodactyls, and most of the species still living are endangered, especially the rhinoceroses, the tapirs, and two of the three species of zebra.

The horses, asses, and zebras are long-legged, running forms with one functional digit in each foot and with high-crowned, molariform (i.e., modified for grinding)

Lowland tapir (Tapirus terrestris). Warren Garst/Tom Stack & Associates

cheek teeth. The tapir is a rather rounded, piglike, semi-amphibious forest and woodland animal with a small proboscis (trunklike snout) and a coat of short, bristly hairs. Tapirs have primitive features, such as four hoofed toes in the forefoot and three in the hind, and they have rather simple molar teeth. Rhinoceroses are massive creatures with a thick and nearly hairless hide, excepting the hairy Sumatran rhinoceros, and three digits on each foot. They bear hornlike structures on the head.

The Perissodactyla are of particular scientific interest because their fossil history is so well-known. The evolution of horses from the tiny "dawn horse" (*Hyracotherium*, formerly *Eohippus*) to the present form is a classic sequence, knowledge of which has played an important role in evolutionary thought. The order also provides a notable example of parallel evolution. Following completely different evolutionary paths, both perissodactyls and artiodactyls (e.g., cattle, antelope, swine) independently evolved features such as high-crowned grinding teeth and elongated limbs with a reduced number of digits, in adaptation to a similar running (cursorial), herbivorous mode of life.

Living perissodactyls are of medium or large size. Asses and tapirs, the smallest representatives of the order, attain a length of approximately two to 2.5 metres (6.6 to 8.2 feet), stand 1 metre (about 3 feet) or more at the shoulder, and weigh up to 250 or 300 kg (550 to 660 pounds). The largest forms are the Indian and square-lipped rhinoceroses (*Rhinoceros unicornis* and *Ceratotherium simum*, respectively), which are four to five metres (13 to 16.4 feet) long, measure up to 2 metres (6.5 feet) at the shoulder, and often weigh more than 1,600 kg (3,500 pounds). *Indricotherium* (or *Paraceratherium*, formerly *Baluchitherium*), known as the giraffe rhinoceros from the Oligocene (about 30 million years ago), was the largest known land mammal, standing about 5.5 metres (18 feet) at the shoulder.

All feed either by grazing (i.e., cropping grasses) or by browsing (taking shoots and leaves from trees and bushes). The Equidae in particular were abundant and important members of the Old World fauna until their numbers were reduced by human beings. Zebras are still numerous and ecologically important in a few parts of Africa. The importance of the domestic horse and the ass in the history of mankind is great indeed. Both have served extensively as pack, draft, and riding animals. The horse is sometimes eaten by people, and its flesh is widely used as pet food. Through centuries of domestication, it has been developed into a number of different breeds.

The living wild Equidae are confined to the Old World. Zebras and the true wild ass (*Equus africanus*) are African, with the zebras confined to the southern and eastern

Morgan stallion with bay coat. © Scott Smudsky

parts, while the ass originally ranged over northern and northeastern Africa.

Although the wild horse (*Equus caballus*), ancestor of the domestic horse, occupied the low country north of the great mountain ranges from Europe across central Asia. It may now be extinct as a wild animal. The half-asses, races of *E. hemionus*, were found in the arid zone of Asia from Persia to the Gobi Desert, as well as in Arabia, Syria, and northwestern India.

The living rhinoceroses are also Old World forms, with two species in Africa and three in Asia. There are three species of tapirs in the New World tropics, one in Middle America and two in South America. The fourth species of tapir is Asiatic.

NATURAL HISTORY

The life cycles of perissodactyls are marked by certain consistent behaviour patterns in communicating and socializing, courting and mating, and raising young.

EXPRESSION AND COMMUNICATION

The Equidae communicate by means of calls and changes in facial expression. Six different sounds are made by Burchell's zebra. A whinny, consisting of a series of two- or three-syllabic "ha" sounds, serves to maintain contact between members of a group. The repertoire includes an alarm call ("i-ha"), an alarm snort, a drawn-out snort of satisfaction, and a squeal of pain and fear. Other species utter similar sounds, the whinny of the horse and the bray of the ass being well-known examples. Characteristic facial expressions have been described for greeting ceremonies (mouth open, ears up), threat (mouth open, ears back), and submission (mouth open, nibbling movements, ears down). In all species studied except the horse, females assume a particular expression ("mating face") when permitting the male to mount.

In the rhinoceroses and tapirs snorting, squealing, bellowing, and, in some forms, whistling sounds play a major role in communication. Visual signals are not well developed in these nonsocial animals, but a few facial expressions are used.

FEEDING

The Perissodactyla are mainly grazers or browsers. The quality and quantity of grasses available to grazing species may vary considerably with the season and the area. The animals may accordingly move great distances to reach attractive sources of food. Migrations of Burchell's zebras to succulent pastures during the rainy season are a feature of the Serengeti Plain in Tanzania and the Etosha National Park in Namibia. The distribution of asses, half-asses, and horses inhabiting arid areas largely follows that of rainfall and pasture.

Because the food of the browsers is fairly readily available throughout the year, species in this category are relatively sedentary. The browsing rhinoceroses may break down trees and shrubs, and use their forelimbs to help get at otherwise inaccessible leaves and twigs. Food is plucked with the lips. In the tapirs, the upper lip is fused with the short proboscis. The rhinoceroses (excluding the white) have a pointed upper lip with a fingerlike process that is used to pluck leaves and twigs. The white rhinoceros, with its broad square muzzle, is the most specialized grazing rhinoceros, feeding on grass.

SOCIAL ORGANIZATION AND TERRITORY

In both the mountain and Burchell's zebras the family group is the basic social unit. It generally consists of a single adult male and two or three adult females with their foals. The groups are stable, apparently because of strong mutual ties among the females rather than because of herding by the male. The stallion is dominant, and there is a hierarchy among the mares, the highest ranking (alpha) animal usually leading the group. Other males are either solitary or live in bachelor groups of two or three, sometimes up to 10. Juveniles leave the family group when they attain sexual maturity at one and a half to two years. When large aggregations occur on favoured grazing grounds, the groups retain their identity. Among Grevy's zebras and wild asses, territorial males and groups of mares and foals and of stallions are found. There is no evidence for territorial behaviour among any of the zebras except Grevy's. Individual groups occupy home ranges that overlap to some degree with those of other groups.

The social organization of other equids is not as well documented. Observers studying the wild horse and half-asses have noted that females and juveniles form a group dominated by a single stallion, which keeps them together by active herding. Unattached males are solitary or live in small herds.

The pattern of social organization among the rhinoceroses is quite different from that of the Equidae. Dominant adult males of the white rhinoceros occupy

Zebras (Equus burchelli) *at a waterhole, an example of coloration disruption.*Gerald Cubitt

territories that, in the KwaZulu/Natal reserves, average about 200 hectares (500 acres). Within its area a male may tolerate subadult or aged bulls, which have subordinate status. Adult females accompanied by their calves inhabit home ranges encompassing the territories of six or seven dominant bulls. Juveniles consort with other juveniles or with calfless females, but groups of more than two usually do not stay together long.

The black rhinoceros is basically solitary. Adults of both sexes usually occupy home ranges of 1,000 hectares (2,500 acres) or more, the size depending on the characteristics of the environment; occasionally the ranges may be as small as 200 hectares (495 acres), however. There is a good deal of overlap in the use of these home ranges.

The Asiatic rhinoceroses also are essentially solitary, but detailed information on the nature of the areas they inhabit is not available. Individual great Indian rhinoceroses are said to occupy tracts as small as 8 to 20 hectares (20 to 50 acres).

Little is known about the social organization or territorial behaviour of the tapirs. All species are reported to be found alone or in pairs.

Male zebras and horses follow mares in estrus. The stallion, after smelling the spot where a mare has urinated or defecated, exhibits "flehmen" (a characteristic display in which the head is lifted and the upper lip raised) and then urinates or defecates on the same spot. In similar fashion, members of stallion groups often urinate or defecate consecutively. Communal dung heaps formed by five to eight animals often arise in this way. The significance of such behaviour is unclear.

Among the Rhinocerotidae excretory products play an important role in marking territories and home ranges. Dominant male white rhinoceroses defecate almost entirely on heaps within their territories. They then scatter the material by kicking vigorously, presumably leaving an individual scent mark in this manner. In addition, they urinate in a ritualized fashion, spraying the urine in powerful jets in a manner peculiar to them and shown by no other sex or age group. Other members of the population also use dung heaps (either in territories or in communal areas, such as along paths) but not exclusively, and they do not scatter dung.

In the black rhinoceros, dung-scattering behaviour does not appear to be exclusive to dominant males. The function of the communal heaps may be mainly to establish the presence of the inhabitant in his home range, and to maintain contact between known animals.

Dung heaps and urine spraying are also observed among other species of rhinoceroses and among tapirs. Their significance is presumably of a similar nature.

Fighting

The pattern of fighting is related to the amount of lethal equipment the various groups possess. The Equidae, unarmoured, do not employ stylized fighting techniques to reduce the danger of serious injury—as among certain other species. Fighting is largely confined to adult males competing for estrous mares. Various techniques occur in the zebras, which may serve as an example of the family. Circling, neck fighting, biting (either in a standing or sitting position), rearing combined with biting and kicking, and kicking on the run all are used, either alone or in combination. No set pattern is followed.

Fights among rhinoceroses consist of charges and striking with the horns, usually accompanied by vocal threats. Goring is not common, the stylized pattern having probably been evolved to minimize the danger of serious injury from the formidable horns.

AMICABLE BEHAVIOUR

Mutual grooming is well known among horses. Two animals stand facing in opposite directions and groom each other by nibbling at the root of the tail and the base of the neck. Burchell's zebra behaves similarly and so, presumably, do other members of the family.

Zebras greet each other simply by nose-to-nose contact, except that adult stallions go through a ceremony involving nose-to-genital contact. Nose-to-nose greeting is also characteristic of tapirs and rhinoceroses. The latter also rub their bodies together.

COURTSHIP AND MATING

Courtship is relatively simple among the social equids. The true ass is apparently exceptional. The partners are strangers when the first approaches are made and the female requires violent subjugation by the male, which bites, kicks, and chases her before she will stand for him. This may be the result of separation of the sexes outside the mating season. The wild horse and Burchell's zebra are not at all violent. The stallion often grooms the mare before attempting to mount. The estrous mare (especially, or exclusively, young mares in the case of Burchell's zebra) adopts a typical posture with legs slightly apart, tail lifted, and, except in the horse, a characteristic facial expression (the "mating face" already mentioned).

The more or less solitary rhinoceroses and tapirs go through a more elaborate courtship, presumably because the partners are strangers. After a chase, the male and female may engage in low-intensity fighting, ending with the male laying his head on the female's rump and then mounting and copulating for an extended period. Several males may mate with an estrous female.

REPRODUCTION

Female equids of all the species for which information is available attain puberty at about one year, but are not normally successfully mated before the age of two to two and one-half years, and possibly as late as three to four years in the case of Grevy's zebra. Zebras probably breed until about 20 years of age. The domestic species are seasonally polyestrous (repeatedly fertile), coming into breeding condition in spring and, unless mated, undergoing repeated estrous cycles at intervals of approximately three weeks until the end of the summer. The wild species studied also tend to mate seasonally, so most young are born in spring and summer.

The gestation period of equids is between 11 and 12 months. In most species a postpartum estrus occurs, usually within two weeks of the birth of the young. Thus, the maximal potential reproductive rate is one young per year. This potential is not always attained. Only about 50 percent of domestic mares that are mated produce foals, and nearly half of a study group of Burchell's zebra mares bore only one foal in three years.

The gestation period of three species of rhinoceroses is about 15 to 17 months. For the Sumatran rhinoceros the period is said to be only seven months. No information is available for the Javan rhinoceros. Female white and black rhinoceroses attain sexual maturity at the age of four to five years and are capable of calving at intervals of approximately two and and one-half years. Rhinoceroses probably breed until between 30 and 40 years old. The white tends to have a mating peak in spring, corresponding with the flush of green grass, and a calving peak in autumn.

The Malayan and South American lowland tapirs have gestation periods of 13 months' duration. The lowland tapir is reported to mate before the onset of the rainy season.

RELATIONS BETWEEN PARENT AND OFFSPRING

The perissodactyls bear well-developed (precocial) young, usually a single offspring. After the mother has assisted in removing the placenta and has licked her offspring in the usual mammalian fashion, the young animal soon attempts to stand. A Burchell's zebra foal has been observed to stand quite firmly 14 minutes after birth, and a black rhinoceros calf 25 minutes after birth.

Newly born equids follow any nearby object during the first few days of life. At this time, zebra mares drive away all other zebras from their foals. The behaviour ensures that the foal will form a bond with its mother during the initial period of imprinting. Foals follow their mothers closely and are groomed frequently.

Although precocial, black rhinoceros calves appear to have a lying-out period, which is an initial period when they rest quietly in thick cover except when being suckled.

White rhinoceroses (Ceratotherium simum). © Digital Vision/Getty Images

Thereafter they follow their mothers closely. A young white rhinoceros tends to walk ahead of the mother and may be guided by her horn.

Most young perissodactyls remain with their mothers until the next offspring is born. A young rhinoceros may, therefore, accompany its mother until it is two and one-half years old, or older. Although grazing starts early, suckling proceeds for a considerable time, perhaps for its psychological rather than its physiological value.

PLAY

As in other mammals, play is a prominent form of behaviour among young perissodactyls. Zebras up to the age of one year frequently engage in running games. Foals gallop wildly about on their own, jumping and kicking up their heels, sometimes chasing other animals, such as gazelles, mongooses, or birds. In groups they play catching games, running after one another in close succession. Mock fighting sometimes takes place. Groups of adults have also been seen to chase foal groups in play, and indeed stallion groups carry out playful gallops. Stallions also engage in play greeting and in mock fights.

Playful romping and mock fighting with the horns are common among rhinoceros calves. Young tapirs play running games.

ROLLING AND WALLOWING

Behaviour for the care of the body is widespread among the perissodactyls. Equids frequently roll in dry, loose soil forming rolling hollows—a common feature of zebra country.

Wallowing may help regulate body temperature. It is probably is mainly a form of self-grooming and is practiced by all species of rhinoceroses. They often spend hours lying in pools during the middle of the day in hot weather. Mud of suitable consistency induces wallowing, which may be followed by sand bathing. Prolonged rubbing on tree trunks or suitable stumps follows a wallow. Old rubbing stumps and stones may take on a shine from repeated use.

Tapirs may have the most pronounced tendency to bathe and wallow, but few details of their behaviour are known. They are also said to enter water when disturbed.

FORM AND FUNCTION

Beginning with the distinctive "odd-toed" form of the foot, perissodactyls bear certain similarities in skeletal structure but also in dentition and digestion.

INTEGUMENT

The skin of rhinoceroses is extraordinarily thick. The great Indian and Javan rhinoceroses are covered with large, practically immovable plates, separated by joints of thinner skin to permit movement. The two species differ in the arrangement of the folds. The hair of all rhinoceroses is sparse or absent except that of young Sumatran rhinoceroses, which have a dense coat of crisp, black hair. The skin of the tapirs is also thick with a sparse covering of short hairs arranged in irregular groups. The equids have a normal hide with a well-developed hairy coat.

The "horns" of the rhinoceroses are noteworthy structures of epidermal origin. The horn is composed of a mass of fused epidermal cells that are impregnated with a tough, fibrous protein (keratin) and that rest on a roughened bony cushion on the fused nasal bones. The male Javan rhinoceros has a short horn about 25 cm (10 inches) long; the horn of the female is rudimentary. The great Indian rhinoceros has a single horn up to 60 cm (25 inches) long. The other species of rhinoceroses have a second horn that stands on a protuberance of the bones (frontals) between the eyes. Hornlike structures were also present in the titanotheres and extinct rhinoceroses.

In all living perissodactyls the terminal digital bones are flattened and triangular, with evenly rounded free edges, and are encased by keratinous hooves derived from the integument. The single hoof of the equids—the only mammals to walk on the tips of single digits—is the most highly developed structure of this kind among mammals. The keratinous wall is analogous to the nail of mammals that have claws or nails.

SKELETON

There is a clear evolutionary tendency in the Equidae for the limbs to become long and slender, with a reduction in the number of digits in the swift-running forms. These changes are accompanied by an increase in rigidity and specialization for movement fore and aft. The vertebral column, meanwhile, acts as a firm girder, with high dorsal (neural) spines on the thoracic vertebrae, above the fore-limbs and ribs. Spines and ribs serve as compression struts above and below.

BACKBONE AND LIMB GIRDLES

The vertebral column balances largely on the forelegs and is pushed from behind by the hindlegs, which are the main propellants. This skeletal structure permits running and also enables great weights to be borne in such animals as the rhinoceroses. There are never fewer than 22 thoraco-lumbar (trunk) vertebrae.

The neck, or cervical, vertebrae are opisthocoelous (i.e., with the bodies, or centra, of the vertebrae hollowed behind to take the convex heads of the succeeding centra). This feature facilitates rotatory movement of the neck and is most highly developed in the horses.

The shoulder blade is long and narrow with a small coracoid process (a ridge to which muscles are attached) and a low spine. There is no clavicle (collarbone). The pelvic girdle has a broad, vertically raised ilium to which are attached the large gluteal (thigh) muscles, important for locomotion, and the abdominal muscles, which carry the weight of the belly.

LIMBS

The upper (proximal) limb segments, the humerus of the forelimb and the femur of the hindlimb, have remained short. In contrast the lower (distal) parts, consisting of an anterior radius and posterior ulna in the forelimb and an anterior tibia and posterior fibula in the hindlimb, have become longer and slimmer. The humerus is short and broad. Its articulation with the radius and ulna only permits fore-and-aft movement. The proximal end of the stout femur has a third projection, or trochanter, in addition to the usual mammalian two, which serves as an additional point of attachment for the large locomotory muscles of the hindlimbs.

The anatomical feature of the order now considered most significant is that the axis of symmetry of the limbs passes through the third or middle toe, the most strongly developed and the one on which most of the weight is borne. This is called the mesaxonic condition and is contrasted with the paraxonic condition of the Artiodactyla, in which the axis passes between the third and fourth toes.

Originally the five toes of the limb were held in the semidigitigrade position (i.e., with the weight of the body being borne on the soles of the toes and on the lower ends of the elongate metacarpal and metatarsal bones of the forefeet and hindfeet). The upper (proximal) ends of these bones were raised above the ground, a condition still to be seen in the tapirs.

As the third digit became increasingly dominant, it became longer and thicker. The upper ends of the third metacarpus and metatarsus broadened and forced the other digits to the side. The first (inner) digit was the first to disappear. The earliest known forms already bore only three digits on the hindfoot. The loss of the first toe on the front foot led to the four-toed condition common in the Eocene. The fifth digit persisted, although it was somewhat weak. The tapirs, with four toes in front and three behind, have retained this early condition.

The fifth digit of the hindfoot was the next to disappear in the evolutionary sequence, and all known forms beyond the lower Oligocene had only three toes in each foot. The living rhinoceroses illustrate this condition. A massive limb with a broad foot is essential in such heavy animals. The feet have cushions of elastic connective tissue well suited to bear the weight of the body.

In the most highly specialized forms, the second and fourth digits also underwent reduction. These digits are retained in the living Equidae only as functionless, vestigial slivers of bone on either side of the third metacarpal and metatarsal.

With reduction in the number of digits, the third has assumed a progressively more vertical position. Its terminal joint, or phalanx, has become larger and the hoof surrounding it bigger and thicker. At the same time the ulna, the smaller bone of the forelimb, decreased in size until, in the modern Equidae, its upper end fused with the radius and its lower end remained merely as part of the articulating surface of the radius with the wrist bones (carpals). In the hindlimb, the fibula became reduced in similar fashion. It articulates with the ankle bones (tarsals) only in a few extinct forms, such as the titanotheres. In the tapirs and rhinoceroses it is slender. In the equids the proximal end remains as a small splint of bone, while the distal end has fused with the tibia.

The arrangement of the small bones of the carpus ("wrist") and tarsus (ankle) is another characteristic feature of perissodactyl limbs. In most other mammalian orders, the carpals and tarsals provide the limbs with regions of flexibility. Their development in the perissodactyls has been toward increasing rigidity, following the trend in the limbs as a whole. The basic mammalian arrangement is one of three rows of bones: a proximal row of three, adjacent to the lower arm and leg bones; an intermediate row of four (the centralia); and a distal row of five (carpalia of the forefoot, tarsalia of the hind), one to each digit. The centralia, carpalia, and tarsalia are numbered one to four or five, beginning on the side of the thumb and big toe. In all orders the number of wrist and ankle bones has been reduced. Usually only one of the centralia, known as the navicular, remains, while there are the same number of carpalia and tarsalia as there are digits.

An interlocking plan is characteristic of the Perissodactyla. In the forefoot, the third distal carpal (the magnum or capitate) is enlarged and interlocks with the proximal carpals. The elongated third metacarpal thrusts up against these interlocked bones. In the equids, distal carpal I (the trapezium) is absent, and the arrangement in the hindfoot is similar. In the most advanced, modern forms metatarsus III thrusts against the enlarged and flattened tarsal III (ectocuneiform), and this in turn is in contact with the large, flat navicular (centrale II and III). The navicular abuts on the flattened astragalus (or talus), the intermediate bone of the proximal row. The articulation between the upper surface of the astragalus and the tibia is pulley-like and permits only fore-and-aft movement of the limb.

TEETH

The full complement of mammalian teeth consists of three incisors, one canine, four premolars, and three molars in each half of each jaw. The arrangement may be expressed by the formula $3 . 1 . 4 . 3 3 . 1 . 4 . 3 = 44$ teeth. The figures represent the number of incisors, canines, premolars, and molars in each half of the upper (above the line) and lower (below) jaws, respectively.

The Condylarthra, a group of mammals that first appeared in the Paleocene (about 65.5 million years ago) and were ancestral to most of the later and recent hoofed mammals, had a full complement of teeth. In many of the early perissodactyls, only the first lower premolar had been lost. The subsequent evolutionary sequence led to losses and specializations of the incisors and canines. Lengthening of the facial part of the skull resulted in the formation of a gap, the diastema, between the incisors and the premolars. The first upper premolar was reduced or lost in consequence. The canines, when present, were situated in this diastema, as they are in male horses.

Among the living perissodactyls, the tapirs have the least specialized battery of teeth. In this, as in many other features, they have remained primitive. The dental formula of the family Tapiridae is: $(2-3) . 1 . 3 . 3 3 . 1 . 4 . 3 = 40-42$ teeth. The first upper premolar is noteworthy in being the only premolar with a milk, or deciduous, predecessor.

The cutting teeth are reduced in the Rhinocerotidae. Incisors and canines are absent in the two African forms. The Asiatic species have one or two upper, but generally no lower, incisors in each half of the jaw. They have no upper canines; the Javan and Sumatran rhinoceroses have one short, sharp lower canine on each side. There are three upper and lower molar teeth in all five species. The white and Sumatran rhinoceroses have three premolars, and the others have three or four premolars. The dental formula for the family is set up, therefore, as follows: 0 . (0–1) . (3–4) . 3(0–2) . 0 . (3–4) . 3 = 24–30 teeth. The dental formula of the Equidae is 3 . 1 . 3 . 3 3 . 1 . (3–4) . 3 = 40–42 teeth.

The form of the premolars and molars is of great interest and their evolutionary history has been studied in some detail. Primitive, browsing members of the order had brachydont cheek teeth (i.e., with low crowns and long, narrow root canals), with separate low, rounded cusps— the bunodont condition. Increasing specialization for grazing resulted in fusion of the cusps into ridges (lophs), thus teeth of this kind are called lophodont. Lower molars typically have two transverse lophs, the protoloph and the metaloph. In the upper molars these ridges are fused with a longitudinal ridge (ectoloph), which runs along the outer edge of the tooth. Further development leads to a convoluted arrangement of the lophs, such teeth being termed selenolophodont.

Associated with these changes in the tooth surfaces is a tendency for the crown to become higher. High-crowned teeth are termed hypsodont. The hollows between the lophs of hypsodont teeth are filled with a deposit of secondary cement, which strengthens the teeth and makes them more resistant to wear. A further evolutionary trend is for premolars to become as large as molars. Where the process of molarization is complete, as in horses, all grinding teeth are identical.

The Tapiridae have primitive brachydont premolars and molars. They possess two simple transverse lophs, and are thus termed bilophodont. They lack secondary cement on the crowns.

The Sumatran rhinoceros, the most primitive of the living rhinoceroses, and the Javan rhinoceros have similar brachydont, lophodont cheek teeth. The great Indian rhinoceros, which is less of a specialized browser, has hypselodont (hypsodont and selenodont) premolars, with a layer of cement on the crowns. The black rhinoceros has brachydont and lophodont teeth, with a thin layer of cement. The white rhinoceros is more specialized, for the cheek teeth are hypselodont and have a thick cement layer.

The grinding teeth of the Equidae are highly specialized, high crowned, with a complicated selenodont surface and thick cement deposits.

Digestive System

The stomach of perissodactyls is small, simple, and undivided. In the horse its capacity is only 8.5 percent of the whole digestive system. The comparable figure for the ox is 71 percent. The intestine is very long and the cecum (blind gut) and colon are huge and sacculated (i.e., with many blind pockets). Here food is macerated and fermented and the fibrous portions are dissolved. The liver has no gall bladder.

CHAPTER 8

HORSES AND OTHER PERISSODACTYLS

I n this chapter the great perissodactyl families — Equidae (the horse, ass, and zebra), Rhinocerotidae (the five species of rhinoceros), and Tapiridae (the four species of tapir) — are described.

EQUIDAE: HORSES AND THEIR RELATIVES

Family of Equidae, order Perissodactyla, includes the modern horses, zebras, and asses, as well as more than 60 species known only from fossils. All modern members of the family are placed in the genus *Equus*. Only subspecies of *E. caballus* (including the myriad domestic breeds) are called horses. Three species (*E. zebra, E. burchelli,* and *E. grevyi*) are called zebras. Various other species (e.g., *E. asinus* and *E. hemionus*) are generally called asses, though various alternate names such as donkey and kiang are also used.

Wild horses once inhabited much of northern Eurasia, primarily in open areas. They were rather small, short-legged animals, compared with their domesticated descendants, standing only about 120 to 130 cm (47 to 51 inches) at the shoulder. In the two millennia BCE, horses from many wild populations were domesticated. Often the remainder of the wild individuals were exterminated. By the early 19th century, two races were still extant: the tarpan (*E. caballus caballus*), found in eastern Europe until the middle of the century, and Przewalski's horse (*E.*

caballus przewalskii, often considered a distinct species, *E. przewalskii*), which inhabited the remote steppe region between China and Mongolia.

The North American wild horses are feral descendants of domestic horses that escaped or were released during the early colonial days.

HORSES

Horses are hoofed, herbivorous mammals of the family Equidae. They comprise a single species, *Equus caballus,* whose numerous varieties are called breeds.

In prehistoric times the wild horse was probably first hunted for food. When its domestication took place is unknown, but it certainly was long after the domestication of the dog or of cattle. It is supposed that the horse was first used by a tribe of Indo-European origin that lived in the steppes north of the chain of mountains adjacent to the Black and Caspian seas. Influenced by climate, food, and humans, the horse rapidly acquired its present form.

The relationship of the horse to humans has been unique. The horse is a partner and friend. It plowed fields and brought in the harvest, hauled goods and conveyed passengers, followed game and tracked cattle, and carried combatants into battle and adventurers to unknown lands. It has provided recreation in the form of jousts, tournaments, carousels, and the sport of riding. The influence of the horse is expressed in the English language in such terms as *chivalry* and *cavalier,* which connote honour, respect, good manners, and straightforwardness.

The horse is the "proudest conquest of Man," according to the French zoologist Le Comte de Buffon. Its place was at its master's side in the graves of the Scythian kings or in the tombs of the pharaohs. Many early human cultures were centred on possession of the horse.

Superstition read meaning into the colours of the horse, and a horse's head suspended near a grave or sanctuary or on the gables of a house conferred supernatural powers on the place. Greek mythology created the centaur, the most obvious symbol of the oneness of horse and rider. White stallions were the supreme sacrifice to the gods, and the Greek general Xenophon recorded that "Gods and heroes are depicted on well-trained horses." A beautiful and well-trained horse was, therefore, a status symbol in ancient Greece. Kings, generals, and statesmen, of necessity, had to be horsemen. The names of famous horses are inseparably linked to those of their famous riders: Bucephalus, the charger of Alexander the Great; Incitatus, once believed to have been made a senator by the Roman emperor Caligula; El Morzillo, Cortés's favourite horse, to whom the Indians erected a statue; Roan Barbery, the stallion of Richard II, mentioned by Shakespeare; Copenhagen, the Duke of Wellington's horse, which was buried with military honours.

The horse has occupied a special place in the realm of art. From the Stone Age drawings to the marvel of the Parthenon frieze, from Chinese Tang dynasty tomb sculptures to Leonardo da Vinci's sketches and Verrocchio's Colleoni, from the Qur'ān to modern literature, the horse has inspired artists of all ages and in all parts of the world.

The horse in life has served its master in travels, wars, and labours and in death has provided many commodities. Long before their domestication horses were hunted by primitive tribes for their flesh, and horsemeat is still consumed by people in parts of Europe and in Iceland and is the basis of many pet foods. Horse bones and cartilage are used to make glue. Tetanus antitoxin is obtained from the blood serum of horses previously inoculated with tetanus toxoid. From horsehide a number of articles are manufactured, including fine shoes and belts. The cordovan leather fabricated by the Moors in Córdoba, Spain, was originally made from horsehide. Stylish fur coats are made of the sleek coats of foals. Horsehair has wide use in upholstery, mattresses, and stiff lining for coats and suits. High-quality horsehair, usually white, is employed for violin bows. Horse manure, which today provides the basis for cultivation of mushrooms, was used by the Scythians for fuel. Mare's milk was drunk by the Scythians, the Mongols, and the Arabs.

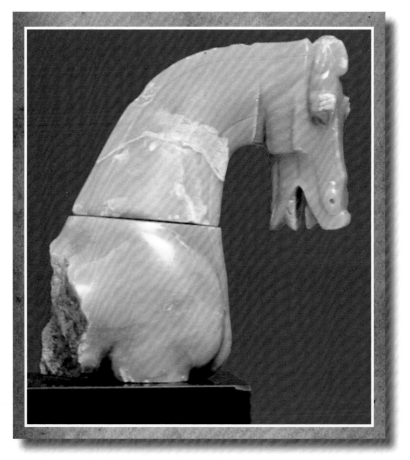

Jade horse head, Chinese, Han dynasty (206 BCE–220 CE). In the Victoria and Albert Museum, London. Height 19 cm (7.5 inches). Courtesy of the Victoria and Albert Museum, London

A mature male horse is called a stallion, the female a mare. A stallion used for breeding is known as a stud. A castrated stallion is commonly called a gelding. Formerly, stallions were employed as riding horses, while mares were kept for breeding purposes only. Geldings were originally used for work and as ladies' riding horses, though they have now generally replaced stallions as riding horses. Young horses are known as foals; male foals are called colts and females fillies.

Anatomical Adaptations

The primitive horse probably stood 12 hands (about 120 cm, or 48 inches) tall at the withers, the high point on the back at the base of the neck, and was dun coloured. Domestic horses gone wild, such as the mustangs of western North America, tend to revert to those primitive features under random mating. They generally are somewhat taller (about 15 hands [about 150 cm, or 60 inches]), usually gray, dun, or brownish in colour, and move in herds led by a stallion.

The horse's general form is characteristic of an animal of speed: the long leg bones pivot on pulley-like joints that restrict movement to the fore and aft, the limbs are levered to muscle masses in such a way as to provide the most efficient use of energy, and the compact body is supported permanently on the tips of the toes, allowing fuller extension of the limbs in running.

The rounded skull houses a large and complex brain, well developed in those areas that direct muscle coordination. While the horse is intelligent among subhuman animals, it is safe to say that the horse is more concerned with the functioning of its acute sensory reception and its musculature than with mental processes. Though much has been written about "educated" horses that appear to exhibit an ability to spell and count, it is generally agreed that in such cases a particularly perceptive animal is responding to cues from its master. But this ability is remarkable enough in its own right—for the cues are often given unconsciously by the human trainer, and detection of such subtle signals requires extremely sharp perception.

The horse, like other grazing herbivores, has typical adaptations for plant eating: a set of strong, high-crowned teeth, suited to grinding grasses and other harsh vegetation, and a relatively long digestive tract, most of which is intestine concerned with digesting cellulose matter from vegetation. Young horses have milk (or baby) teeth, which they begin to shed at about age two and a half. The permanent teeth, numbering 36 to 40, are completely developed by age four to five years. In the stallion these teeth are arranged as follows on the upper and lower jaws: 12 incisors that cut and pull at grasses; four canines, remnants without function in the modern horse and usually not found in mares; 12 premolars and 12 molars, high prisms that keep moving out of the jaw to replace the surfaces worn off in grinding food.

Under domestication the horse has diversified into three major types, based on size and build: draft horses, heavy limbed and up to 20 hands (200 cm, or 80 inches) high; ponies, by convention horses under 14.2 hands (about 147 cm, or 58 inches) high; and light horses—the saddle or riding horses—which fall in the intermediate size range. Domestic horses tend to be nearsighted, less hardy than their ancestors, and often high-strung, especially thoroughbreds, where intensive breeding has been focused upon speed to the exclusion of other qualities. The stomach is relatively small, and, since much vegetation must be ingested to maintain vital processes, foraging is almost constant under natural conditions. Domestic animals are fed several (at least three) times a day in quantities governed by the exertion of the horse.

Senses

The extremely large eyes placed far back on the elongated head admirably suit the horse for its chief mode of defense: flight. Its long neck and high-set eyes, which register a much wider range than do the eyes of a human being, enable the horse to discern a possible threat even while eating low grasses. Like human vision, the horse's vision is binocular, but only in the narrow area directly forward, and evidence suggests that it does not register colour. While visual acuity is high, the eyes do not have variable focus, and objects at different distances register only on different areas of the retina, which requires tilting movements of the head. The senses of smell and hearing seem to be keener than in human beings. As the biologist George Gaylord Simpson put it in *Horses* (1961):

> *Legs for running and eyes for warning have enabled horses to survive through the ages, although subject to constant attack by flesh eaters that liked nothing better than horse for supper.*

Colour and Pattern

From the dun of the primitive horse has sprung a variety of colours and patterns, some highly variable and difficult to distinguish. Among the most important colours are black, bay, chestnut (and sorrel), palomino, cream, and white.

The black colour is a true black, although a white face marking (blaze) and white ankles (stockings) may occur. The brown horse is almost black but has lighter areas around the muzzle, eyes, and legs. Bay refers to several shades of brown, from red brown and tan to sandy. Bay horses have a black mane, tail, and (usually) stockings. Chestnut is similar to bay but with none of the bay's black overtones. Lighter shades of chestnut are called sorrel.

Appaloosa mare with bay colouring. © Scott Smudsky

The palomino horse runs from cream to bronze, with a flaxen or silvery mane and tail. The cream is a diluted sorrel, or very pale yellow, nearly white. White in horses is variable, ranging from aging grays to albinos with blue eyes and pink skin and to pseudoalbinos with a buff mane or with brown eyes. The chief patterns of the white horse are gray, roan, pinto, and appaloosa. Gray horses are born dark brown or black and develop white hairs as they age, becoming almost all white in advanced years. Roan refers to white mixed with other colours at birth: blue roan is white mixed with black; red roan is mixed white and bay; and strawberry roan is white and chestnut. The pinto is almost any spotted pattern of white and another colour. Other names, such as paint, calico, piebald, skewbald, overo, and tobiano, refer to subtle distinctions in type of colour or pattern. Appaloosa is another extremely variable pattern, but the term generally refers to a large white patch over the hips and loin, with scattered irregular dark spots.

Nutrition

The horse's natural food is grass. For stabled horses, the diet generally consists of hay and grain. The animal should not be fed immediately before or after work, to avoid digestive problems. Fresh water is important, especially when the horse is shedding its winter coat, but the animal should never be watered when it is overheated after working. Oats provide the greatest nutritional value and are given especially to foals. Older horses, whose teeth are worn down, or those with digestive troubles, can be provided with crushed oats. Chaff (minced straw) can be added to the oat ration of animals that eat greedily or do not chew the grain properly. Crushed barley is sometimes substituted in part for oats. Hay provides the bulk of the horse's ration and may be of varying composition according to locale. Mash is bran mixed with water and with various invigorating additions or medications. It may be given to horses with digestive troubles or deficient eating habits. Corn (maize) is used as a fattening cereal, but it makes the horse sweat easily. Salt is needed by the horse at all times and especially when shedding. Bread, carrots, and sugar are tidbits often used to reward an animal by the rider or trainer. In times of poverty horses have adapted to all sorts of food—potatoes, beans, green leaves, and in Iceland even fish—but such foods are not generally taken if other fare is available. A number of commercial feed mixes are available to modern breeders and owners. Such mixes contain minerals, vitamins, and other nutrients and are designed to provide a balanced diet when supplemented with hay.

Behaviour

The horse's nervous system is highly developed and gives proof to varying degrees of the essential faculties that are the basis of intelligence: instinct, memory, and judgment. Foals, which stand on their feet a short while after birth and are able to follow their mothers within a few hours, even at this early stage in life exhibit the traits generally ascribed to horses. They have a tendency to flee danger. They express fear sometimes by showing panic and sometimes by immobility. Horses rarely attack and do so either when flight is impossible or when driven to assault a person who has treated them brutally.

Habit governs a large number of their reactions. Instinct, together with a fine sense of smell and hearing, enables them to sense water, fire, even distant danger. An extremely well-developed sense of direction permits the horse to find its way back to its stables even at night or after a prolonged absence. The visual memory of the horse prompts it to shy repeatedly from an object or place where it had earlier experienced fear. The animal's auditory memory, which enabled ancient army horses or hunters to follow the sounds of the bugles, is used in training. When teaching, the instructor always uses the same words and the same tone of voice for a given desired reaction. Intelligent horses soon attach certain movements desired by their trainers to particular sounds and even try to anticipate their rider's wishes.

While instinct is an unconscious reaction more or less present in all individuals of the same species, the degree of its expression varies according to the individual and its development. Most horses can sense a rider's uncertainty, nervousness, or fear and are thereby encouraged to disregard or even deliberately disobey the rider. Highbred animals, which give evidence of greater intelligence than those of low breeding, are capable not only of acts of vengeance and jealousy against their riders but also of expressions of confidence, obedience, affection, and fidelity. They are less willing than a lowbred horse to suffer rough handling or unjust treatment.

Cunning animals have been known to employ their intelligence and physical skill to a determined end, such as opening the latch of a stall or the lid of a chest of oats.

Reproduction and Development

The onset of adult sex characteristics generally begins at the age of 16 to 18 months. The horse is considered mature, according to the breed, at approximately three years and adult at five. Fecundity varies according to the breed and may last beyond age 20 with thoroughbreds and to 12 or 15 with other horses. The gestation period is 11 months, 280 days being the minimum in which the foal can be born with expectation to live. As a rule a mare produces one foal per mating, twins occasionally, and triplets rarely. The foal is weaned at six months.

The useful life of a horse varies according to the amount of work it is required to do and the maintenance furnished by its owner. A horse that is trained carefully and slowly and is given the necessary time for development may be expected to serve to an older age than a horse that is rushed in its training. Racehorses that enter into races at the age of two rarely remain on the turf beyond eight. Well-kept riding horses, on the contrary, may be used more than 20 years.

The life span of a horse is calculated at six to seven times the time necessary for his physical and mental development; that is, 30 to 35 years at the utmost, the rule being about 20 to 25 years. Ponies generally live longer than larger horses. There are a number of examples of horses that have passed the usual limit of age. The veterinary university of Vienna conserves the skeleton of a thoroughbred mare of 44 years of age. There have been reports made of horses living to the early 60s in age.

Diseases and Parasites

Horses are subjected to a number of contagious diseases, such as influenza, strangles, glanders, equine encephalomyelitis, and swamp fever. Their skin is affected by parasites, including certain mites, ticks, and lice. Those with sensitive skin are especially subject to eczemas and abscesses, which may result from neglect or contamination. Sores caused by injuries to the skin from ill-fitting or unclean saddles and bridles are common ailments. The horse's digestive tract is particularly sensitive to spoiled feed, which causes acute or chronic indigestion, especially in hot weather. Worms can develop in the intestine and include the larvae of the botfly, pinworms, tapeworms, and roundworms (ascarids). Overwork and neglect may predispose the horse to pneumonia and rheumatism. The ailment known as roaring is an infection of the larynx that makes the horse inhale noisily; a milder form causes the horse to whistle. Chronic asthma, or "broken wind," is an ailment that is considered to be all but incurable. A horse's legs and feet are sensitive to blows, sprains, and overwork, especially if the horse is young or is worked on hard surfaces. Lameness may be caused by bony growths, such as splints, spavins, and ringbones, by soft-tissue enlargements, known as windgalls, thoroughpins, and shoe boils, and by injury to the hooves, including sand crack, split hoof, tread thrush, and acute or chronic laminitis.

BREEDS OF HORSES

The first intensively domesticated horses were developed in Central Asia. They were small, lightweight, and stocky. In time, two general groups of horses emerged: the

PRZEWALSKI'S HORSE

Przewalski's horse (*Equus caballus przewalskii*) is the last wild horse sub-species surviving into the 21st century. It was discovered in western Mongolia in the late 1870s by the Russian explorer N.M. Przhevalsky. Several expeditions since 1969 have failed to find this horse, which probably crossed with half-wild domesticated horses and lost its distinct features. Specimens have been kept and bred in zoos, and Mongolia in the late 20th century attempted to reintroduce them into the wild.

Przewalski's horse is yellowish or light red (sometimes called dun) in colour, with a dark mane and tail and, usually, a dorsal stripe. The mane is short and erect with no forelock. The low withers blend into a narrow back, and the croup is short and steep. About 12 to 14 hands (122 to 142 cm [48 to 56 inches]) tall, Przewalski's horse resembles a coarse domestic pony.

southerly Arab-Barb types (from the Barbary coast) and the northerly, so-called cold-blooded types. When, where, and how these horses appeared is disputed. Nevertheless, all modern breeds—the light, fast, spirited breeds typi-fied by the modern Arabian, the heavier, slower, and calmer working breeds typified by the Belgian, and the intermediate breeds typified by the Thoroughbred—may be classified according to where they originated (e.g., Percheron, Clydesdale, and Arabian), by the principal use of the horse (riding, draft, coach horse), and by their out-ward appearance and size (light, heavy, pony).

Light Horses

Light horses are typified by the Arabian, English Thoroughbred, and various American breeds. The long history of the Arabian horse is obscured by legend, but this great breed—prized for its stamina, intelligence, and character—is known to have been developed in Arabia by the 7th century CE. It is a compact horse with a small head, protruding eyes, wide nostrils, marked withers, and a short back. It usually has only 23 vertebrae, while 24 is the usual number for other breeds. Its legs are strong with fine hooves. The coat, tail, and mane are of fine silky hair. While many colours are possible in the breed, gray prevails. The most famous stud farm is in the region of Najd, Saudi Arabia, but many fine Arabian horses are bred in the United States.

The history of the English Thoroughbred is a long one. Records indicate that a stock of Arab and Barb horses was introduced into England as early as the 3rd century. Conditions of climate, soil, and water favoured development, and selective breeding was long encouraged by those interested in racing. Under the reigns of James I and Charles I, 43 mares (the Royal Mares) were imported into England, and a record, the General Stud Book, was begun in which are inscribed only those horses that may be traced back to the Royal Mares in direct line, or to only three other horses imported to England: the Byerly Turk (imported in 1689), the Darley Arabian (after 1700), and the Godolphin Barb (also known as the Godolphin Arabian, imported about 1730). The English Thoroughbred has since been introduced to most countries, where it is bred for racing or used to improve local breeds. The Thoroughbred has a small fine head, a deep chest, and a straight back. Its legs have short bones that allow a long easy stride, and its coat is generally bay or chestnut, rarely black or gray.

Asian breeds were strongly influenced by Arabian or Persian breeds, which together with the horses of the steppes produced small, plain-looking horses of great intelligence and endurance. Among them are the Tartar, Kirghis, Mongol, and Cossack horses. A Persian stallion and a Dutch mare produced the Orlov trotter in 1778, named after Count Orlov, the owner of the stud farm where the mating took place.

The Anglo-Arab breed originated in France with a crossing of English Thoroughbreds to pure Arabians. The matings produced a horse larger than the Arabian and smaller than the Thoroughbred, of easy maintenance, and capable of carrying considerable weight in the saddle. Its coat is generally chestnut or bay.

Among American breeds, the Standardbred, a breed that excels at the pace and trot, ranks as one of the world's finest harness racers. A powerful, long-bodied horse, the Standardbred was developed during the first half of the 19th century and can be traced largely to the sire Messenger, a Thoroughbred imported from Britain in 1788 and mated to various brood mares in New York, New Jersey, and Pennsylvania.

The quarter horse was bred for races of a quarter of a mile and is said to descend from Janus, a small Thoroughbred stallion imported into Virginia toward the end of the 18th century. It is 14.2 to 16 hands (144 cm [57 inches] to 163 cm [64 inches]) high, with sturdily muscled hindquarters, essential for the fast departure required in short races. It serves as a polo pony equally well as for ranch work.

The Morgan horse originated from a stallion given to Justin Morgan of Vermont around 1795. This breed has become a most versatile horse for riding, pulling carriages, farm labour, and cattle cutting. It was the ideal army charger. It stands about 15 hands (about 50 cm, or 60 inches) high and is robust, good-natured, willing, and intelligent. Its coat is dark brown or liver chestnut.

Appaloosa is a colour breed said to have descended in the Nez Percé Indian territory of North America from wild mustangs, which in turn descended from Spanish horses brought to the New World by explorers. The

Appaloosa is 14.2 to 15.2 (144 cm [57 inches] to 54 cm [61 inches]) hands high, of sturdy build and of most diverse use; it is especially good in farm work.

American breeders have also developed several horses that have specialized gaits. These gaited breeds include the American saddle horse, the Tennessee walking horse, and the Missouri fox trotting horse. The American saddle horse has a small head and spectacular high-stepping movements. It is trained for either three or five gaits. The three-gaited horses perform the walk, trot, and canter. The five-gaited horses in addition perform the rack, a quick, high-stepping four-beat gait, and the slow gait, a somewhat slower form of the rack. Because they are used mainly for shows, their hooves are kept rather long, and the muscles of the tail are often clipped so that the base of the tail is carried high. Chestnut and bay are the usual

Hackney horse performing its typical high-stepping trot during a driving competition. © Sally Anne Thompson/Animal Photography

colours. The Tennessee walking horse—a breed derived partially from the Thoroughbred, Standardbred, Morgan, and American saddle horse—serves as a comfortable riding mount used to cover great distances at considerable speed. Its specialty is the running walk, a long and swift stride. Bay is the most common colour. The Missouri fox trotting horse, a breed developed to cover the rough terrain of the Ozark region, is characterized by an unusual gait, called the fox trot, in which the front legs move at a walk while the hind legs perform a trot. The most common colours for this breed are sorrel and chestnut sorrel.

The English Hackney is a light carriage horse, influenced by the Thoroughbred, capable of covering distances of 19 to 24 km (12 to 15 miles) per hour at the trot and canter. It measures 15.2 to 15.3 hands (154 cm [60.8 inches] to 155 cm [61.2 inches]) high and is appreciated for its high knee action.

The Cleveland Bay carriage horse, up to 17 hands (173 cm [68 inches]) high and generally bay in colour, is similar to the Yorkshire Coach horse. Both breeds are now used for the sport of driving.

Other versatile breeds include the German Holstein, Hanoverian, and East Prussian (Trakehner, which serve equally well for riding, light labour, and carriage. These horses, 16 to 18 hands (163 cm [64 inches] to 183 cm [72 inches]) high and of all colours, are now mostly bred for sport.

The Andalusian, a high-stepping, spirited horse, and the small but enduring Barb produced the Lipizzaner, which was named after the stud farm founded near Trieste, Italy, in 1580. Originally of all colours, the Lipizzaner is gray or, now exceptionally, bay. It is small, rarely over 15 hands (about 150 cm, or 60 inches) high, of powerful build but slender legs, and with long silky mane and tail. Intelligence and sweetness of disposition as well as gracefulness destined it for academic horsemanship, notably as practiced at the Spanish Riding School of Vienna.

Heavy Breeds

The horses used for heavy loads and farm labour descended from the ancient war horses of the Middle Ages. These breeds—including the English Shire (the world's largest horse), Suffolk, and Clydesdale; the French Percheron; the Belgian horse; the German Noriker; and the Austrian Pinzgauer—are now little used for their original purpose, having been almost entirely replaced by the tractor. They usually measure well over 16 hands (163 cm [64 inches]) high, some more than 19 hands (193 cm [76 inches]). They are of all colours, sometimes spotted, and generally have an extremely calm temperament.

Ponies

Ponies are any horses other than Arabians that are shorter than 14.2 hands (144 cm [57 inches]). They are generally very sturdy, intelligent, energetic, and sometimes stubborn. The coat is of all colours, mainly dark, and the mane and tail are full. Ponies are used for pulling carriages and pack loads

An Icelandic horse moving swiftly at the tölt, a smooth four-beat, lateral running walk. © Pall Stefansson/Iceland Review

and as children's riding horses or pets. There are numerous varieties, including the Welsh, Dartmoor, Exmoor, Connemara, New Forest, Highland, Dale, Fell, pony of the Americas, Shetland (under seven hands (71 cm [28 inches]) high), Iceland, and Norwegian. Ponies of the warmer countries include the Indian, Java, Manila, and Argentine.

Originating in the South Tyrol, the Haflinger is a mountain pony, enduring, robust, and versatile, used for all farm labour, for pulling a carriage or sledge, and for pack hauling. It is chestnut with a flaxen mane and tail.

EVOLUTION OF THE HORSE

The evolutionary lineage of the horse is among the best-documented in all paleontology. The history of the horse family, Equidae, began during the Eocene Epoch, which lasted from about 55.8 to 33.9 million years ago. During the early Eocene there appeared the first ancestral horse, a hoofed, browsing mammal designated correctly as *Hyracotherium* but more commonly called *Eohippus*, the "dawn horse." Fossils of *Eohippus*, which have been found in both North America and Europe, show an animal that stood from 4.2 to 5 hands (43 cm [17 inches] to 51 cm [20 inches]) high, diminutive by comparison to the modern horse, with an arched back and raised hindquarters. The legs ended in padded feet with four functional hooves on the forefeet and three on the hindfeet—quite unlike the unpadded, single-hoofed foot of modern equines. The skull lacked the large, flexible muzzle of the modern horse, and the size and shape of the cranium indicate that the brain was far smaller and less complex than that of today's horse. The teeth, too, differed significantly from those of the modern equines, being adapted to a fairly general browser's diet. *Eohippus* was, in fact, so unhorselike that its evolutionary relationship to the modern equines was at first unsuspected. It was not until paleontologists had unearthed fossils of later extinct horses that the link to *Eohippus* became clear.

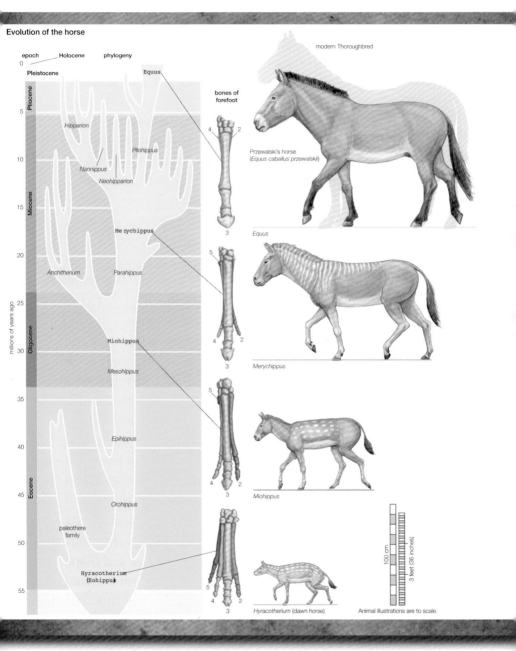

Evolution of the horse

epoch — Holocene — phylogeny

bones of forefoot

modern Thoroughbred

Przewalski's horse
(*Equus caballus przewalskii*)

Equus

Merychippus

Miohippus

Hyracotherium (dawn horse)

Animal illustrations are to scale.

100 cm
3 feet (36 inches)

Evolution of the horse over the past 55 million years. The present-day Przewalski's horse is believed to be the only remaining example of a wild horse (i.e., the last remaining modern horse to have evolved by natural selection). Numbered bones in the forefoot illustrations trace the gradual transition from a four-toed to a one-toed animal. Encyclopædia Britannica, Inc.

243

The line leading from *Eohippus* to the modern horse exhibits the following evolutionary trends: increase in size, reduction in the number of hooves, loss of the foot pads, lengthening of the legs, fusion of the independent bones of the lower legs, elongation of the muzzle, increase in the size and complexity of the brain, and the development of crested, high-crowned teeth suited to grazing. This is not to imply that there was a steady, gradual progression in these characteristics leading inevitably from those of *Eohippus* to those of the modern horse. Some of these features, such as grazing dentition, appear abruptly in the fossil record, rather than as the culmination of numerous, gradual changes. *Eohippus*, moreover, gave rise to many now-extinct branches of the horse family, some of which differed substantially from the line leading to the modern equines.

Although *Eohippus* fossils occur in both the Old and New worlds, the subsequent evolution of the horse took place chiefly in North America. During the remainder of the Eocene, the prime evolutionary changes were in dentition. *Orohippus*, a genus from the middle Eocene, and *Epihippus*, a genus from the late Eocene, resembled *Eohippus* in size and in the structure of the limbs. But the form of the cheek teeth—the four premolars and the three molars found in each half of both jaws—had changed somewhat. In *Eohippus* the premolars and molars were clearly distinct, the molars being larger. In *Orohippus* the fourth premolar had become similar to the molars, and in *Epihippus* both the third and fourth premolars had become molarlike. In addition, the individual cusps that characterized the cheek teeth of *Eohippus* had given way in *Epihippus* to a system of continuous crests or ridges running the length of the molars and molariform premolars. These changes, which represented adaptations to a more specialized browsing diet, were retained by all subsequent ancestors of the modern horse.

Fossils of *Mesohippus*, the next important ancestor of the modern horse, are found in the early and middle Oligocene of North America (the Oligocene Epoch lasted from about 33.9 to 23 million years ago). *Mesohippus* was far more horselike than its Eocene ancestors. It was larger (averaging about six hands (61 cm [24 inches]) high); the snout was more muzzlelike; and the legs were longer and more slender. *Mesohippus* also had a larger brain. The fourth toe on the forefoot had been reduced to a vestige, so that both the forefeet and hindfeet carried three functional toes and a foot pad. The teeth remained adapted to browsing.

By the late Oligocene, *Mesohippus* had evolved into a somewhat larger form known as *Miohippus*. The descendants of *Miohippus* split into various evolutionary branches during the early Miocene (the Miocene Epoch lasted from about 23 to 5.3 million years ago). One of these branches, known as the anchitheres, included a variety of three-toed, browsing horses comprising several genera. Anchitheres were successful, and some genera spread from North America across the Bering land bridge into Eurasia.

It was a different branch, however, that led from *Miohippus* to the modern horse. The first representative of this line, *Parahippus*, appeared in the early Miocene. *Parahippus* and its descendants marked a radical departure in that they had teeth adapted to eating grass. Grasses were at this time becoming widespread across the North American plains, providing *Parahippus* with a vast food supply. Grass is a much coarser food than succulent leaves and requires a different kind of tooth structure. The cheek teeth developed larger, stronger crests and became adapted to the side-to-side motion of the lower jaw necessary to grind grass blades. Each tooth also had an extremely long crown, most of which, in the young animal, was buried beneath the gum line. As grinding wore down the exposed surface, some of the buried crown grew out. This high-crowned tooth structure assured the animal of having an adequate grinding surface throughout its normal life span. Adaptations in the digestive tract must have occurred as well, but the organs of digestion are not preserved in the fossil record.

The change from browsing to grazing dentition was essentially completed in *Merychippus*, which evolved from *Parahippus* during the middle and late Miocene. *Merychippus* must have looked much like a modern pony. It was fairly large, standing about 10 hands (102 cm [40 inches]) high, and its skull was similar to that of the modern horse. The long bones of the lower leg had become fused. This structure, which has been preserved in all modern equines, is an adaptation for swift running. The feet remained three-toed, but in many species the foot pad was lost, and the two side toes became rather small. In these forms, the large central toe bore the animal's weight. Strong ligaments attached this hoofed central toe to the bones of the ankles and lower leg, providing a spring mechanism that pushed the flexed hoof forward after the impact of hitting the ground. *Merychippus* gave rise to numerous evolutionary lines during the late Miocene. Most of these, including *Hipparion*, *Neohipparion*, and *Nannippus*, retained the three-toed foot of their ancestors. One line, however, led to the one-toed *Pliohippus*, the direct predecessor of *Equus*. *Pliohippus* fossils occur in the early to middle Pliocene beds of North America (the Pliocene Epoch lasted from about 5.3 to 2.6 million years ago).

Equus—the genus to which all modern equines, including horses, asses, and zebras, belong—evolved from

Pliohippus toward the end of the Pliocene. *Equus* shows even greater development of the spring mechanism in the foot and exhibits straighter and longer cheek teeth. This new form was extremely successful and had spread from the plains of North America to South America and to all parts of the Old World by the early Pleistocene (the Pleistocene Epoch lasted from about 2.6 million to 11,700 years ago). *Equus* flourished in its North American homeland throughout the Pleistocene. Then, about 10,000 to 8,000 years ago, *Equus* disappeared from North and South America. Scholars have offered various explanations for this disappearance, including the emergence of devastating diseases or the arrival of human populations (which presumably hunted the horse for food). Despite these speculations, the reasons for the demise of *Equus* in the New World remain uncertain. The submergence of the Bering land bridge prevented any return migration of horses from Asia, and *Equus* was not reintroduced into its native continent until the Spanish explorers brought horses in the early 16th century.

During the Pleistocene the evolution of *Equus* in the Old World gave rise to all the modern members of the genus. The modern horse, *Equus caballus*, became widespread from central Asia to most of Europe. Local types of horses, all breeds of this single species, undoubtedly developed, and three of these—Przewalski's horse from central Asia, the tarpan from eastern Europe and the Ukrainian steppes, and the forest horse of northern Europe—are generally credited as being the ancestral stock of the domestic horse. According to this line of thinking, Przewalski's horse and the tarpan formed the basic breeding stock from which the southerly "warm-blooded" horses developed, while the forest horse gave rise to the heavy, "cold-blooded" breeds.

ASSES

Asses, or wild asses, are two species of hoofed grazers belonging to the horse family, Equidae. The two species are the African wild ass (*Equus africanus*), sometimes referred to as the true ass, and the related Asiatic wild ass, sometimes called the Asian wild ass or the half-ass (*E. hemionus*), which is usually known by the local names of its various subspecies: for example, kulan (*E. h. kulan*, Mongolia) and khur (*E. h. khur*, India and Pakistan). The Syrian wild ass (*E. h. hemippus*) is extinct. The donkey (*E. asinus*; described later in this section) is a domesticated descendant of *E. africanus*.

Asses are small, sturdy animals, ranging from 90 to 150 cm (3 to 5 feet) high at the shoulder. The African wild ass is bluish gray to fawn. The Asiatic wild ass, lighter in colour, is reddish to yellow-gray. Both have whitish muzzles and underparts, short, dark, erect manes lacking a forelock, and tufted tails. Most asses have a dark stripe from the mane back onto the tail, but only the Nubian ass (*E. a. africanus*) regularly has a prominent stripe across the shoulders, as does the donkey. The Asiatic wild ass differs from the African wild ass in its extremely long, slender legs, shorter ears (intermediate between those of the horse and donkey), and larger hooves. The bray of the Asiatic wild ass lacks the alternating low tones heard in the "hee-haw" of the African wild ass. The ass is a swift runner: kulans have been clocked at 64.4 km (40 miles) per hour. In ancient times Asiatic wild asses, especially the onager, were tamed and trained for work. These lighter-bodied animals were eventually rejected in favour of the sturdier donkey.

Desert dwellers, wild asses often inhabit exceptionally arid regions that cannot support other large mammals. African wild asses are territorial, mature males (stallions) maintaining areas in which they are dominant over other asses. The only strong social bond is between the female and her foals, herds being formed only when individuals travel together casually. Kulans live in herds consisting of one stallion and several females with their young. These family groups join to form large herds during the winter season.

KIANGS

The kiang (*Equus kiang*) is a species of Asian wild ass found in the cold, arid highlands of Nepal, India, and Pakistan and in Qinghai and Gansu provinces and the western Tibet Autonomous Region in China at elevations above 4,000 metres (13,000 feet). The kiang's coat is reddish in summer and brown in winter, and it has white underparts that do not change with the seasons. The kiang is the largest species of wild ass, standing 140 cm (55 inches) at the shoulder and weighing between 250 and 440 kg (550 and 970 pounds). In some areas, populations have declined because of competition with livestock. In areas where they do not compete with humans, however, the kiang has thrived.

ONAGERS

The onager (*Equus onager*) is a species of Asian wild ass that ranges from northwest Iran to Turkmenistan. The onager is pale-coloured and has a short erect mane and fairly large ears. It stands 1.5 metres (4.5 feet) at the shoulder and weighs about 250 kg (550 pounds). The onager was domesticated in ancient times but has been replaced by the domestic horse and donkey. It now is found in limited numbers and may be approaching extinction. The name *onager* is sometimes used for the Asian wild ass (*Equus hemionus*).

*Onager (*Equus onager*) and foal.* Kenneth W. Fink/Bruce Coleman Inc.

The Persian onager (*Equus onager*) lives in a lower semi-desert or desert environment. It is now extremely rare and is unlikely to survive outside northeastern Iran and the Badkhyz Reserve in Turkmenistan. A small population lives in the semidesert salt plains of the Kavir Protected Region in Iran.

The Indian wild ass, or khur, is a closely related, probably identical, form that is sometimes distinguished as the subspecies *E. h. khur*. A fairly small population occupies salt flats in the Rann of Kachchh in Gujarat state, a remnant of the thousands found there at the end of World War II.

DONKEYS

Donkeys (*Equus asinus*), also called burros, are domestic asses belonging to the horse family, Equidae, and descended from the African wild ass (*Equus africanus*).

MULES

A mule is the hybrid offspring of a male ass (jackass, or jack) and a female horse (mare). The less-frequent cross between a female ass and a male horse results in a hinny, or hinney, which is smaller than a mule. Mules were beasts of burden in Asia Minor at least 3,000 years ago and are still used today in many parts of the world because of their ability to withstand hardships and perform work under conditions too severe for many other draft and pack animals. Mules are usually sterile.

The mule resembles the horse in height, uniformity of coat, and shape of neck and croup. It resembles the ass in its short, thick head, long ears, thin limbs, small hooves, and short mane. The coat is usually brown or bay. In size, mules range widely from about 12 to 17.5 hands (120 to 180 cm, or 50 to 70 inches) in height and from 275 to 700 kg (600 to 1,500 pounds) in weight.

The donkey is known to have been used as a beast of burden since 4000 BCE. The average donkey stands 101.6 cm (40 inches) at the shoulder, but different breeds vary greatly. The Sicilian donkey reaches only about 61 cm (24 inches), while the large ass of Majorca stands at about 157.5 cm (62 inches), and the American ass has been measured to 167.6 cm (66 inches). In colour the donkey ranges from white to gray or black and usually has a dark stripe from mane to tail and a crosswise stripe on the shoulders. The mane is short and upright and the tail, with long hairs only at the end, is more cowlike than horselike. The very long ears are dark at the base and tip. Although slower than horses, donkeys are surefooted and can carry heavy loads over rough terrain. In some parts of the world where horses cannot easily survive or where extreme poverty prevents locals from owning horses, donkeys are the main beasts of burden and source of transportation.

Although the names *donkey* and *burro* are interchangeable, the term *burro* is widely used in the southwestern United States to describe small donkeys, *burro* being the word for donkey in the Spanish language. Feral donkeys, found in various parts of the world, are descendants of escaped or abandoned domestic animals. In the western United States, many authorities consider that the large population of feral burros is driving the desert bighorn sheep to extinction by competing for the limited resources of its very arid habitat. On tropical islands where plants evolved in the absence of large mammalian herbivores, feral donkeys pose a real threat of extinction for native plants. Efforts to remove donkeys from habitats where they are not native has generated a great deal of controversy, pitting animal rights groups against biologists and other conservation groups who see donkeys as an alien species and a threat to biodiversity conservation.

ZEBRAS

Zebras are three species of strikingly black-and-white-striped mammals of the horse family Equidae (genus *Equus*). Burchell's, or plains, zebra (*E. burchellii*), is found in rich grasslands over much of eastern and southern Africa. Grevy's zebra (*E. grevyi*) lives in arid, sparsely wooded areas in Kenya and a few small areas in Ethiopia. Finally, the mountain zebra (*E. zebra*) inhabits dry upland plains in Namibia and a few scattered areas in western South Africa.

Zebras are closely related to domestic horses. They are large, single-hoofed ungulates built for speed and long-distance migrations. Zebras typically stand about 120–140 cm (47–55 inches) at the shoulder. Male Grevy's zebras are larger than females. In Burchell's and the mountain zebra, the sexes are nearly the same size. Zebras exhibit no other sexual dimorphism except for males having spade-shaped canines used in fighting.

The teeth of all three species are adapted for grazing. Zebras possess strong upper and lower incisors for cropping grasses and large high-crowned teeth for processing silicate-rich grasses that wear down molars.

The three species are easily distinguished by the pattern of their stripes. In Burchell's zebras, the stripes are wide and widely spaced. Some races have lighter "shadow stripes" between the main stripes. The northern races of this species are more fully striped than the southern ones, in which the striping of the lower legs tends to give way to white. The mountain zebra has smaller stripes than Burchell's zebra; its stripes are closely spaced on its head and shoulders but widely spaced on its haunches. The mountain zebra also has a peculiar gridlike pattern of stripes on the rump. The Grevy's zebra has a white belly and the narrowest and most closely spaced stripes of the three species. Where stripes converge on the shoulders, all zebras have triangular chevrons. Grevy's zebra is the only species with a second chevron on the rump where the stripes converge. In all zebra species, the stripes are like fingerprints, allowing scientists to easily identify individuals.

Two types of mating systems are observed in zebras. Like the horse, the mountain and Burchell's zebras live in small family groups consisting of a stallion and several mares with their foals. The females that form the harem are unrelated. The harem remains intact even when the stallion leading the harem is replaced by another male. When moving, stallions usually remain in the rear but still maintain control over the movement of the herd.

In Grevy's zebra, males are territorial. Males create dung piles, or middens, to mark territorial boundaries that typically follow physical features such as streambeds. Increased reproductive success is enjoyed by males that occupy territories through which females must pass in order to gain access to safe drinking areas or prime grazing sites. Females and bachelor males form unstable groups without any clear dominance hierarchy. Adult males and females do not form lasting bonds, but related females may occupy the same grazing areas. Grevy's stallions maintain territories as large as 10–15 square km (4–6 square miles). However, females and bachelor male groups use annual home ranges of several thousand square kilometres. Territoriality has evolved because resources are widely scattered and easily defendable.

With plentiful food, small groups may coalesce into large herds, but the smaller groups still retain their identities. Zebras often form mixed herds with other mammals such as wildebeests and giraffes, which gain protection from predators by the alertness of the zebras. Zebras with young colts avoid predators such as hyenas by forming a cluster around the mother and young rather than bolting. A stallion will attack hyenas and wild dogs if his harem is threatened. Unless hyenas hunt in large groups, their attacks on zebras are often unsuccessful.

Available surface water is a critical need of zebras during the hot dry season. Both Grevy's and mountain zebras excavate pits in dry streambeds to obtain subsurface water, and they defend these waterholes against strangers. After the zebras have moved on, the drinking holes are used by other animals such as oryxes, springboks, Burchell's zebras, kudus, giraffes, hyenas, and lions.

Like other perissodactyls, zebras digest their food in the cecum, a blind sac at the far end of the small intestine where complex compounds such as cellulose are acted upon by symbiotic bacteria. Cecal digestion is less efficient for digesting grasses than ruminant digestion, but zebras compensate by ingesting more forage than do ruminants. This forage often includes grass stems and leaves too high in fibre or low in protein for ruminants to digest effectively and meet metabolic needs. Food travels rapidly through the cecum, and forage passes faster through a zebra than, for example, a wildebeest. Thus, even though zebras are less efficient than wildebeests in extracting protein from their food, they can extract more protein from low-quality grasses because of their faster rate of digestion and assimilation. The selective advantage of this approach is that zebras can subsist on range grasses unsuitable for antelope, an especially important adaptation during periods of drought or seasonal declines in forage quality. The disadvantage is that zebras must spend a considerable part of their day feeding to maintain the high rate of intake. The increased time spent foraging exposes them to greater risks of predation.

RHINOCEROSES

Rhinoceroses (family Rhinocerotidae), or rhinoceri, are five species of giant, horn-bearing herbivores that include some of the largest living land mammals. Only African and Asian elephants are larger than the two largest rhinoceros species—the white, or square-lipped (*Ceratotherium simum*), and the Indian, or greater one-horned, rhinoceros (*Rhinoceros unicornis*). The white and the black (*Diceros bicornis*) rhinoceros live in Africa; the Indian, the Javan (*Rhinoceros sondaicus*), and the Sumatran rhinoceros (*Dicerorhinus sumatrensis*) live in Asia. The precarious state of the five surviving species (all are endangered) is in direct contrast to the early history of this group as one of the most successful lineages of hoofed mammals. Today the total population of all five species combined is probably less than 25,000. Rhinoceroses today are restricted to eastern and southern Africa and to subtropical and tropical Asia.

Rhinoceroses are characterized by the possession of one or two horns on the upper surface of the snout. These horns are not true horns but are composed of keratin, a fibrous protein found in hair. Modern rhinoceroses are large animals, ranging from 2.5 metres (8 feet) long and 1.5 metres (5 feet) high at the shoulder in the Sumatran rhinoceros to about 4 metres (13 feet) long and nearly 2 metres (7 feet) high in the white rhinoceros. Adults of larger species weigh 3,000–5,000 kg (3–5 tons). Rhinoceroses are noted for their thick skin, which forms platelike folds, especially at the shoulders and thighs. All rhinos are gray or brown in colour, including the white rhinoceros, which tends to be paler than the others. Aside from the Sumatran rhinoceros, they are nearly or completely hairless, except for the tail tip and ear fringes, but some fossil species were covered with dense fur. The feet of the modern species have three short toes, tipped with broad, blunt nails.

Most rhinoceroses are solitary. Individuals usually avoid each other, but the white rhinoceros lives in groups of up to 10 animals. In solitary species the home territory is crisscrossed with well-worn trails and often marked at the borders with urine and piles of dung.

Rhinoceroses have poor eyesight but acute senses of hearing and smell. Most prefer to avoid humans, but males, and females with calves, may charge with little provocation. The black rhinoceros is normally ill-tempered and unpredictable and may charge any unfamiliar sound or smell. Despite their bulk, rhinoceroses are remarkably agile. The black rhinoceros can attain a speed of about 45 km (30 miles) per hour, even in thick brush, and can turn around rapidly after missing a charge. Like elephants, rhinoceroses communicate using infrasonic frequencies that are below the threshold of human hearing. The use of infrasonic frequencies is likely an adaptation for rhinoceroses to keep in touch with each other where they inhabit dense vegetation and probably for females to advertise to males when females are receptive to breeding.

Rhinoceroses are by far the largest of the perissodactyls, an order of hoofed mammals that also includes the horses and zebras. One of the features of very large body size in mammals is a low reproductive rate. In rhinoceroses, females do not conceive until about six years of age. Gestation is long (16 months in most species), and they give birth to only one calf at a time. The period of birth between calves can range from 2 to 4.5 years. Thus, the loss of a number of breeding-age females to poachers can greatly slow the recovery of rhinoceros populations. However, an Indian rhinoceros female will conceive again quickly if she loses her calf. In this species tigers kill about 10–20 percent of calves. Tigers rarely kill calves older than one year, so those Indian rhinoceroses that survive past that point are invulnerable to nonhuman predators.

The three Asian species fight with their razor-sharp lower outer incisor teeth, not with their horns. In Indian rhinoceroses such teeth, or tusks, can reach 13 cm (5 inches) in length among dominant males and inflict lethal wounds on other males competing for access to breeding females. The two African species, in contrast, lack these long tusklike incisors and instead fight with their horns.

The rhinoceros's horn is also the cause of its demise. Powdered rhinoceros horn has been a highly sought commodity in traditional Chinese medicine—not as an aphrodisiac, as is often widely reported, but as an antifever agent. Substitute agents have been found, particularly pig bone and water buffalo horn, but rhinoceros horn commands tens of thousands of dollars per kilogram in Asian markets. Today poaching remains a serious problem throughout the range of all five species of rhinoceros.

The term *rhinoceros* is sometimes also applied to other, extinct members of the family Rhinocerotidae, a

Indricotherium, *detail of a restoration painting by Charles R. Knight.*
Courtesy of the American Museum of Natural History, New York

diverse group that includes several dozen fossil genera, among them the woolly rhinoceros (*Coelodonta antiquitatis*). Early rhinoceroses resembled small horses and lacked horns. (Horns are a relatively recent development in the lineage.) The largest land mammal ever to have lived was not an elephant but *Indricotherium*, a perissodactyl that was 6 metres (20 feet) long and could browse treetops like a giraffe.

WHITE RHINOCEROSES

The white rhinoceros (*Ceratotherium simum*), also called the square-lipped rhinoceros, is the largest of the five rhinoceros species at 4 metres (13 feet) long and nearly 2 metres (7 feet) high and one of two African species of rhinoceros. The white rhinoceros can weigh up to 1,600 kg (3,500 pounds); it is the only rhinoceros species in which males are noticeably larger than females. The white rhinoceros is a grazing species and has a broad, square muzzle. It prefers short grasses 7–10 cm (3–4 inches) high. The animal makes much use of shade trees for resting. The white rhinoceros tends to be paler than the other species of rhinoceroses. It lives in groups of up to 10 individuals and fights with its horns.

The range of the white rhinoceros is not contiguous. South of the Zambezi River it was once extremely common over a fairly large area of bushveld. The white rhinoceros population in southern Africa was reduced to less than one hundred individuals about 1900 but today numbers well over 17,000, one of the most remarkable success stories in African conservation. Some of these animals have been redistributed to several other parks and reserves in southern Africa. A northern race formerly inhabited the southern Sudan and adjacent areas of

Uganda and the Congo (Kinshasa), extending westward into the Central African Republic. However, it now numbers only about 20 individuals in the Garamba National Park in Congo (Kinshasa).

BLACK RHINOCEROSES

The black rhinoceros (*Diceros bicornis*) is the the third largest rhinoceros and one of two African species of rhinoceros. The black rhinoceros typically weighs between 700 and 1,300 kg (1,500 and 2,900 pounds); males are the same size as females. It stands 1.5 metres (5 feet) high at the shoulder and is 3.5 metres (11.5 feet) long. The black rhinoceros occupies a variety of habitats, including open plains, sparse thorn scrub, savannas, thickets, and dry forests, as well as mountain forests and moorlands at high altitudes. It is a selective browser, and grass plays a minor role in its diet. Where succulent plants, such as euphorbias, are abundant in dry habitats, it can survive without flowing water. Where water is available, drinking is regular and frequent; black rhinoceroses also dig for water in dry riverbeds. They are normally ill-tempered and unpredictable and may charge any unfamiliar sound or smell. Four subspecies are recognized, including one from Namibia that lives in near-desert conditions.

The black rhinoceros was originally widespread from the Cape of Good Hope to southwestern Angola and throughout eastern Africa as far as Somalia, parts of Ethiopia, and the Sudan. Its range also extended westward through the northern savanna zone to Lake Chad, northern Cameroon, Burkina Faso, Côte d'Ivoire, and Guinea. Black rhinoceroses were abundant about 1900; some estimates put their numbers at over one million

Black rhinoceros (Diceros bicornis) in a zoo. Encyclopædia Britannica, Inc.

individuals. Rampant poaching reduced the total population to some 2,400 by 1995, but since then conservation
efforts have brought the numbers up to more than four
thousand. Black rhinoceroses now occupy a much smaller
area, within which they are found in scattered pockets,
many of them in parks and reserves. The species still
occurs in northern Namibia, Zimbabwe, Mozambique,
and Malawi. Populations kept in well-guarded small sanctuaries and game ranches have expanded rapidly. The
challenge now is to protect free-ranging black rhinoceroses in much larger reserves, such as the Selous Game
Reserve in Tanzania, a park the size of Switzerland.
Tanzania and Kenya have more black rhinoceroses than
any other country, but the future of the animals outside
parks and reserves is rather bleak.

INDIAN RHINOCEROSES

The Indian rhinoceros (*Rhinoceros unicornis*), also called the greater one-horned rhinoceros, is the largest of the three Asian rhinoceroses. The Indian rhinoceros weighs between 1,800 and 2,700 kg (4,000 and 6,000 pounds). It stands 2 metres (7 feet) high at the shoulder and is 3.5 metres (11.5 feet) long. The Indian rhinoceros is more or less equivalent in size to the white rhinoceros of Africa and is distinguishable from the Javan rhinoceros by its greater size, the presence of a large horn, tubercles on its skin, and a different arrangement of skin folds. The Indian rhinoceros occupies the world's tallest grasslands, where at the end of the summer monsoon in October grasses reach 7 metres (23 feet) tall. They are primarily grazers, except during the winter when they consume a larger proportion of browse. The Indian rhinoceros fights with its razor-sharp lower outer incisor teeth, not with its horn. Such teeth, or tusks, can reach 13 cm (5 inches) in length among dominant males and inflict lethal wounds on other males competing for access to breeding females.

The Indian rhinoceros previously occupied an extensive range across northern India and Nepal from Assam state in the east to the Indus River valley in the west. Today, this species is restricted to about 11 reserves in India and Nepal. Nearly four thousand individuals remain in the wild, and only two populations, those of Kaziranga National Park in Assam state and Royal Chitwan National Park, Nepal, contain more than five hundred individuals. Because this species reaches high densities on dynamic, nutrient-rich floodplains, rhinoceros populations recover quickly when these habitats—and the rhinoceroses themselves—are protected from poaching. In Kaziranga, Indian rhinoceroses numbered only 12 individuals about 1900, but today over 1,200 are estimated for this reserve. Similarly, the Chitwan population declined to 60–80 animals in the late 1960s after the eradication of malaria in the Chitwan Valley, the conversion of natural habitat to rice farming, and rampant poaching. By 2000 the population had climbed back to such an extent that rhinoceroses were transferred to other reserves in Nepal and India where they had once occurred but had been extirpated.

The Indian rhinoceroses' dung piles, or middens, are of interest not only as places where scent is deposited and as communication posts but also as sites for the establishment of plants. Indian rhinoceroses can deposit as much as 25 kg (55 pounds) in a single defecation, and more than 80 percent of defecations occur on existing latrines rather than as isolated clusters. By defecating the ingested seeds of fruits from the forest floor, rhinoceroses are important in helping shade-intolerant trees to colonize open areas. The Indian rhinoceroses' dung piles support interesting collections of over 25 species of plants whose seeds are ingested by rhinoceroses and germinate in the nutrient-rich dung.

JAVAN RHINOCEROSES

The Javan rhinoceros (*Rhinoceros sondaicus*), also called the lesser one-horned rhinoceros, is one of three Asian species of rhinoceros. Although only a few Javan rhinoceroses have ever been measured or weighed, the Javan rhinoceros is believed to be about the size of the black rhinoceros, with a weight between 700 and 1,300 kg (1,500 and 2,900 pounds). It fights with its razor-sharp lower outer incisor teeth, not with its horn. The Javan rhinoceros inhabits forests, marshy areas, and regions of thick bush and bamboo. It is an active climber in mountainous country. Javan rhinoceroses are mainly browsers and often feed on pioneer plants that dominate in gaps in the forest created by fallen trees. This species once occupied the islands of Java, Borneo, and Sumatra, the Malay Peninsula, and a region extending northward through Burma (Myanmar) into Assam and eastern Bengal. Perhaps no more than 60 remain in the wild: about 50 animals live in Ujung Kulon National Park in the western tip of the island of Java in Indonesia, and a relict population of less than 10 animals lives in Cat Loc, Vietnam, making this species among the most endangered of all mammals. Rhinoceroses of the Vietnam population are thought to be much smaller in body mass than those of the Javan population.

SUMATRAN RHINOCEROSES

The Sumatran rhinoceros (*Dicerorhinus sumatrensis*) is one of three Asian species of rhinoceros and the smallest living rhinoceros. Both females and males typically weigh less than 850 kg (1,870 pounds); they are 2.5 metres (8 feet) long and 1.5 metres (5 feet) high at the shoulder. Sumatran rhinoceroses are the most ancient of the five rhinoceros species and the most unusual in that they are covered in long body hair. This species was originally found from Assam throughout Burma (Myanmar), much of Thailand, Indochina (Cambodia, Laos, and Vietnam), Malaysia, Sumatra, and Borneo. Today, the Sumatran rhinoceros numbers no more than 300 individuals in the wild, scattered among a few protected areas in the Malay Peninsula, Sumatra, and Sabah in east Malaysia.

The Sumatran rhinoceros inhabits forests, marshy areas, and regions of thick bush and bamboo. It is an active climber in mountainous country. The Sumatran rhinoceros is mainly a browser and often feeds on pioneer plants that dominate in gaps in the forest created by fallen trees.

TAPIRS

Tapirs (genus *Tapirus*) are four species of hoofed mammals, the only extant members of the family Tapiridae, order Perissodactyla. They are found in tropical forests of Malaysia and the New World. Heavy-bodied and rather short-legged, tapirs are 1.8 to 2.5 metres (about 6 to 8 feet) long and reach about 1 metre (3.3 feet) at the shoulder. The eyes are small, the ears are short and rounded, and the snout extends into a short fleshy proboscis, or trunk, that hangs down over the upper lip. The feet have three functional toes, the first (inner) being absent, and the fifth reduced in front and absent in the hind foot. Body hair is short and usually sparse but fairly dense in the mountain tapir (*T. pinchaque,* formerly *T. roulini*). There is a short, bristly mane in the Central American, or Baird's, tapir (*T. bairdii*) and the South American lowland tapir (*T. terrestris*). This geographic distribution, with three species in Central and South America and one in Southeast Asia, is peculiar. Fossil remains from Europe, China, and North America show that tapirs were once widespread, but the extinction of intermediate forms has isolated the living species.

The three New World species are plain dark brown or gray, but the Malayan tapir (*T. indicus*) is strongly patterned, with black head, shoulders, and legs and white rump, back, and belly. The young of all tapirs are dark brown, streaked and spotted with yellowish white. A single young (rarely two) is produced after a gestation of about four hundred days.

Tapirs are shy inhabitants of deep forest or swamps, traveling on well-worn trails, usually near water. When disturbed, they usually flee, crashing through undergrowth and often seeking refuge in water. Their main enemy wherever they are found is the human. In South America the jaguar is a principal predator, and in Asia the tiger is another predator. Despite declining numbers caused largely by habitat destruction, tapirs are hunted for food and sport in many parts of their range.

CHAPTER 9

PROBOSCIDEANS

Proboscideans are a group of mammals that includes elephants and their extinct relatives such as mammoths and mastodons. Although only three species of elephant are extant today, more than 160 extinct proboscidean species have been identified from remains found on all continents except Australia and Antarctica. Most of these were called gomphotheres, which belonged to a different family from elephants. Elephants and mammoths both belong to the only surviving proboscidean family, Elephantidae.

Within the elephant family, Asian elephants (genus *Elephas*) and mammoths (genus *Mammathus*) are more closely related to one another than African elephants (genus *Loxodonta*) are to either. Molecular studies have recently corroborated the morphological studies that have long suggested this. The mastodons that roamed North America until 10,000 years ago are more distantly related and belong to a separate family, Mammutidae.

American mastodon   woolly mammoth   African savanna elephant

Illustration comparing a mastodon, a woolly mammoth, and an elephant. Encyclopædia Britannica, Inc.

CHARACTERISTICS OF ORDER PROBOSCIDEA

Elephants, mastodons, and mammoths all have upper incisor teeth that emerge from the skull as tusks. The first proboscideans, however, had three small sets of incisors in each jaw. *Moeritherium*, a tapir-sized mammal that lived some 35 million years ago, had upper and lower incisors representing an early stage in proboscidean tusk development. Some proboscideans, called "shovel-tuskers," developed a pair of long and broad lower incisors used for digging. Many, including the gomphotheres, had upper and lower pairs of tusks, whereas others had tusks only in the lower jaw.

The earliest proboscideans date to the late Paleocene Epoch (61 to 54.8 million years ago) in northeastern Africa. They stood less than a metre (3.3 feet) at the shoulder and did not possess a trunk. Because the trunk is made of soft tissue that does not fossilize, paleontological evidence for it comes from knowledge of the elephant's cranium, which contains an opening (external naris) low on the forehead where the trunk begins. Generally in mammals the external naris is situated near the front of the mouth, whereas in elephants the naris is enlarged, deepened, and located higher and farther back. Another important clue for the presence of a trunk is an enlarged opening (infraorbital canal) below the eye socket through which blood and lymph vessels and nerves pass to nourish and innervate the trunk. The combination of an elevated and enlarged external naris and an enlarged infraorbital canal is interpreted as an indication that an extinct species may have possessed a trunk. Skulls with the single narial opening are theorized to have inspired the myth of the Cyclops.

The living mammals most closely related to proboscideans are the manatees and the dugongs—marine mammals of the order Sirenia. Proboscideans and sirenians are together classified as tethytherians, in reference to the ancient sea of Tethys, where both groups are hypothesized to have originated. On land the closest proboscidean relative is the hyrax (order Hyracoidea), a small rodentlike animal of Africa and southwestern Asia. Tethytheria and Hyracoidea are grouped together as Uranotheria.

ELEPHANTS

The elephant is the largest living land animal, characterized by its long trunk (elongated upper lip and nose), columnar legs, and huge head with temporal glands and wide, flat

African elephant (Loxodonta africana). Anthony Mercieca/Root Resources

ears. Elephants are grayish to brown in colour, and their body hair is sparse and coarse. They are found most often in savannas, grasslands, and forests but occupy a wide range of habitats, including deserts, swamps, and highlands in tropical and subtropical regions of Africa and Asia.

The African savanna, or bush, elephant (*Loxodonta africana*) weighs up to 8,000 kg (9 tons) and stands 3 to 4 metres (10 to 13 feet) at the shoulder. The African forest elephant (*Loxodonta cyclotis*), which lives in rain-forests, was recognized as a separate species in 2000 and is smaller than the savanna elephant. It has slender, downward-pointing tusks. The common belief that there existed "pygmy" and "water" elephants has no basis; they are probably varieties of the African forest elephants.

The Asian elephant (*Elephas maximus*) weighs about 5,500 kg (5.5 tons) and has a shoulder height of up to 3.5

Asian elephant (Elephas maximus). E.S. Ross

metres (11.5 feet). The Asian elephant includes three subspecies: the Indian, or mainland (*E. m. indicus*), the Sumatran (*E. m. sumatranus*), and the Sri Lankan (*E. m. maximus*). African elephants have much larger ears, which are used to dissipate body heat.

FORM AND FUNCTION

The trunk, or proboscis, of the elephant is one of the most versatile organs to have evolved among mammals. This structure is unique to members of the order Proboscidea, which includes the extinct mastodons and mammoths. Breathing, drinking, and eating are all vital functions of the trunk. Tusks are used for defense, offense, digging, lifting objects, gathering food, and stripping bark to eat from trees. They also protect the sensitive trunk, which is tucked between them when the elephant charges.

THE TRUNK (PROBOSCIS)

Anatomically, the trunk is a combination of the upper lip and nose; the nostrils are located at the tip. The trunk is large and powerful, weighing about 130 kg (290 pounds) in an adult male and capable of lifting a load of about 250 kg. However, it is also extremely dexterous, mobile, and sensitive, which makes it appear almost independent of the rest of the animal. The proboscis comprises 16 muscles. A major muscle covering the top and sides functions to raise the trunk; another covers the bottom. Within the trunk is an extremely complex network of radiating and transverse muscle fascicles that provide fine movement. A total of nearly 150,000 muscle fascicles have been counted in cross-sections of trunk. The trunk is innervated by two proboscidean nerves, which render it extremely sensitive. Bifurcations of this nerve reach most portions of the trunk, especially the tip, which is equipped with tactile bristles at regular intervals. At the end of the trunk are flaplike projections enabling it to perform amazingly delicate functions, such as picking up a coin from a flat surface or cracking a peanut open, blowing away the shell, and putting the kernel in the mouth. African elephants have two such extremities (one above and one below); Asian elephants have one. An Asian elephant most often curls the tip of its trunk around an item and picks it up in a method called the "grasp," whereas the African elephant uses the "pinch," picking up objects in a manner similar to that of a human's use of the thumb and index finger. The trunk of the African elephant may be more extendable, but that of the Asian elephant is probably more dexterous.

Elephants use the trunk like a hand in other ways as well. Tool use in elephants involves holding branches and scratching themselves in places that the trunk and tail cannot reach. Large branches are sometimes wielded, and objects may be thrown in threat displays. When elephants meet, one may touch the face of the other, or they will intertwine trunks. This "trunk-shake" can be compared to a human handshake in that it may be associated with similar functions such as assurance and greeting or as a way of assessing strength.

Most breathing is performed through the trunk rather than the mouth. Elephants drink by sucking as much as 10 litres (2.6 gallons) of water into the trunk and then squirting it into the mouth. They eat by detaching grasses, leaves, and fruit with the end of the trunk and using it to place this vegetation into the mouth. The trunk is also used to collect dust or grass for spraying onto themselves, presumably for protection against insect bites and the sun. If danger is suspected, elephants raise and swivel the

trunk as if it were "an olfactory periscope," possibly sniff-
ing the air for information.

SOUND PRODUCTION AND WATER STORAGE

Elephants produce two types of vocalization by modifying
the size of the nostrils as air is passed through the trunk.
Low sounds are the growl, rolling growl, snort, and roar;
high sounds are the trump, trumpet, pulsated trumpet,
trumpet phrase, bark, gruff cry, and cry. Rumbling sounds
initially thought to be caused by intestinal activity are now
known to be produced by the larynx and are considered
to be similar to purring in cats. Vocalizations originate in
the larynx and a special structure associated with it, the
pharyngeal pouch. In the vast majority of mammals, the
throat contains nine bones connected in a boxlike structure, the hyoid apparatus, that supports the tongue and
the voice box (larynx). Elephants have only five bones in
the hyoid apparatus, and the gap formed by the missing
bones is filled by muscles, tendons, and ligaments. These
looser attachments allow the larynx a great degree of freedom and enable the formation of the pharyngeal pouch
just behind the tongue. This unique structure facilitates
sound production and has voluntary muscles that allow
the pouch to be used as a resonating chamber for calls
emitted at frequencies below the range of human hearing. These low-frequency (5–24 hertz) calls are responded
to by other elephants up to 4 km (2.5 miles) away. Low-
frequency sound waves travel through the ground as well
as the air, and results of experiments indicate that elephants can detect infrasonic calls as seismic waves.
Elephants can produce a variety of other sounds by beat-
ing the trunk on hard ground, a tree, or even against their
own tusks.

In addition to sound production, the pharyngeal pouch
is presumed to be used for carrying water. For centuries

people have observed that on hot days and in times when there is no water nearby, elephants insert their trunks into their mouths, withdraw liquid, and spray themselves with it. The source of this liquid and the ability of elephants to withdraw it have posed a mystery even though the pharyngeal pouch was described in 1875. Two plausible sources of the liquid are the stomach and the pharyngeal pouch. Stomach contents, however, are acidic and would irritate the skin. In addition, the sprayed liquid contains small food particles commonly found in the pharyngeal pouch, as opposed to digested food from the stomach. Finally, repeated field observations attest that elephants can spray themselves while walking or running. As it would be difficult to suck liquid from the stomach while running, the most likely explanation for the liquid's source is the pharyngeal pouch. Another possible function of the pouch is heat absorption, especially from the sensitive brain area above it.

Tusks and Teeth

Elephant tusks are enlarged incisor teeth made of ivory. In the African elephant both the male and the female possess tusks, whereas in the Asian elephant it is mainly the male that has tusks. When present in the female, tusks are small, thin, and often of a uniform thickness. Some male Asian elephants are tuskless and are known as *muknas*. Tusk size and shape are inherited. In times of drought, elephants dig water holes in dry river beds by using their tusks, feet, and trunks.

Elephants have six sets of cheek teeth (molars and premolars) in their lifetime, but they do not erupt all at once. At birth an elephant has two or three pairs of cheek teeth in each jaw. New teeth develop from behind and slowly move forward as worn teeth fragment in front and either fall out or are swallowed and excreted. Each new set is successively

IVORY

Ivory is a variety of dentin of which the tusk of the elephant is composed, prized for its beauty, durability, and suitability for carving. The tusk is the upper incisor and continues to grow throughout the lifetime of the male and female African elephant and of the male Indian elephant; the female Indian elephant has no tusks or small ones. The teeth of the hippopotamus, walrus, narwhal, sperm whale, and some types of wild boar and warthog are recognized as ivory but have little commercial value because of their small size. Elephant tusks from Africa average about 2 metres (6 feet) in length and weigh about 23 kg (50 pounds) each. Tusks from Asian elephants are somewhat smaller. The elephant's tusk grows in layers, the inside layer being the last produced. About a third of the tusk is embedded in the bone sockets of the animal's skull. The head end of the tusk has a hollow cavity that runs for some distance along its interior, but the tusk gradually becomes entirely solid, with only a narrow nerve channel running through its centre to the tip of the tusk.

There are two main types of elephant ivory, hard and soft. Hard ivory generally comes from elephants in the western half of Africa, soft ivory from those in the eastern half. A hard ivory tusk is darker in colour and is more slender and straighter in form than a soft tusk. Internally, a hard tusk has more colour and is more brittle than a soft tusk, which is an opaque white and has a somewhat fibrous texture.

Ivory is an extremely durable material and is not easily damaged or destroyed. It will not burn and is scarcely affected by immersion in water. Ivory is similar to a hard wood in some of its properties. It is quite dense, it polishes beautifully, and it is easily worked with woodworking tools. Most of the ivory used commercially comes from Africa, but commercial sales of ivory have declined since the 19th and the early 20th centuries because of the shrinking numbers of African elephants. The once-flourishing ivory markets of Europe have largely shifted to South and East Asia, where skilled artisans still carve ivory into figurines and other aesthetic objects. The white tops of piano keys ("ivories") and white billiard balls were formerly made of ivory, but these objects are now made of plastics or other synthetic materials.

longer, wider, and heavier. The last molars can measure nearly 40 cm (almost 16 inches) long and weigh more than 5 kg (about 11 pounds). Only the last four molars or their remains are present after about 60 years of age. Sometimes tooth loss is the cause of death, as it brings on starvation.

LIFE CYCLE

Elephants live in small family groups led by old females (cows). Where food is plentiful, the groups join together. Most males (bulls) live in bachelor herds apart from the cows. Males and females both possess two glands that open between the eye and ear. Elephants of all ages and sexes secrete a fluid called temporin out of this orifice. Males, however, enter a "musth period," during which they secrete a fluid differing in viscosity from the fluid secreted when they are not in musth. Serum testosterone during musth is higher than in a nonmusth elephant, and the animal's behaviour is erratic. They are uncontrollable (*musth* is Hindi for "intoxicated"), sometimes even by their own handlers (mahouts). Musth is the time for establishing reproductive hierarchy, which can differ from the usual social hierarchy in that a male in musth outranks nonmusth males. In the wild, males are usually at their prime physical state during musth and ordinarily do most of the breeding.

Elephants are able to assess the reproductive status of one another by using their keen sense of smell. Inside the skull, elephants possess from seven to nine nasal turbinals with specialized sensitive tissues for olfaction. (Humans have only three turbinals; dogs have five.) When a female is in estrus, or when a male is in musth, an elephant apparently can detect airborne hormones. Once "collected," the information is then passed to the Jacobson's organ, located on the roof of the mouth. This organ conveys the molecules to the brain for analysis. Hormones are also sniffed directly from urine and feces.

Gestation is the longest of any mammal (18–22 months). The newborn elephant is about a metre (3.3 feet) tall and weighs about 100 kg (220 pounds). It suckles by using the mouth, not the trunk, at mammary glands located in the chest region. Weaning is a long process and sometimes continues until the mother can no longer tolerate the pokes of her offspring's emerging tusks. After weaning, many hours of each day are spent eating. An adult elephant consumes about 100 kg (220 pounds) of food and 100 litres (26 gallons) of water per day. These amounts can double for a hungry and thirsty individual. Such consumption makes elephants an important ecological factor, because they substantially affect and even alter the ecosystems they live in.

Elephants migrate seasonally according to the availability of food and water. Memory plays an important role during this time, as they remember locations of water supplies along migration routes. Intelligence has also been observed in conjunction with memory. One elephant, using its tusks and trunk, stripped bark from a nearby tree and chewed it until it made a large ball, then plugged a waterhole it had previously dug and covered the plug with sand. Subsequently, the elephant was seen to uncover the sand, unplug the hole, and drink—a behaviour that could be interpreted as tool-making.

Although unable to jump or gallop, elephants can reach a top speed of 40 km (25 miles) per hour. Their feet are well adapted to carrying their great weight. The heel is partially elevated, and below it is a thick fatty, fibrous wedge of tissue protected by thick skin. It is not easy for elephants to lie down and get up; they sleep lying down for three to four hours during the night. While standing, elephants doze for short periods but do not sleep deeply.

Elephants can live to 80 years of age or more in captivity but live to only about 60 in the wild. Evidence does not substantiate the existence of so-called "elephant graveyards," where elephants supposedly gather to die.

IMPORTANCE TO HUMANS

For many centuries the Asian elephant has been important as a ceremonial and draft animal. Technically, elephants have not been domesticated, for they have not been subjected to selective breeding for "improvement" of traits desired by humans, as has been the practice with cattle, horses, and dogs. Historical records of tamed Asian elephants date to the Indus civilization of the 3rd millennium BCE. At Mohenjo-Daro and Harappa, Pakistan, soapstone carvings depict elephants with cloth on their backs, which indicates use by humans. Mahouts and oozies (elephant trainers in India and Myanmar, respectively) are skilled people who remain in direct contact with the animals for many years. The handlers take care of all the elephants' needs, and the bond between man and beast becomes very strong. *Hastividyarama*, an age-old handbook for elephant tamers, spells out prescribed training procedures in detail and is still used today in some parts of Asia. Commanded by its mahout, the elephant was once basic to Southeast Asian logging operations. It remains a symbol of power and pageantry but has been largely supplanted by machinery. At the beginning of the 21st century, Thailand and Myanmar each had about five thousand mingled with modern use as tourist attractions.

The most famous historical event using elephants in war was that of Hannibal, the young commander of the Carthaginians who crossed the Alps from Spain into Italy. He left Cartagena, Spain, in 218 BCE with 37 elephants — 36 African forest elephants and one Asian — each under its own well-trained mahout. The Asian, Hannibal's personal elephant named Surus (meaning "Syrian"), was the only one that survived to reach Italy.

African elephants were also tamed during the 19th century, in what was the Belgian Congo. Training of these forest elephants was initiated by King Leopold II of Belgium and was conducted by Indian mahouts with Asian elephants. African elephants are now used mainly for transporting tourists in Garamba National Park, where they are valuable in providing revenue to sustain its activities.

CONSERVATION

At the beginning of the 21st century, fewer than 50,000 Asian elephants remained in the wild. Threatened by habitat loss and poaching, Asian and African elephants are listed as endangered species. From 1979 to 1989 the number of African elephants in the wild was reduced by more than half, from 1.3 million to 600,000, owing in part to commercial demand for ivory. However, in some parts of Africa elephants are abundant, and culling is practiced in some reserves to prevent habitat destruction. A nine-year ban on the ivory trade was lifted in 1997, and Botswana, Namibia, and Zimbabwe were allowed to sell limited stocks of ivory from government warehouses to Japan. In 2000 South Africa joined the three southern African nations in selling limited amounts of ivory from existing stocks.

CHAPTER 10

LAGOMORPHS AND GRAZING MARSUPIALS

Lagomorphs are members of the mammalian order Lagomorpha, which is made up of the relatively well-known rabbits and hares (family Leporidae) and also the less frequently encountered pikas (family Ochotonidae). Rabbits and hares characteristically have long ears, a short tail, and strong hind limbs that provide a bounding locomotion. In contrast, the smaller pikas have shorter, rounded ears, no external tail, and less–well-developed hind limbs associated with scampering locomotion. Marsupials are some 250 species of mammals belonging to the infraclass Metatheria (sometimes called Marsupialia), a group characterized by premature birth and continued development of the newborn while attached to the nipples on the lower belly of the mother. The pouch, or marsupium, from which the group takes its name, is a flap of skin covering the nipples. Although prominent in many species, it is not a universal feature—in some species the nipples are fully exposed or are bounded by mere remnants of a pouch. The young remain firmly attached to the milk-giving teats for a period corresponding roughly to the latter part of development of the fetus in the womb of a placental mammal (eutherian).

LAGOMORPHS

All lagomorphs (meaning "hare-shaped") are small to medium-sized terrestrial herbivores. They superficially resemble rodents and in older classifications were even included in the order Rodentia, as both possess a set of continuously growing incisor teeth. It is now recognized that these two orders have long separate evolutionary histories. A distinctive feature setting lagomorphs apart from rodents is the presence of a second pair of peglike incisors set directly behind the large, continuously growing pair in the upper jaw. Another trait of all lagomorphs is their production of two kinds of feces—solid round droppings and soft black greaselike pellets. The soft feces are produced in the cecum and contain up to five times the vitamin content of hard feces; these are reingested. This double-digestion process, known as coprophagy, allows lagomorphs to use nutrients missed during the first passage through the digestive tract and thus ensures that maximum nutrition is derived from the food they eat.

Lagomorphs proverbially are known for their high rates of reproduction, and many species produce many large litters per year. However, there are also several species that breed only once per year or have only extremely small litters. One common and interesting feature of lagomorph reproduction is how inattentive the mothers are to their young. Nearly absentee parents, most lagomorph mothers visit their young to nurse only once a day, and the duration of nursing is quite short. However, lagomorph milk is among the richest of that of all mammals, and the young grow rapidly and are generally weaned in about a month. Lagomorphs are frequently abundant and play an important role in many terrestrial communities as prey species in food chains. They are also noted for their effect on native vegetation.

The pikas (family Ochotonidae) are represented by one genus (*Ochotona*) and about 29 species found in the mountains of western North America and much of Asia. The two North American pikas and about half of Asian

Black-tailed jackrabbits (Lepus californicus) *are widespread on the western plains of North America.* © G.C. Kelley/Photo Researchers

pikas occupy rocky habitat, where they live without making burrows. The other Asian pikas are burrowers that live in steppe and meadow habitats.

The rabbits and hares, or leporids (family Leporidae), are clearly separable from family Ochotonidae, the only other family in the order Lagomorpha. Morphologically, rabbits and hares have a more arched skull than pikas, correlated with development of bounding locomotion and a relatively upright posture of the head. Strengthened hind limbs and pelvic girdle and elongation of the limbs are also evident. Family Leporidae consist of 30 species of hare in one genus (*Lepus*) and 28 species of rabbit in 10 genera (*Pentalagus, Pronolagus, Romerolagus, Caprolagus, Oryctolagus, Sylvilagus, Brachylagus, Bunolagus, Poelagus, Nesolagus*). The most commonly recognized rabbits are the European rabbit (*O. cuniculus*) and the cottontail rabbits of the Western Hemisphere (genus *Sylvilagus*).

The vernacular names *hare* and *rabbit* are frequently misapplied to particular species. Jackrabbits of North America, for example, are actually hares, while the hispid hare (*Caprolagus hispidus*) of Nepal and India is a rabbit, and the mouse hare is another name for the pika.

RABBITS

Rabbits are ground dwellers that live in environments ranging from desert to tropical forest and wetland. Their natural geographic range encompasses the middle latitudes of the Western Hemisphere. In the Eastern Hemisphere rabbits are found in Europe, portions of Central and Southern Africa, the Indian subcontinent, Sumatra, and Japan. The European rabbit (*Oryctolagus cuniculus*) has been introduced to many locations around the world, and all breeds of domestic rabbit originate from the European. Nearly half of the world's 28 rabbit species are in danger of extinction, many of which are among the most vulnerable of all mammals.

The long ears of rabbits are most likely an adaptation for detecting predators. In addition to their prominent ears, which can measure up to 6 cm (more than 2 inches) long, rabbits have long, powerful hind legs and a short tail. Each foot has five digits (one reduced); rabbits move about on the tips of the digits in a fashion known as digitigrade locomotion. Full-bodied and egg-shaped, wild rabbits are rather uniform in body proportions and stance. The smallest is the pygmy rabbit (*Brachylagus idahoensis*), at only 20 cm (8 inches) in length and 0.4 kg (0.9 pound) in weight, while the largest grow to 50 cm (20 inches) and more than 2 kg (4.4 pounds). The fur is generally long and soft, and its colour ranges through shades of brown, gray, and buff. Exceptions are the black Amami rabbit (*Pentalagus furnessi*) of Japan and two black-striped species from Southeast Asia. The tail is usually a small puff of fur, generally brownish but white on top in the cottontails (genus *Sylvilagus*) of North and South America.

NATURAL HISTORY

While the European rabbit is the best-known species, it is probably also the least typical, as there is considerable variability in the natural history of rabbits. Many rabbits dig burrows, but cottontails and hispid hares do not. The European rabbit constructs the most extensive burrow systems, called warrens. Nonburrowing rabbits make surface nests called forms, generally under dense protective cover. The European rabbit occupies open landscapes such as fields, parks, and gardens, although it has colonized habitats from stony deserts to subalpine valleys. It is the most social rabbit, sometimes forming groups in warrens of up to 20 individuals. However, even in European rabbits social behaviour can be quite flexible, depending on habitat and other local conditions, so that at times the primary social unit is a territorial breeding pair. Most rabbits are relatively solitary and sometimes territorial, coming together only to breed or occasionally to forage in small groups. During territorial disputes rabbits will sometimes "box," using their front limbs. Rabbits are active throughout the year; no species is known to hibernate. Rabbits are generally nocturnal, and they also are relatively silent. Other than loud screams when frightened or caught by a predator, the only auditory signal known for most species is a loud foot thump made to indicate alarm or aggression. A notable exception is the volcano rabbit of Mexico, which utters a variety of calls.

Instead of sound, scent seems to play a predominant role in the communication systems of most rabbits. They possess well-developed glands throughout their body and rub them on fixed objects to convey group identity, sex, age, social and reproductive status, and territory ownership. Urine is also used in chemical communication. When danger is perceived, the general tendency of rabbits is to freeze and hide under cover. If chased by a predator, they engage in quick, irregular movement, designed more to evade and confuse than to outdistance a pursuer. Skeletal adaptations such as long hind limbs and a strengthened pelvic girdle enable their agility and speed (up to 80 km [50 miles] per hour).

Rabbits must consume plant material in large quantities to ensure proper nutrition, and thus they have large digestive tracts. In addition, their diet, consisting primarily of forbs and grasses, contains large amounts of cellulose, which is hard to digest. Rabbits solve this problem by passing two distinctive types of feces: hard droppings and soft black viscous pellets, the latter of which are immediately eaten (coprophagy). This double-digestion process ensures that that maximum nutrition is derived from the food they eat.

Most rabbits produce many offspring (kittens) each year, although scarcity of resources may cause this potential to be suppressed. A combination of factors allows the high rates of reproduction commonly associated with rabbits. Rabbits generally are able to breed at a young age, and many regularly conceive litters of up to seven young, often doing so four or five times a year. In addition, females (does) exhibit induced ovulation, their ovaries releasing eggs in response to copulation rather than according to a regular cycle. They can also undergo postpartum estrus, conceiving immediately after a litter has been born.

Newborn rabbits are naked, blind, and helpless at birth (altricial). Mothers are remarkably inattentive to their young and are almost absentee parents, commonly nursing their young only once per day and for just a few minutes. Therefore, the milk of rabbits is highly nutritious so as to allow the young grow rapidly. Most are weaned in about a month. Males (bucks) do not assist in rearing the kittens.

Both wild and domestic rabbits are of economic importance to people. Wild lagomorphs are popular with hunters for sport as well as for food and fur. Rabbit meat, known for its delicate flavor, remains an important source of protein in many cultures. Domestic rabbits are raised for meat and skins, the latter being used as pelts and for making felt. Domestication of the European rabbit probably started during Roman times in North Africa or Italy, and today there are more than 50 established strains of domestic rabbit, all selectively bred from this one species. Their attractive appearance and quiet manner have made domestic rabbits good and relatively undemanding pets. Because they are easily raised in captivity, rabbits are also important as laboratory animals for medical and scientific purposes. However, rabbits may also carry and transmit to humans diseases such as tularemia, or rabbit fever.

Because of their frequent local abundance, rabbits (and hares) are important in many terrestrial food chains. They are preyed upon by a wide variety of mammals and birds that rely upon them as dietary staples. Wolves, foxes, bobcats, weasels, hawks, eagles, and owls all take their toll. Rabbits can have such a profound influence on native and cultivated vegetation that they are considered pests in some circumstances. Extreme examples have occurred where the European rabbit has been introduced. Wild European rabbits were introduced to Australia in 1859, and within 10 years they were causing extensive agricultural damage. Early rates of spread were phenomenal (up to 350 km [220 miles] per year), and within 60 years the southern half of the continent had been occupied, with widespread damage to crops and decreases—even extinctions—of native Australian flora and fauna the result.

Attempts to control the rabbit have been largely futile. For instance, a viral disease (myxomatosis) naturally existing in certain South American cottontails was found to be lethal to European rabbits. The virus was introduced to the Australian population during the early 1950s, and although the initial wave of infection killed nearly all rabbits in Australia (99 percent), subsequent waves proved to be less effective, as the rabbits quickly developed immunity and the virus became less virulent. Ongoing research in Australia continues to seek methods for controlling the rabbit population.

DIVERSITY AND EVOLUTION

There is no single taxonomic group that constitutes the rabbit. Rather the name refers to an accumulation of 10 genera in the family Leporidae whose characteristics are intermediate between hares and pikas, the other members of order Lagomorpha. The best-known and most recognizable of the 28 rabbit species are the European rabbit and the 16 or so species of North and South American cotton-tails. The European rabbit originally occupied the Iberian Peninsula and northwestern Africa, but it was widely introduced throughout western Europe two thousand years ago. More recently this species has been intro-duced to oceanic islands throughout the world, parts of Chile and Argentina, and also New Zealand and Australia, where it thrives. Most cottontails are North American and prefer open or brushy habitats, although some live in tropical forests and others are semiaquatic (the swamp rabbit, *S. aquaticus*, and the marsh rabbit, *S. palustris*). Two other genera of rabbit also live in North America. The volcano rabbit, or *zacatuche* (*Romerolagus diazi*), inhabits dense undergrowth of bunchgrass in pine forests in the high mountains surrounding Mexico City. A population of only about six thousand remains in fragments of habitat. The pygmy rabbit (*Brachylagus idahoensis*) is closely related to the cottontails and occupies mature sagebrush habitat throughout the northern Great Basin of the United States.

Five rabbit species live in Africa. The bunyoro rabbit (*Poelagus majorita*) has a broad range in Central Africa, while the three species of rockhares (genus *Pronolagus*) are all found in Southern Africa. Each is locally common and inhabits rocky areas associated with grass or woodlands. The riverine rabbit (*Bunolagus monticularis*) is endemic to the Karoo region of South Africa, where it inhabits dense vegetation along seasonal rivers and is endangered because of habitat destruction throughout its range.

In Asia the hispid hare (*Caprolagus hispidus*) is similarly endangered and occupies the dense, tall grassland (com-monly referred to as elephant grass) along the southern Himalayan foothills of Nepal, Bangladesh, and India. The Amami rabbit lives only in forests on two small islands (Amami and Tokunoshima) of southern Japan. Its frag-mented population of about three thousand animals is declining owing to habitat destruction and predation by introduced mongooses and by feral dogs and cats. The rabbits most threatened with extinction, however, are found in Southeast Asia. The Sumatran rabbit (*Nesolagus netscheri*) is known to live in the island's southwestern montane forests. Although there has been only one confirmed sighting of this animal since 1916, pictures of the rabbit have been captured with automated cameras. Another striped rabbit (*N. timminsi*) distantly related to the Sumatran rabbit was discovered in the Annamite mountains of Laos and Vietnam during the late 1990s.

The family Leporidae (rabbits and hares) has been relatively unchanged since the Eocene Epoch about 40 million years ago, when its fossil record first became well documented. Rabbits had entered North America by that time, and they underwent most of their development there. By about seven million years ago (the Miocene Epoch), they had become reestablished in Asia and had moved into Europe, which led to the present distribution.

HARES

Hares are the largest lagomorphs. Depending on the species, the body is about 40–70 cm (16–28 inches) long, with feet up to 15 cm (5.9 inches) long and ears up to 20 cm (7.9 inches) that apparently help dissipate excess body heat. In general, hares have longer ears and longer hind feet than rabbits. While the tail is relatively short, it is longer than that of rabbits. Although usually gray-brown throughout the year, hares living in northern latitudes may turn white in winter (in the far north some remain white all year). One such "varying hare" is the smallest member of genus *Lepus*, the snowshoe hare (*L. americanus*) of North America. Most *Lepus* species have very high rates of reproduction, with multiple large litters being produced each year. Young hares (leverets) are typically born fully furred and with their eyes open and are able to hop a few minutes after birth. Throughout their range, hares are important in the diets of various carnivorous birds, mammals, and reptiles. One of the more dramatic ecological patterns known is the boom-and-bust cycle of snowshoe hare populations in the boreal forests of North America. Populations peak

The Alpine, or blue, hare (Lepus timidus) *lives in Scandinavia and Siberia.* Gordon Langsbury/Bruce Coleman Ltd.

every eight to 11 years and then sharply decline, with densities decreasing up to one hundred-fold. Predation is believed to be responsible for this regular pattern. Lynx populations correlate with those of the snowshoe hare but with a one- to two-year time lag. Lynx eat increasing numbers of hares as they become more common, but, owing to the high rate of predation, lynx numbers drop following the resultant crash in the number of hares. Once hare populations begin to recover, lynx numbers build again, and the cycle is repeated. As hares are almost exclusively herbivorous, they can also dramatically damage natural vegetation or crops when their populations are high. Like rabbits, hares provide people with food and fur.

Hares are the most widespread lagomorph genus, occupying most of North America, Europe, Asia, and Africa. A typical species is the European hare (*L. europaeus*) of central and southern Europe, the Middle East, and Asia westward into Siberia. The mountain hare (*L. timidus*) of Asia, the Arctic hare (*L. arcticus*), and the snowshoe hare live in the far north. Several species of jackrabbit (including *L. californicus* and *L. alleni*) are found in the extensive deserts of North America. Many species are abundant throughout their range, including the European hare, which has been introduced into many places, including South America, New Zealand, and Australia, where it has become a pest. In contrast, several hares are endangered, such as the Tehuantepec jackrabbit (*L. flavigularis*) of southern Mexico, the broom hare (*L. castroviejoi*) of northern Spain, and the Hainan hare (*L. hainanus*), which lives on Hainan Island off the coast of southern China.

PIKAS

The 29 species of pika are remarkably uniform in body proportions and stance. All are small, short-legged,

American pika (Ochotona princeps). Kenneth W. Fink/Root Resources

round-eared, and virtually tailless egg-shaped mammals. Their fur is long and soft and is generally grayish-brown in colour, although a few species are rusty red. Unlike those of rabbits and hares, the hind limbs are not appreciably longer than the forelimbs. The feet, including the soles, are densely furred, with five toes in front and four behind. Most pikas weigh between 125 and 200 grams (4.5 and 7.1 ounces) and are about 15 cm (6 inches) in length.

Pikas are normally found in mountainous areas at high elevations. Two species reside in North America, the rest being found primarily throughout Central Asia, and 23 of them live entirely or partly in China, especially the Tibetan plateau. There are two distinctly different ecological niches occupied by pikas. Some live only in piles of broken rock (talus), whereas others inhabit meadow or steppe environments, where they construct burrows. The North American species and roughly half of the Asian species live in rocky habitats and do not make burrows. Rather, their nests are made deep in a labyrinth of talus adjoining alpine meadows or other suitable vegetation. The collared pika (*O. collaris*) of Alaska and northern Canada has been found on the isolated nunataks (crags or peaks surrounded by glaciers) in Kluane National Park, and *O. macrotis* has been recorded at 6,130 metres (20,113 feet) on the slopes of the Himalayas. The pika with the largest distribution, the northern pika (*O. hyperborea*), ranges from the Ural Mountains to the east coast of Russia and Hokkaido Island of northern Japan. Although the northern pika is considered a typical talus-dwelling species, it also is known to inhabit rocky terrain in coniferous forests, where it makes burrows under fallen logs and tree stumps.

There are dramatic differences between pikas that inhabit rocky terrain and those that construct burrows in open habitats. Rock dwellers are generally long-lived (up to seven years) and occur at low density, their populations tending to be stable over time. In contrast, burrowing pikas rarely live more than one year, and their widely fluctuating populations may be 30 or more times as dense. These dense populations fluctuate widely. The contrast between rock-dwelling and burrowing pikas extends to their reproduction. Rock-dwelling pikas normally initiate only two litters per year, and generally only one of these is successfully weaned. It is believed that the second litter is successful only when the first offspring are lost early in the breeding season. Litter size of most rock dwellers is low, but burrowing pikas may produce multiple large litters each season. The steppe pika (*O. pusilla*) has been reported to have litters of as many as 13 young and breed up to five times in a year.

The degree of social behaviour also varies. Rock-dwelling pikas are relatively asocial, claiming widely spaced, scent-marked territories. They communicate their presence to one another by frequently uttering a short call (generally an "eenk" or "ehh-ehh"). Thus, rock-dwelling pikas are able to keep track of neighbours, directly encountering them only once or twice a day. Such encounters normally result in aggressive chases. In contrast, burrowing pikas live in family groups, and these groups occupy and defend a mutual territory. Within the group, social encounters are numerous and generally amicable. Pikas of all ages and both sexes may groom each other, rub noses, or sit side-by-side. Aggressive encounters, normally in the form of long chases, ensue only when an individual from one family group trespasses on the territory of another. Burrowing pikas also have a much larger vocal repertoire than rock-dwelling pikas. Many of these calls signal cohesion within family groups, especially among young from sequential litters or between males and juveniles. All pikas utter short alarm calls when predators are sighted. Males give a long call, or song, during the mating season.

Unlike rabbits and hares, pikas are active during the day, with the exception of the nocturnal steppe pikas (*O. pusilla*). Being largely alpine or boreal species, most pikas are adapted to living in cold environments and cannot tolerate heat. When temperatures are high, they confine their activity to early morning and late afternoon. Pikas do not hibernate, and they are generalized herbivores. Where snow blankets their environment (as is often the case), they construct caches of vegetation called haypiles to provide food during winter. A characteristic behaviour of rock-dwelling pikas during summer is their repeated trips to meadows adjoining the talus to harvest plants for the haypile. One often repeated but untrue tale is that pikas lay their hay on rocks to dry before storing it. Rather, pikas carry their provisions straight to their haypile unless disturbed. Similar to other lagomorphs, pikas practice coprophagy to provide additional vitamins and nutrients from their relatively poor-quality forage.

Most pikas live in areas far away from people, yet, given the high densities reached by some burrowing pikas, they have been considered pests on the Tibetan plateau, where pikas are thought to reduce forage for domestic livestock and to damage grasslands. In response, government agencies in China have poisoned them over great expanses. Recent analyses, however, have shown that such control efforts may be misguided, as the pika is a keystone species for biodiversity in this region. Four Asian pikas—three in China and one in Russia and Kazakhstan—are listed as endangered species. One of these, Koslov's pika (*O. koslowi*) from China, was originally collected by the Russian explorer Nikolai Przewalski in 1884, and approximately one hundred years passed before it was seen again. Not only is this species apparently rare, but it may be in danger of being poisoned as part of control efforts directed at plateau pikas.

Pikas have a variety of common names, most applied to particular forms or species. The names *mouse hare* and *cony* are sometimes used, although the pika is neither mouse nor hare, and *cony* may be confused with the unrelated hyrax—the biblical coney. The genus name originates from the Mongolian *ochodona*, and the term *pika* comes from the vernacular *piika* of the Tunguses, a tribe from northeastern Siberia. *Ochotona* is the sole living genus of the family Ochotonidae, and its members lack several special skeletal modifications present in hares and rabbits (family Leporidae), such as a highly arched skull, relatively upright posture of the head, strong hind limbs and pelvic girdle, and elongation of limbs. The family Ochotonidae was clearly differentiated from the other lagomorphs as early as the Oligocene Epoch. *Ochotona* first appeared in the fossil record in the Pliocene in eastern Europe, Asia, and western North America. Its origin was probably in Asia. By the Pleistocene, *Ochotona* was found in the eastern United States and as far west in Europe as Great Britain.

This extensive spread was followed by restriction to its present range. One fossil pika (genus *Prolagus*) apparently lived during historical time. Its remains have been found on Corsica, Sardinia, and adjacent small islands. Earlier fossil material has been found on the mainland of Italy. Apparently it was still present up to two thousand years ago but was driven to extinction, likely owing to habitat loss and to competition and predation from introduced animals.

MARSUPIALS

The largest and most varied assortment of marsupials— some two hundred species—is found in Australia, New Guinea, and neighbouring islands, where they make up most of the native mammals found there. In addition to the larger species such as kangaroos, wallabies, wombats, and the koala, there are numerous smaller forms, many of which are carnivorous, the Tasmanian devil being the largest of this group (family Dasyuridae). About 70 species live in the Americas, mainly in South and Central America, but one, the Virginia opossum (*Didelphis virginiana*), ranges through the United States into Canada. The largest living marsupial is the red kangaroo (*Macropus rufus*), males of which can grow to about 2 metres (6.6 feet) in height, 3 metres (10 feet) from muzzle to tail tip, and a weight of up to 90 kg (about 200 pounds). The smallest are the planigales (*see* marsupial mice), especially *Planigale ingrami*, measuring barely 12 cm (4.7 inches) in total length. The vast majority of marsupials range from the size of a squirrel to that of a medium-size dog.

NATURAL HISTORY

Structural and behavioral parallels between marsupial mammals and placental mammals are in some cases quite striking. Such resemblances are examples of convergent evolution, a tendency for organisms to adapt in similar ways to similar habitats. Thus, there are marsupials that look remarkably like moles, shrews, squirrels, mice, dogs, and hyenas. Others are the ecological counterparts, less in structure than in habits, of cats, small bears, and rabbits. Even the larger grazing marsupials, which resemble

Spotted-tailed quoll, or native cat (Dasyurus maculatus). Hans and Judy Beste/Ardea Photographics

no placental mammal at all, can be thought of as filling the same ecological role (niche) as deer and antelope found elsewhere. The niches that marsupials fill are closely associated with structure. The burrowing species, such as the marsupial mole and the wombats, have powerful foreclaws with which they can tunnel into the ground for food and for shelter. Terrestrial forms, such as the kangaroos and wallabies, possess well-developed hind limbs that serve both as formidable weapons and as catapults by which they can bound over the plains. The gliders have a membrane along either flank, attached to the forelegs and hind legs, that enables these arboreal animals to glide down from a high perch. A few marsupials, such as tree kangaroos, koalas, and some species of cuscus, spend most of their lives in trees. The water opossum, or yapok (*Chironectes minimus*), of Central and South America is semiaquatic.

The diets of marsupials are as varied as the niches they occupy. Many dasyurids live chiefly on insects and other small animals. Dunnarts (genus *Sminthopsis*) are so hyperactive—like shrews—that, to supply their high energy needs, they must devour their own weight in food (chiefly insects) each day. The numbat uses its remarkable wormlike tongue to lap up termites and ants. Many Australian possums, bandicoots, and American opossums have a mixed diet of plant matter and insects. Wombats and many other marsupials are strictly vegetarian. The small honey possum (*Tarsipes rostratus*) is specialized to feed on the nectar of flowers, and other marsupials too may serve as important pollinators in this way. Few large carnivores have ever evolved in Australia, because of the low productivity of its environment. The most recent large carnivorous marsupials, the Tasmanian devil (*Sarcophilus harrisii*) and the now-extinct thylacine, or Tasmanian wolf (*Thylacinus cynocephalus*), were both displaced on the mainland by the dingo.

The marsupials are notably less intelligent than placental mammals, a fact that is attributable in part to a simpler brain. Compared with that of placentals, the brain of marsupials differs markedly in both structure and bulk. Most notably it lacks a corpus callosum, the part of the placental brain that connects the two cerebral halves. In addition, the marsupial brain is smaller relative to overall body size; a quoll has about half as much brain tissue as a placental cat of similar skull size. It is not surprising, therefore, to find a repertory of behaviour that differs somewhat from that of placentals. One peculiarity that may stem from this underdevelopment is restricted vocal ability. Although marsupials are not entirely silent, few of them emit loud sounds of excitement or distress; apparently, none utters grunts of contentment or even cries of hunger when young. What vocalizing they do is more limited and less variable than that of placentals. The ferocious-sounding rutting roars of male koalas (*Phascolarctos cinereus*) are a dramatic and unexpected exception.

There seems to be little permanent social organization among most marsupials beyond the short-lived pair bonds during mating. Many of the grazing marsupials, such as the kangaroos and wallabies, move in feeding groups called mobs, but these associations are not true social groups, as there is no attention paid to any leaders or elders. Only the lesser gliders (genus *Petaurus*) are known to have permanent, cohesive social groupings.

The life cycle of marsupials exhibits peculiarities that have long been considered primitive compared with those of placental mammals but are more likely an adaptation to low-productivity environments. The uterine cycle of the female marsupial has no secretory phase, and the uterine wall is not specialized for the implantation of the embryos, although a transitory placenta does exist in the bandicoots. The period of intrauterine development in marsupials ranges from about 12 days in the bilby (*Macrotis lagotis*) to 38 days in the swamp wallaby (*Wallabia bicolor*). The young, born in a vulnerable embryonic condition, make their own way to the shelter, warmth, and nourishment of the pouch; in pouchless marsupials the young simply cling to the teats. Those fortunate enough to survive this arduous journey may succeed in attaching themselves to the mother's nipples, which then swell and become firmly fastened—almost physically fused—to the mouth tissues of the young. In this condition the young continue their development for weeks or months, after which they are weaned and begin to look after themselves. Frequently the partially developed young outnumber the available teats, and the excess individuals perish.

PALEONTOLOGY AND RECENT HISTORY

Fossil evidence indicates clearly that the marsupials originated in the New World. Although the oldest fossils referable to marsupials are found in North American strata from the Late Cretaceous Period (99.6 to 65.5 million years ago), it is probable that South America is equally or more likely their place of origin. Their presence in Australia and nearby islands is thought to have occurred as a result of passage over presumed land connections with South America via Antarctica. Whether this took place before the rise of the placental mammals or placentals also reached Australasia but died out early on is a subject of lively controversy. By about 65 million years ago, Australasia was isolated from all other continental masses, and here marsupials evolved into many diverse forms, some of which apparently rivaled the mastodons in bulk. In South America they survived alongside placentals, forming a significant part of the Neotropical mammalian fauna. Marsupials briefly populated Europe, Asia, and North Africa.

In Australia it is disputed whether aboriginal hunting, and particularly burning of the landscape, contributed to the disappearance of several large species (megafauna) during the Pleistocene Epoch (2.6 million to 11,700 years ago). It is certain, however, that Europeans brought methods of hunting and trapping, large-scale land clearing, and the introduction of foxes, rabbits, cats, and sheep, which soon drove several species of kangaroos and bandicoots to extinction. Many others, including the koala and the Tasmanian devil, were driven close to the same fate. Through human agency, however, marsupials have been introduced to nearby islands of Australia and especially to New Zealand. In New Ireland the grey cuscus (*Phalanger orientalis*) was introduced more than 10,000 years ago, and the same species was transported to Timor more than four thousand years ago. In Australia the brushtail possum (*Trichosurus vulpecula*) is an example of a marsupial that has readily adapted to changing conditions brought about by people, having become plentiful in some urban centres. Its adaptability to different locales is attributed to its tolerance for a variety of food, including household refuse. The Virginia opossum has experienced similar success in North America for the same reason.

KANGAROOS

A kangaroo is any of six large species of Australian marsupials noted for hopping and bouncing on their hind legs. The term *kangaroo*, most specifically used, refers to the eastern gray kangaroo, the western gray kangaroo, and the red kangaroo, as well as to the antilopine kangaroo and two species of wallaroo. Less specifically, *kangaroo* refers to all 13 species in the genus *Macropus*, some of which are called wallabies. In its broadest usage, *kangaroo* refers to any member of the family Macropodidae, which comprises about 54 species, including tree kangaroos and the quokka; rat kangaroos belong to a "sister" family, Potoroidae. The Macropodidae are found in Australia (including Tasmania and other offshore islands, such as Kangaroo Island), New Guinea, and the islands east to the Bismarcks. Several species have been introduced into New Zealand.

FORM AND FUNCTION

With the exception of tree kangaroos (genus *Dendrolagus*), all members of the kangaroo family (Macropodidae) rely on long, powerful hind legs and feet for hopping and leaping, their predominant forms of locomotion. Their long tails, thickened at the base, are used for balancing. This feature is most obvious in the large kangaroos, which use the tail as a third leg when standing still. Each long, narrow hind foot has four toes, the large fourth toe bearing most of the animal's weight. The second and third toes are united and merely vestigial, a condition known as syndactyly. The short forelimbs, having five unequal digits, are used almost like human arms, but all digits of the "hand" are sharp-clawed, and the thumb is not opposable. The head is relatively small; the ears are (in most macropodids) large and rounded; and the mouth is small, with prominent lips. The pelage is generally soft and woolly; in many species it is grizzled, and stripes may be present on the head, back, or upper limbs. All macropodids are herbivorous and have a chambered stomach that is functionally similar to those of such ruminants as cattle and sheep. Ecologically, they occupy the niche filled elsewhere by grazing and browsing animals (larger species tend to be grazers, smaller ones browsers). Several smaller species have become extinct or are gravely endangered, probably because of predation by introduced foxes. The wedge-tailed eagle (*Aquila audax*) is one of the macropodids' few natural predators.

MARSUPIUM

A marsupium is a specialized pouch for protecting, carrying, and nourishing newborn marsupial young. A marsupium is found in most members of the order Marsupialia (class Mammalia). In some marsupials (e.g., kangaroos) it is a well-developed pocket, while in others (e.g., dasyurids) it is a simple fold of skin; a few species lack any type of marsupium. It contains the teats, to which the incompletely developed young remain attached for a considerable period, during which time they could not survive unprotected.

The term *marsupium* is sometimes used for functionally similar structures in other animals. The mammary pouch of the echidna (order Monotremata) is a simple fold of skin which develops during the breeding season. In mollusks such as oysters (class Bivalvia), the marsupium is a modified gill structure that holds the eggs and larvae. In the crustacean orders Isopoda and Amphipoda, a marsupium, or brood pouch, is formed by extensions from the thoracic limbs.

Reproduction and Development

In all species, the pouch is well developed, opens forward, and contains four teats. The young kangaroo ("joey") is born at a very immature stage, when it is only about 2 cm (1 inch) long and weighs less than a gram (0.04 ounce). Immediately after birth, it uses its already clawed and well-developed forelimbs to crawl up the mother's body and enter the pouch. The joey attaches its mouth to a teat, which then enlarges and holds the young animal in place. After continuous attachment for several weeks, the joey becomes more active and gradually spends more and more time outside the pouch, which it leaves completely at seven to 10 months of age.

Female macropodids of many species enter into heat within a few days after giving birth, mating and conception thus occurring while the previous offspring is still in the pouch. After only one week's development, the microscopic embryo enters a dormant state, called diapause, that lasts until the first joey begins to leave the pouch or until conditions are otherwise favourable. The development of the second embryo then resumes and proceeds to birth after a gestation period of about 30 days. Therefore, the teats are for a while feeding young of very different developmental stages, during which time different teats produce two different compositions of milk. This is thought to be an adaptation for recovering population numbers quickly after a drought, when breeding ceases and the diapause state is prolonged. In the gray kangaroos, which live in wooded country with a more predictable environment, this system does not exist; there is no diapause, and the pouch is occupied by one young at a time.

Teeth

The larger species of kangaroos have complex, high-crowned teeth. The four permanent molars on each side of both jaws erupt in sequence from front to back and move forward in the jaw, eventually being pushed out at the front. Thus, an old kangaroo may have only the last two molars in place, the first two (and the premolar) having long since been shed. The molars possess cross-cutting ridges, so that tough grass is sheared between opposing teeth. The molars of smaller macropodids are much simpler. The large kangaroos continue growing throughout life, especially the males (most markedly in the red kangaroo), whereas the smaller macropodids do not.

BEHAVIOUR

Kangaroos have an irregular activity rhythm; generally, they are active at night and during periods of low light, but it is quite possible to find them out in the open in bright sunlight. During hot weather, kangaroos lick their forearms, which promotes heat loss by evaporation.

Kangaroos travel and feed in groups ("mobs") whose composition shifts, but they are not truly social, since the individual members move at liberty. One member can send the mob into a wild rout—individuals bounding off in all directions—by thumping its tail on the ground in a signal of alarm. In any mob, the largest male ("old man," or "boomer") dominates during the mating season. Males fight for access to females by biting, kicking, and boxing. These methods are also used by kangaroos to defend themselves against predators. With their agile arms, they can spar vigorously. They can also use the forepaws to grip an enemy while rocking back on their tails and then swiftly dropping their huge clawed hind feet. This tactic has been known to disembowel dogs and humans. When chased by hunters with dogs, kangaroos often make for water, where they have been known to turn and press down on the dog with their forepaws in an attempt to drown it.

Overall, however, kangaroos have benefited from human presence. Aboriginal hunters regularly burned large areas of forest and grassland, opening up the country for large grazers at the expense of smaller browsers. European pastoralists then cleared further tracts of dense vegetation and provided permanent sources of water in arid and seasonal habitats. By the late 20th century, the number of kangaroos in Australia had increased to the point that a major industry came to be based on them. The three most abundant species, the eastern gray, western gray, and red kangaroos, together number in the tens of millions. Every year millions of these three species, and thousands of medium-size species such as whiptail wallabies (*M. parryi*), are harvested. Their skins are made into rugs and clothing, and their meat, formerly used as pet food, is now increasingly sold for human consumption. The kangaroo's status as a national symbol makes harvests politically controversial. Kangaroos are also killed because they compete for forage with livestock. Other threats are feral dogs and dingoes.

DESCRIPTIONS OF SELECTED SPECIES

The eastern gray kangaroo (*Macropus giganteus*) is found mostly in the open forests of eastern Australia and Tasmania. It is replaced by the western gray kangaroo (*M. fuliginosus*) along the southern coast into the southwest of Western Australia. The ranges of the two species overlap in western New South Wales and western Victoria. Both species, but especially the eastern, prefer lightly forested country, at least for refuge, but they go out into the open plains for grazing. Western grays are stockier and more brownish; there are different subspecies in the southwest, on Kangaroo Island, and on the Nullarbor Plain. Each of these may in fact be distinct species. Eastern grays may grow up to 2.1 metres (6.9 feet) in length, and some males can weigh as much as 90 kg (about 200 pounds). In contrast, western grays are shorter, with an average length of 1.6 metres (5.25 feet), and some males can weigh up to 54 kg (about 120 pounds).

Gray kangaroos can clear more than 9 metres (30 feet) at a bound—13.5 metres (45 feet) has been recorded—and can attain a speed of 55 km (34 miles) per hour. Research has revealed a remarkable advantage to bipedal hopping. Although at low speeds kangaroos expend more energy than do quadrupeds of the same size, the red kangaroo (*M. rufus*) actually uses less energy at 10.1 km (6 miles) per hour than at 6.5 km (4 miles) per hour and less still at higher speeds. This seems to be related to the storage of elastic strain energy in its tendons and muscles. In addition, the heavy tail swings downward as the legs are moving backward, which helps to counteract the natural pitching motion of the head and upper body—another energy-saving device.

The red kangaroo is found throughout Australia's interior grasslands and is the largest and most powerful macropodid. An old male may attain a head and body length of 1.5 metres (5 feet), have a tail 1 metre (3.3 feet) long, and stand 2 metres (6.6 feet) tall. Males can weigh 90 kg (200 pounds), but females are much smaller. Usually males are red and females are blue-gray, but there are generally a few red females and gray males in most populations. In regions such as western New South Wales, where red kangaroos and both species of grays can be found in the same general area, the red kangaroo is easily distinguished by its longer arms, convex face, whitish underparts, prominent black and white whisker marks on the muzzle, and bald patch on the nose (rhinarium). Gray kangaroos are more uniformly coloured, and the nose is haired.

The antilopine kangaroo (*M. antilopinus*), sometimes called the antilopine wallaroo, replaces the red kangaroo in the plains of the tropical north, from Cape York Peninsula in the east to the Kimberleys in the west. It is smaller than the red kangaroo and more wallaroo-like in general appearance, although it is more slenderly built. Males can grow to be 1.8 metres (5.9 feet) long and can weigh as much as 70 kg (154 pounds), whereas females are smaller, often weighing less than 30 kg (66 pounds). The antilopine kangaroo is an extremely fast hopper. The wallaroo, or euro (*M. robustus*), is a smaller, stockier animal quite closely related to the red kangaroo and like it in that the sexes are coloured differently (black in the male, reddish in the female), though this is not universal. The rhinarium is larger than in the red kangaroo. This wallaroo lives in hilly country throughout mainland Australia except in the far north, where it is replaced by the smaller Woodward's, or black, wallaroo (*M. bernardus*).

WALLABIES

A wallaby is any of several middle-sized marsupial mammals belonging to the kangaroo family, Macropodidae. Wallabies are found chiefly in Australia.

The 11 species of brush wallabies (genus *Macropus,* subgenus *Protemnodon*) are built like the big kangaroos but differ somewhat in dentition. Their head and body length is 45 to 105 cm (18 to 41 inches), and the tail is 33 to 75 cm (13 to 29.5 inches) long. A common species is the red-necked wallaby (*M. rufogriseus*), with reddish nape and shoulders, which inhabits brushlands of southeastern Australia and Tasmania; this species is often seen in zoos. The pretty-faced wallaby, or whiptail (*M. elegans,* or *M. parryi*), with distinctive cheek marks, is found in open woods of coastal eastern Australia.

Bridled nail-tailed wallaby (Onychogalea fraenata). © Mitch Reardon—National Audubon Society Collection/Photo Researchers

The six named species of rock wallabies (*Petrogale*) live among rocks, usually near water. They are prettily coloured in shades of brown and gray and are distinguished by stripes, patches, or other markings. They are extremely agile on rocky terrain. The three species of nail-tailed wallabies (*Onychogalea*) are named for a horny growth on the tail tip. They are handsomely striped at the shoulder. Because they rotate their forelimbs while hopping, they are often called organ-grinders. Two species are endangered.

The two species of hare wallabies (*Lagorchestes*) are small animals that have the movements and some of the habits of hares. Often called pademelons, the three species of scrub wallabies (*Thylogale*) of New Guinea, the Bismarck Archipelago, and Tasmania are small and stocky, with short hind limbs and pointy noses. They are hunted for meat and fur. A similar species is the short-tailed scrub wallaby, or quokka (*Setonix brachyurus*); this species is now restricted to two offshore islands of Western Australia.

The three named species of forest wallabies (*Dorcopsulus*) are native to the island of New Guinea. The dwarf wallaby is the smallest member of the genus and the smallest known member of the kangaroo family. Its length is about 46 cm (18 inches) from nose to tail, and it weighs about 1.6 kg (3.5 pounds).

RAT KANGAROOS

A rat kangaroo is any of nine species of Australian and Tasmanian marsupials constituting a subfamily, Potoroinae, of the kangaroo family, Macropodidae. (Some authorities recognize a separate family, Potoroidae.) They differ from other kangaroos in skull and urogenital anatomy and in having large canine teeth. All are rabbit-sized or smaller. Rat kangaroos live in undergrowth. At night they forage for grass, tubers, and underground fungi; some also eat grubs and worms.

The four species of short-nosed rat kangaroos (genus *Bettongia*), also called boodies, have pinkish noses and short ears. The two long-nosed rat kangaroos, or potoroos (*Potorous*), have shorter tails and more pointed faces.

The rufous rat kangaroo (*Aepyprymnus rufescens*) is the largest of the rat kangaroos and has a whitish but not distinct hip stripe. The tail attains a length of 35 cm (14 inches) or more.

The musky rat kangaroo (*Hypsiprymnodon moschatus*) is the only member of the Macropodidae that has a naked tail and retains the first digit of the hind foot. It is therefore classified by some taxonomists as a separate subfamily, Hypsiprymnodontinae.

BANDICOOTS

The bandicoots are about 22 species of Australasian marsupial mammals comprising the family Peramelidae. Bandicoots are 30 to 80 cm (12 to 31 inches) long, including the 10- to 30-cm (4- to 12-inch) sparsely haired tail. The body is stout and coarse haired, the muzzle tapered, and the hind limbs longer than the front. The toes are reduced in number; two of the hind digits are united. The teeth are sharp and slender. The pouch opens rearward and encloses six to 10 teats. Unlike other marsupials, bandicoots have a placenta (lacking villi, however). Most species have two to six young at a time; gestation takes 12–15 days.

Bandicoots occur in Australia, Tasmania, New Guinea, and nearby islands. They are terrestrial, largely nocturnal, solitary animals that dig funnellike pits in their search for insect and plant food. Farmers consider them pests; some species are endangered, and all have declined.

The long-nosed bandicoot (*Perameles*, or *Thylacis, nasuta*), a vaguely ratlike brown animal whose rump may be black-barred, is the common form in eastern Australia. The three species of short-nosed bandicoots, *Isoodon* (incorrectly *Thylacis*), are found in New Guinea, Australia, and Tasmania. Rabbit-eared bandicoots, or bilbies, are species of *Thylacomys* (sometimes *Macrotis*); now endangered, they are found only in remote colonies in arid interior Australia. As the name implies, they have big narrow ears, long hind legs, and bushy tails. The 35-cm- (14-inch-) long pig-footed bandicoot (*Chaeropus ecaudatus*) of interior Australia has feet that are almost hooflike, with two toes functional on the forefoot, one on the hind foot. This herbivorous creature, resembling a little deer, is an endangered species and may well be extinct; it was last observed locally in the 1920s.

KOALAS

The koala (*Phascolarctos cinereus*), also called the koala bear, is a tree-dwelling marsupial of coastal eastern Australia. The koala is about 60 to 85 cm (24 to 33 inches) long and weighs up to 14 kg (31 pounds) in the southern part of its range (Victoria) but only about half that in subtropical Queensland to the north. Virtually tailless, the body is stout and gray, with a pale yellow or cream-coloured chest and mottling on the rump. The broad face has a wide, rounded, leathery nose, small yellow eyes, and big fluffy ears. The feet are strong and clawed; the two inner digits of the front feet and the innermost digit of the hind feet are opposable for grasping.

The koala feeds quite selectively on the leaves of certain eucalyptus trees. Generally solitary, individuals move within a home range of more than a dozen trees, one of

Koala (Phascolarctos cinereus). Anthony Mercieca—The National
Audubon Society Collection/Photo Researchers

which is favoured over the others. If koalas become too numerous in a restricted area, they defoliate preferred food trees and, unable to subsist on even closely related species, decline rapidly. To aid in digesting as much as 1.3 kg (3 pounds) of leaves daily, the koala has an intestinal pouch (cecum) about 2 metres (7 feet) long, where symbiotic bacteria degrade the tannins and other toxic and complex substances abundant in eucalyptus. This diet is relatively poor in nutrients and provides the koala little spare energy, so the animal spends long hours simply sitting or sleeping in tree forks, exposed to the elements but insulated by thick fur. Although placid most of the time, koalas produce loud, hollow grunts.

The koala is the only member of the family Phascolarctidae. Unlike those of other arboreal marsupials, its pouch opens rearward. Births are single, occurring after a gestation of 34 to 36 days. The youngster (called a joey) first puts its head out of the pouch at about five months of age. For up to six weeks, it is weaned on a soupy predigested eucalyptus called pap that is lapped directly from the mother's anus. Pap is thought to be derived from the cecum. After weaning, the joey emerges completely from the pouch and clings to the mother's back until it is nearly a year old. A koala can live to about 15 years of age in the wild, somewhat longer in captivity.

Formerly killed in huge numbers for their fur, especially during the 1920s and '30s, koalas dwindled in number from several million to a few hundred thousand. In the southern part of their range, they became practically extinct except for a single population in Gippsland, Victoria. Some were translocated onto small offshore islands, especially Phillip Island, where they did so well that these koalas were used to restock much of the original range in Victoria and southern New South Wales. Though once again widespread, koala populations are now scattered and separated by urban areas and farmland, which makes them locally vulnerable to extinction. Another problem is the infection of many populations with *Chlamydia*, which makes the females infertile.

MARSUPIAL MOLES

Marsupial moles are two species of small marsupial mammals of the genus *Notoryctes* that make up the family Notoryctidae. Found in hot sandy wastes of south-central and northwestern Australia, the 18-cm (7-inch) *N. typhlops* and the 10-cm (4-inch) *N. caurinus* (by some not separated from *N. typhlops*) are remarkably like true moles. The forefeet bear triangular claws used in digging, and the skin of the blunt snout and stubby tail is leathery. The eyes are poorly developed and virtually hidden in the long silky fur, which is silvery to yellowish red or pinkish, with an iridescent sheen—much like that of the golden moles of Africa. These creatures are intensely active one moment, then suddenly fall asleep. They burrow just beneath the soil surface, hunting for grubs and earthworms. Unlike true moles, they do not leave tunnels behind them when feeding; they therefore often come up for air.

MARSUPIAL MICE

A marsupial mouse is any one of many small rat- or mouse-like marsupial animals, belonging to the family Dasyuridae, found in Australia and New Guinea. The species vary in body length from 5 to 22 cm (2 to 9 inches), and all have tails, often brushlike, that are about as long as their bodies. Their coat is generally solid gray, buff, or brown; a few species are speckled. All marsupial mice are predatory, most are nocturnal, and they are really more like shrews than mice.

They subsist on insects and small vertebrates, although the broad-footed marsupial mice (*Antechinus* species) are also known to eat nectar. The fat-tailed dunnart (*Sminthopsis crassicaudata*) stores excess fat in its tail. Members of all genera except *Antechinus* will go into torpor when food is scarce. The crest-tailed marsupial mouse, or mulgara (*Dasycercus cristicauda*), an arid-land species valued for killing house mice, gets all of its water from the bodies of its prey.

Reminiscent of jerboas—long-tailed and big-eared with stiltlike hind legs—are the two species of *Antechinomys,* also of the Australian outback. The two species of brush-tailed marsupial mice, or tuans (*Phascogale*), are grayish above and whitish below in colour; the distal half of the long tail is thickly furred and resembles a bottle brush when the hairs are erected. Tuans are arboreal but may raid poultry yards. In both appearance and behaviour the flat-skulled marsupial mice, or planigales (*Planigale*), are similar to the true shrews (*Sorex*). The *Red Data Book* lists the eastern jerboa marsupial, or kultarr (*Antechinomys laniger*), of Australia as endangered; several other marsupial mice are considered rare.

NUMBATS

Numbats (*Myrmecobius fasciatus*), also called banded anteaters, are marsupial mammals of the family Dasyuridae (though some authorities classify it as a family in its own right, Myrmecobiidae). They forage by day for termites in forests of southwestern Australia. Formerly widespread across southern Australia, the numbat is now restricted to the southwestern corner of the country and is regarded as an endangered species. It has a squat body and small, pointed head, together about 20 cm (8 inches) long, and a 15-cm (6-inch) bushy tail. Its coat is gray-brown to reddish brown, with about eight transverse white stripes on the rump. The teeth are small, and there are extra molars—50–52 teeth in all. The tongue is extensible and sticky, and the forefeet are strong-clawed, for digging. The numbat is pouchless; it normally has four young a year. It is the official animal emblem of the Australian state of Western Australia.

PHALANGERS

Phalangers are several species of Australasian marsupial mammals. They are called possums in Australia and Tasmania.

True phalangers are of the family Phalangeridae, which includes the cuscus. They are tree-dwelling animals: the clawless innermost hind digit and, sometimes, the first and second digits of the forefoot are opposable, making it possible for the animal to grasp branches. The second and third digits of the hind foot are united. The tail is long and prehensile. The pouch opens forward; there are usually two to four teats. The first incisor tooth is long and stout; the side teeth are tiny. The coat is often woolly, and many species are striped. Total length ranges from 55 to 125 cm (22 to 50 inches).

Phalangers are native to the forests of Australia, Tasmania, New Guinea, and islands west to Celebes and east to the Solomons. All are herbivorous, feeding on fruits, leaves, and blossoms. Some species also eat insects and small vertebrates. Phalangers are active chiefly at night. Most bear their young—usually only one but sometimes up to three—in tree hollows and unused birds' nests; a few build leafy nests of their own.

Several species are endangered: they are the prey of snakes and cats, they have been trapped for their fur, and they are threatened by loss of habitat. In Australia some species, such as the scaly-tailed possum (*Wyulda squamicaudata*), are now protected. The common brush-tailed possum (*Trichosurus vulpecula*), however, the most widely distributed Australian and Tasmanian marsupial, is considered a pest, and in some areas steps have been taken to control its population growth. The two other species of brush-tailed possum, the northern brush-tailed possum (*T. arnhemensis*) and the mountain brush-tailed possum (*T. caninus*), are also relatively common.

Species of other marsupial families, such as Phascolarctidae, Petauridae, Burramyidae, and Tarsipedidae, are often referred to as phalangers and have sometimes been included in the Phalangeridae family. Several of these phalangers are arboreal gliders who use flaps of skin along their flanks as sails with which to ride from tree to tree.

GLIDERS

Gliders, also called flying phalanger or flying possums, are about six species of small phalangers—marsupial mammals of Australasia—that volplane from tree to tree like flying squirrels. Most have well-developed flaps of skin along the flanks; these become sails when the limbs are extended. An eastern Australian species, which feeds on nectar and insects, is the pygmy glider, or feathertail (*Acrobates pygmaeus*), only 15 cm (6 inches) in total length; it has narrow side flaps, and its 8-cm- (2.5-inch-) long tail is stiffly haired laterally—a "feather" that helps it to navigate. The 25-cm- (10-inch-) long pen-tailed phalanger (*Distoechurus pennatus*) of New Guinea lacks the flaps; its tail is furry at the base but otherwise featherlike.

The three species of lesser, or sugar, gliders (*Petaurus*) are 25 to 80 cm (10 to 36 inches) long. An example is the short-headed glider (*P. breviceps*) found from New Guinea to Tasmania; it is blue-gray with a dark centre stripe and has a long bushy tail. These animals can glide 55 metres (180 feet). The greater glider (*Schoinobates volans*) of eastern

Australia may be 105 cm (42 inches) long; it often glides 100 metres (328 feet) or more. It has adapted to eating leaves and is sometimes classified with ring-tailed possums and the koala in a separate family, Phascolarctidae.

WOMBATS

Wombats are three species of large terrestrial Australian marsupials making up the family Vombatidae. Like woodchucks, wombats are heavily built and virtually tailless burrowers with small eyes and short ears. Wombats, however, are larger, measuring 80 to 120 cm (31 to 47 inches) long. Chiefly nocturnal and strictly herbivorous, they eat grasses and, in the case of the common wombat (*Vombatus ursinus*), the inner bark of tree and shrub roots. Wombats are considered pests by farmers because they dig in cultivated fields and pastures and because their burrows may harbour rabbits.

The common wombat has coarse dark hair and a bald, granular nose pad. It is common in woodlands of hilly country along the Dividing Range in southeastern Australia, from southeastern Queensland through New South Wales and Victoria into South Australia, and in Tasmania. In historic times dwarf forms lived on small islands in the Bass Strait, but these have become extinct because of habitat destruction by grazing cattle.

The hairy-nosed wombats (genus *Lasiorhinus*) are more sociable. They make a grassy nest at the end of a large underground burrow 30 metres (100 feet) long that is shared with several other wombats. They have silky fur and pointed ears, and the nose is entirely hairy, without a bald pad. The southern hairy-nosed wombat (*L. latifrons*) is smaller than the common wombat. It lives in semiarid country mainly in South Australia, extending through the Nullarbor Plain into the southeast of Western Australia.

The extremely rare Queensland, or northern, hairy-nosed wombat (*L. barnardi*) is larger and differs in cranial details. It is protected by law, and most of the population lives within Epping Forest National Park in central Queensland, where there are only 60 to 80 remaining. Two other populations of hairy-nosed wombats became extinct in the late 19th or early 20th century, one near St. George in southwestern Queensland and the other at Deniliquin on the Murray River in New South Wales; these closely resembled the Queensland species.

The skull of the wombat is flattened, and its bones are extremely thick. Unlike other marsupials, wombats have continuously growing rootless teeth adapted to a hard-wearing diet. The two incisor teeth in each jaw are rodentlike; there are no canine teeth. Wombats almost invariably bear one young at a time, which develops for five months or longer in a pouch that opens rearward. They become sexually mature at two years of age in the common wombat and three in the hairy-nosed wombats.

CONCLUSION

The grazing (and browsing) animals are extremely important members of the global ecosystem. They are a crucial link in the food chain—converting the energy stored in plants into living tissue that is, in turn, consumed by the carnivores that run grazers down and devour them, by the scavengers that pick over their carcasses, and by the insects, invertebrates, and microbes that break down what is left and return it to the earth. Many of the grazers, especially sheep and goats, cattle, and swine, are important sources of food and clothing for humans and have been domesticated for this purpose for thousands of years. Others, such as many of the deer and antelopes, not being as suited to domestication as their more tractable kin, have been left to roam in the wild, where they are hunted for their meat and skin. Still others occupy a fascinating ground that spans both domestication and wildness—among these, the reindeer, the bison, and many lagomorphs. Meanwhile, horses, asses, and camels (as well as llamas and alpacas) have long been domesticated as beasts of burden and for personal transportation.

Today, the big grazing animals of Africa, from large antelopes and giraffes to hippopotamuses, elephants, and rhinoceroses, are valued as living symbols of the natural beauty of that great continent. In Australia, kangaroos and other marsupials serve much the same function in that unique part of the world. Even in crowded and developed areas of Asia, Europe, and North America, many types of deer have adapted to living in the wild, as well as in close proximity to humans. In all cases, the grazers are vivid reminders of the delicate balance among all living creatures and their environments.

buffalo wallow A shallow undrained depression occurring on the Great Plains, often containing water in wet seasons, and generally thought to have been produced or deepened by the rolling and wallowing of herds of buffalo in mud and dust.

cecum Pouch or large tubelike structure in the lower abdominal cavity that receives undigested food material from the small intestine and is considered the first region of the large intestine.

coprophagy The feeding on or eating of dung or excrement that is normal behaviour among many insects, birds, and other animals.

cud The portion of food that is brought up into the mouth by ruminating animals from their first stomach to be chewed a second time.

dentin A calcareous material similar to bone but harder and denser that composes the principal mass of a tooth.

dewlap Pendulous fold of skin under the neck of bovine animals, or a corresponding fold on various other animals.

digitigrade Walking upon the digits with the posterior part of the foot more or less raised.

disruptive coloration Disruptive patterns, often a part of camouflage coloration, that create a visual disruption by forming a pattern that does not correspond with the body's shape.

domestication Process of hereditary reorganization of wild animals and plants into forms more accommodating to the interests of people.

ecotone A transition area between two adjacent ecological communities (as forest and grassland) usually exhibiting competition between organisms common to both.

ecotype A population of a species that survives as a distinct group through environmental selection and isolation and that is comparable with a taxonomic subspecies.

extant Still in existence.

foot-and-mouth disease Highly contagious viral disease of cloven-footed mammals (including cattle), spread by ingestion and inhalation.

forb An herb other than grass; a broadleaf herb.

gregarious Tending to live in a flock, herd, or community rather than alone.

inguinal Of, relating to, or in the region of the groin.

lek In animal behaviour, communal area in which two or more males of a species perform courtship displays.

midden An accumulation of refuse about a dwelling place; a refuse heap.

molariform Resembling a molar tooth especially in shape.

morphological Referring to the study of form or structure.

musth A periodic state of murderous frenzy of the bull elephant usually connected with the rutting season and marked by the exudation of a dark brown odorous ichor from tiny holes above the eyes.

predation Mode of life in which one animal, the predator, eats an animal of another species, the prey, immediately after killing it or, in some cases, while it is still alive.

proboscus The flexible, conspicuously long snout of some mammals (as tapirs, shrews); especially the trunk of an elephant.

pronking High, stiff-legged bounds with bowed back and lowered neck, during which the hair of the rump patch and spinal crest merge to form a big white patch.

rumination The act or process of regurgitating and rechewing previously swallowed food.

rut Recurring period of sexual excitement in mammals.

territory In ecology, any area defended by an organism or a group of similar organisms for such purposes as mating, nesting, or feeding.

velvet The soft and highly vascular hairy skin that envelops and nourishes the antlers of deer during their rapid growth but later peels off or is rubbed off by the animal.

ARTIODACTYLS AND PERISSODACTYLS

Information on even-toed ungulates can be found in
I.W. Cornwall, *Bones for the Archaeologist*, rev. ed. (1974),
on the morphology and identification of bones including
artiodactyls; J. Dorst and P. Dandelot, *A Field Guide to
the Larger Mammals of Africa*, 2nd ed. (1972), giving sum-
marized descriptions, habits, ecology, and distribution
maps for all African artiodactyls; R.F. Ewer, *Ethology of
Mammals* (1968, reissued 1973), a comprehensive text
with much information on artiodactyl behaviour; V.
Geist, "The Evolution of Horn-Like Organs," *Behaviour*,
27:175–214 (1966), on the functional implications of
horn shape; G.B. Schaller, *The Deer and the Tiger* (1967,
reprinted 1984), a study of the life of Indian artiodactyls;
C.A. Spinage, *The Book of the Giraffe* (1968), much information well presented for the general reader; W.P. Taylor
(ed.), *The Deer of North America* (1956, reissued 1969), on
all aspects of the life of North American deer; J.Z. Young,
The Life of Vertebrates, 3rd ed. (1981), containing a chapter
on artiodactyls; and F.E. Zeuner, *A History of Domesticated
Animals* (1963), a useful source for much information difficult to find elsewhere.

Information on odd-toed ungulates is contained in
J. Sidney, "The Past and Present Distribution of Some
African Ungulates," *Trans. Zool. Soc. Lond.*, vol. 30 (1965), a
comprehensive account; C.A.W. Guggisberg, *S.O.S. Rhino*
(1966), a readable general account of the living rhinoceroses, their biology and conservation; and G.G. Simpson,

Horses: The Story of the Horse Family in the Modern World and Through Sixty Million Years of History (1951, reissued 1970), an interesting account of the natural history and evolution of the Equidae. Myron J. Smith, *Equestrian Studies* (1981), is a comprehensive, classified bibliography of more than 4,600 equestrian studies in English.

For further studies of horses, *see* Margaret C. Self, *The Horseman's Encyclopedia*, rev. ed. (1963, reprinted 1978), an invaluable collection of information on domestic horses; and *A Standard Guide to Horse and Pony Breeds*, general ed. Elwyn Hartley Edwards (1980), providing information on 150 breeds and types. *The Horseman's International Book of Reference*, ed. by Jean Froissard and Lily Powell Froissard (1980), is an authoritative source consisting of contributions of international experts. Special aspects are examined in David P. Willoughby, *Growth and Nutrition in the Horse* (1975); R.H. Smythe, *The Horse: Structure and Movement*, 2nd ed., rev. by Peter C. Goody (1972); George H. Waring, *Horse Behavior: The Behavioral Traits and Adaptations of Domestic and Wild Horses, Including Ponies* (1983); and Moyra Williams, *Horse Psychology*, rev. ed. (1976).

ELEPHANTS

Jeheskel Shoshani (ed.), *Elephants*, rev. ed. (2000), begins with a discussion of elephant evolution and general biology and then goes on to cover topics including behaviour, communication, conservation, the role of elephants in human culture, and the ivory trade.

LAGOMORPHS

Joseph A. Chapman and John E.C. Flux, eds., *Rabbits, Hares, and Pikas: Status Survey and Conservation Action Plan*

(1990), is a taxonomically arranged review of the biology and status of the world's lagomorphs. Ronald M. Nowak, *Walker's Mammals of the World* (6th ed., 1999), photographically illustrates an article on each living lagomorph genus. J.C. Sandford, *The Domestic Rabbit*, 5th ed. (1996), describes the 50-plus breeds and all aspects of raising domestic rabbits. Harry V. Thompson and Carolyn M. King (eds.), *The European Rabbit: The History and Biology of a Successful Colonizer* (1994), thoroughly examines the biology of the European rabbit worldwide.

MARSUPIALS

Sources of information on Australasian marsupials include Ronald Strahan (ed.), *Mammals of Australia*, rev. ed. (1998); Timothy Flannery, *Mammals of New Guinea*, rev. and updated (1995); Peter Menkhorst, *A Field Guide to Mammals of Australia* (2001); and Hugh Tyndale-Biscoe, *Life of Marsupials* (1973). *The Amazing Marsupials* (1986), written and produced by Robert Raymond, is a video documentary that portrays a variety of Australian species.

INDEX

A

abomasum, 30, 31, 32
addax, 105–106
Aepycerotini tribe, 72–74
African bush pig, 29
African elephants, 267, 271, 272, 274, 275, 279
African forest elephant, 270, 279
African gazelles, 99–100
African savanna (bush) elephant, 270
African wild ass or true ass, 205–206, 208, 212, 248–249, 250
Alcelaphini tribe (alcelaphines), 33, 119–126
alpaca, 3–4, 179, 184–187, 188, 189
Amami rabbit, 284, 288–289
American bison, 157–160
American opossum, 298
American saddle horse, 239, 240
anchitheres, 245
Andalusian horse, 240
Andean deer, 53
Anglo-Arab horse, 238
antelopes, 1, 8, 9–10, 11, 13, 16, 18–19, 24, 28, 31, 33, 70–126
   duikers, 84–87
   dwarf antelope tribe, 87–94
   gazelle tribe, 94–104
   hartebeest tribe, 119–126
   horse antelope tribe, 104–112

   impalas, 72–74
   nilgais, 83–84
   reedbuck and waterbuck tribe, 112–118
   spiral-horned antelope tribe, 74–82
antilopine kangaroo, 301, 307
Antilopini tribe, 70, 94–104
antlers, 9, 15, 23–25, 35–36, 37–38, 40–41, 53
aoudad, 148
Appaloosa horse, 231–232, 238–239
aquatic life adaptations, 23, 199, 200
Arabian camel, 179, 180–181
Arabian horse, 236–237
Arabian oryx, 18, 108
Arctic hare, 291
argali, 20, 130–131
artiodactyls, 1–34
   abundance and distribution, 1–3
   form and function, 21–34
   importance to humans, 3–5
   natural history, 5–20
   ranges, 18–20
   social behaviour, 6–9
Asian elephant, 267, 271, 274, 275, 278–279
Asian elk, 57
Asian gazelles, 98–99
Asian horses, 237–238

X

Y

Z